D1309323

Programming
Excel® Services

Alvin Bruney

PUBLISHED BY
Microsoft Press
A Division of Microsoft Corporation
One Microsoft Way
Redmond, Washington 98052-6399

Library of Congress Control Number: 2007926320

Printed and bound in the United States of America.

1 2 3 4 5 6 7 8 9   QWT   2 1 0 9 8 7

Distributed in Canada by H.B. Fenn and Company Ltd.

A CIP catalogue record for this book is available from the British Library.

Microsoft Press books are available through booksellers and distributors worldwide. For further infor-
mation about international editions, contact your local Microsoft Corporation office or contact Microsoft
Press International directly at fax (425) 936-7329. Visit our Web site at www.microsoft.com/mspress.
Send comments to mspinput@microsoft.com.

Microsoft, ActiveX, Excel, Internet Explorer, MSDN, SharePoint and Windows are either registered
trademarks or trademarks of Microsoft Corporation in the United States and/or other countries. Other
product and company names mentioned herein may be the trademarks of their respective owners.

The example companies, organizations, products, domain names, e-mail addresses, logos, people, places,
and events depicted herein are fictitious. No association with any real company, organization, product,
domain name, e-mail address, logo, person, place, or event is intended or should be inferred.

This book expresses the author's views and opinions. The information contained in this book is provided
without any express, statutory, or implied warranties. Neither the authors, Microsoft Corporation, nor its
resellers, or distributors will be held liable for any damages caused or alleged to be caused either directly
or indirectly by this book.

Acquisitions Editor: Ben Ryan
Developmental Editor: Devon Musgrave
Project Editor: Lynn Finnel
Editorial Production Services: Publishing.com
Copy Editor: Roger LeBlanc
Technical Reviewer: Bill Ryan

Body Part No. X13-76792

Dedication

This book is for Kathyann, a light in my tunnel.

This book is also for Boob E. Tube. I hope you can read and understand this.
Daddy loves you and mommy.

To Dominique & Valentine Zamore:

Gone but not forgotten, rest in peace.

To Mommy and Daddy:

Thank you for the discipline. Thank you for the drive to challenge myself.
Thank you for the giving me the ability to think independently and differently.

To The One:

Thank you for the gift of life.

Contents at a Glance

Table of Contents

What do you think of this book? We want to hear from you!

Microsoft is interested in hearing your feedback so we can continually improve our books and learning resources for you. To participate in a brief online survey, please visit:

www.microsoft.com/learning/booksurvey/

What do you think of this book? We want to hear from you!

Microsoft is interested in hearing your feedback so we can continually improve our books and learning resources for you. To participate in a brief online survey, please visit:

www.microsoft.com/learning/booksurvey/

Acknowledgments

A book—especially any good book—is the sum of its polished parts. Some parts are more visible than others, but each part is equally important. Peer review is one less visible piece that adds polish and shine to an otherwise dry idea. Peer review is as important as the idea itself because it validates the idea, shapes it, and provides form and function—making it better and allowing it to go further. I'd like to say thanks to the following people for their peer review work:

Bill Ryan, thank you for taking the time to peer review the code for this book. Bill is a Device Application Development MVP and a Senior Consultant with Magenic Technologies, working in its Atlanta office. Bill started out peer reviewing and eventually became the technical editor for the book.

Jon Skeet, thank you for taking the time to peer review the code for this book. Jon is a software engineer doing his bit "in the trenches" while helping the community as a C# MVP.

Brian Desmond, thank you for taking the time to peer review the code for this book. Brian is a Directory Services MVP currently working on his own book.

In case you are interested in being an MVP, here is a link to the Web site: *http://mvp.support.microsoft.com.*

I like to think that a book isn't simply written, it is hand-assembled much like a puzzle is constructed, one precious piece at a time. The writing is only one part; the other parts are arguably just as important. I would like to take the time to thank the following people, who are responsible for the other parts of this wonderful effort:

Ben Ryan, program manager for developer books at Microsoft; Curtis Philips, courtesy of Publishing.com, for production; Andrea Fox, proofreader; Roger LeBlanc, copy editor; Bill Ryan, technical reviewer; Lynn Finnel, project editor; and Devon Musgrave, developmental editor. This book shines because of you all.

To those who touched this project and were not mentioned, a hearty thank you as well.

Alvin Bruney

Introduction

As an IT pro, you might have already felt the rumble of Excel Services within your IT circles. Or your clients might have gotten wind of something big on the horizon. Either way, the momentum is building, churning, and evolving in a way that will cause significant shifts in the technology that powers Microsoft Office applications. And you need to be prepared to handle that change because it promises to reshape the very way customers and businesses interact with these types of applications in the enterprise.

Excel Services is a new technology built and conditioned to support and extend spreadsheet-based applications. One of the defining points of this new technology is that it is designed to use Microsoft Office SharePoint Server (MOSS) 2007. In addition, the programmable parts of Excel Services are hooked into the .NET Framework so that user-interface pieces can be created to either sit on the client desktop or roam the Web through the browser.

Programming Excel Services describes the Excel Services product that is part of MOSS 2007 in complete detail. The material covers Excel Services using techniques and approaches common to .NET technology. This is no accident; MOSS 2007 is built on .NET technology. Where appropriate, and as necessary, the written discussion is complemented by code snippets written in Microsoft Visual Basic .NET and C#.

Programming Excel Services provides a fresh perspective on software as a solution. In that regard, it is substantially different from most resources that cover the subject. The book, as a whole, is designed to encourage you to think outside the box. It departs from the run-of-the-mill resource recipes for learning a new product. For instance, this resource shows you how to use Excel Services to overcome fundamental flaws in business processes today. Consider a user who changes a spreadsheet and forwards it to each member of her team for review. This type of approach is fundamentally flawed because it leads to out-of-sync spreadsheets that grow difficult to manage. The cure for this ailment is software as a solution—that is, the ability to use software to encourage the adoption of a better process, such as peer collaboration on a single, versioned copy of the spreadsheet. And this is where *Programming Excel Services* delivers, because it encourages the developer to solve the problem rather than just remedy a symptom.

Who This Book Is For

The book is recommended for the enterprise developer who is interested in building applications that take advantage of Excel Services. To gain the most from this book, the reader should have development experience in Visual Basic .NET, C#, or both. SharePoint experience, though helpful, is not a requirement. The material in the book speaks directly to experienced developers who are new to Excel Services. Inexperienced developers might find certain parts of the book a challenge. The book does not cater to developers with little to no experience in

.NET. And such developers will probably find themselves lost at times although much of the material will no doubt be useful to them.

Although this book is not intended as a SharePoint tutorial, parts of SharePoint that are necessary to host Excel Services are explained in great detail to include installation, configuration, and code implementation. However, you should not buy this book to learn SharePoint Server 2007. The book is primarily an Excel Services resource. It is important to understand this.

There is much emphasis on the Microsoft Visual Studio Extensions for SharePoint templates, and rightly so, because this new tool boosts productivity and uses the Visual Studio IDE, which is familiar to the target audience. However, it does go against the grain as far as existing resources are concerned. Expect to be more productive using these techniques. Expect to build more sophisticated applications using these techniques, with the same look and feel as applications built in ASP.NET.

As a whole, the book outlines radically different ways of working that unleash what was formerly impossible. To accomplish this within the constraints of a 300-page book, these chapters necessarily assume that the reader has a solid grasp of .NET programming techniques and is well rounded in the science of programming. Advanced chapters are designed to push the envelope of what is possible, so the reader needs to be at least familiar with the bounds and constraints of the .NET paradigm.

How This Book Is Organized

The book is structured using a simple format. Chapter 1 is fairly high level and is aimed at decision makers, architects, and technical leads who need to assess the product for use in the enterprise. The chapter contains no code snippets. The language and tone is kept intentionally moderate to suit the target audience.

Chapters 2 through 5 examine the building blocks of Excel Services. These chapters target the enterprise developer, and the language is technical. Each component building block is described in complete detail, with a suitable mix of theory and code. However, where appropriate, the emphasis is on code.

Chapter 6 focuses on Web Part development. The target audience is the enterprise developer. As the material will point out, SharePoint relies heavily on Web Parts. The book shows by example the techniques that can be used to design, build, and deploy .NET Web Parts in SharePoint Server 2007. The chapter is fairly advanced and requires a solid understanding of some of the more advanced topics in .NET. The reader might find the going a bit difficult without a good grasp of some of these concepts and techniques.

Chapter 7 demonstrates how to leverage the Excel Services product in the enterprise. The coverage includes integration with ASP.NET applications, examination of the more complex features of the product, and Microsoft Office automation examples. Excel Services does not run in a vacuum, so any suitable resources must take this into consideration. In the real world, developers are expected to integrate custom applications into SharePoint, and this chapter walks the reader through this process.

System Requirements

You'll need the following hardware and software to build and run the code samples for this book:

- Microsoft Windows XP with Service Pack 2, along with Microsoft VPC 2004, Microsoft Windows Server 2003 with Service Pack 1, or Microsoft Windows 2000 with Service Pack 4

- Microsoft Office SharePoint Server 2007

- Microsoft Visual Studio 2005 Standard Edition or Microsoft Visual Studio 2005 Professional Edition

- Microsoft SQL Server 2005 Express Edition (included with Visual Studio 2005) or Microsoft SQL Server 2005

- 600-MHz Pentium or compatible processor (1-GHz Pentium recommended)

- 192 MB of RAM (256 MB or more recommended)

- Video monitor (800 × 600 or higher resolution) with at least 256 colors (1024 × 768 High Color 16-bit recommended)

- Microsoft mouse or compatible pointing device

Code Samples

The downloadable code includes projects for most chapters that cover the code snippets and examples referenced in the chapter. All the code samples discussed in this book can be downloaded from the book's companion content page at the following address:

http://www.microsoft.com/mspress/companion/9780735624078/

On the code download page you might notice an "Extras" folder containing a few additional projects. These projects provide alternative connection approaches that you might find helpful and demonstrate how to source events and automate Microsoft Office applications

For code snippets, indentation follows the Visual Studio 2005 standard. In addition, and where appropriate, lines of code that wrap contain further indentation for readability purposes.

Support for This Book

Every effort has been made to ensure the accuracy of this book and the companion content. As corrections or changes are collected, they will be added to a Microsoft Knowledge Base article.

Microsoft Press provides support for books and companion content at the following Web site:

http://www.microsoft.com/learning/support/books/

Questions and Comments

If you have comments, questions, or ideas regarding the book or the companion content, or questions that are not answered by visiting the site just mentioned, please send them to Microsoft Press via e-mail to

mspinput@microsoft.com

Or via postal mail to

Microsoft Press
Attn: Programming Excel Services *Editor*
One Microsoft Way
Redmond, WA 98052-6399

Please note that Microsoft software product support is not offered through the above addresses.

Chapter 1
An Introduction to Excel Services

Every now and then, a product hits the market that causes a significant shift in the way software is designed and built. Excel Services is one such product; it completely changes the way Microsoft Office applications are written. This chapter will focus on introducing and explaining the Excel Services architecture that drives this fundamental shift in thinking so that you can gain an appreciation for the product. The focus is less on code and more on painting Excel Services in broad strokes, thereby allowing you to grasp the grand design. Later on, we intend to probe the basic building blocks that drive this new technology. We will then work our way up to some of the more advanced concepts of building and integrating sometimes disparate applications on top of the common infrastructure backbone exposed by Office SharePoint Server 2007.

Excel Services is a new technology that allows developers to load, calculate, and display Excel workbooks on Office SharePoint Server 2007. In some respects, Excel Services behaves much like a development framework that allows developers to build applications based on Excel workbooks. The concept of providing a framework for developers is certainly not new—think the .NET Framework. However, the way in which this technology is exposed is fundamentally different from legacy approaches. This radically different architecture enables new applications that target Office and SharePoint to be efficient, robust, and scalable. Legacy Office applications can scarcely make that claim ring true.

Excel Services is built on ASP.NET 2.0 and Office SharePoint Server 2007. The architectural decision to use Excel Services on the .NET and Microsoft Office SharePoint Server (MOSS) platforms is significant because it means that Excel Services benefits from the flexibility and performance capabilities of these highly regarded platforms. Consider that SharePoint is a mature technology that provides, among other things, collaboration, content management, and business intelligence capabilities while ASP.NET provides a framework for building Web application software. Excel Services, a part of MOSS, provides for some exciting ways to build and deploy enterprise software with internal support for key SharePoint functionality and application extensibility.

> **Planning**   Because of the use of the ASP.NET platform, you should expect applications built using Excel Services to require less code effort, benefit from rapid application development (RAD) technology, incorporate best practices at the architectural and design level, and be built to remain well-behaved under increased load. Because of the SharePoint platform, you should expect applications built using Excel Services to be configurable, require less administrative effort, and be inherently distributed in nature.

However, it's extremely important for .NET developers to approach Excel Services from a SharePoint perspective. It is a mind shift that ultimately improves the quality and effort of application development for MOSS 2007. SharePoint is a product designed to be assembled out-of-the-box and configured appropriately. This is markedly different from an ASP.NET mindset where products must be built from the ground up using blocks of code. Following this new mindset, most of your development efforts will focus on extending the SharePoint product. Much of this book is designed along these lines—that is, the material forces you to think from a SharePoint perspective. An ASP.NET developer must resist the inherent urge to use the .NET Framework to build standalone application functionality for SharePoint because that urge is unhealthy. Rather, an ASP.NET developer should seek to build functionality that supplements what is already offered by SharePoint.

One of the fundamentals that we intend to focus on is the bridge between MOSS and Office applications. In that regard, it's important to point out that Excel Services targets Excel workbooks only. The depth and breadth of application products and features are not directly available to Excel Services. For instance, Excel Services contains no internal support for Outlook automation. That is certainly no setback, as you will soon learn that the Excel workbook itself plays a pivotal role in exposing Office functionality because it is able to dovetail with so many other Office applications.

For instance, an Excel workbook can invoke search functionality, create charts, display Pivot-Tables, read XML files, query data stores, provide Web service functionality, and do so much more. If Excel Services functions as a bridge between the Excel workbook and SharePoint server, it must mean that traveling this bridge indirectly exposes Office functionality to Web applications that are hosted on SharePoint. And this is the angle that will be explored going forward—that is, learning to build real-world software that is integrated with SharePoint. Chapter 7, "Advanced Concepts with Excel Services," illustrates some exciting integration ideas by example.

Along the way, you'll gain an appreciation for the tools and strategies employed by Excel Services to retrieve data and manipulate workbooks. Excel Services allows you to connect to data across different back ends while maintaining the connection information in a secure way—see Chapter 4, "Excel Calculation Service." You'll learn how to protect intellectual property using features specifically built in to the workbooks—see Chapter 7. You'll define the boundaries between Excel Services and its full-blown counterpart, Office Excel 2007–see Chapter 2, "Excel Web Services." But most importantly, you will learn to think in a new way using new tools to tackle old problems.

Excel Services Architecture Overview

Figure 1-1 introduces the Excel Services architecture at a high level.

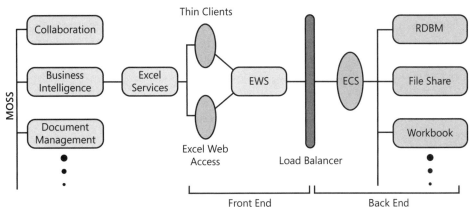

Figure 1-1   Excel Services architecture big picture overview.

MOSS 2007 contains several key components shown by the leftmost vertical section of Figure 1-1. Our focus is the Excel Services layer within the Business Intelligence component. The Excel Services placement within the hierarchy is significant because it is designed to address the Business Intelligence need at an enterprise level. This book considers the other pieces, such as collaboration and the document management items in the lower leftmost vertical section of the figure, only within the context of Excel Services.

The architecture solves a particular subset of problems associated with Business Intelligence. These problems span the spectrum of issues across the Office platform to include browser-affined user-interface applications, lack of workbook security, version control issues, poor scalability, and terrible enterprise-level performance. Even with an abundance of new software tools, more fundamental headaches such as harvesting data from disparate back ends, analysis of dissimilar pieces of information, and poor control over out-of-sync data threaten to counter the advances of data analysis. Excel Services was designed to provide a solution for the broad spectrum of technical and business issues that conspire to derail the field of Business Intelligence.

The new architecture provides more than a face-lift for the long list of eyesores that stifle the forward movement of Business Intelligence today. Excel Services provides solutions at the design level–that is, you can now design applications that allow for both horizontal and vertical scaling. The new architecture based on the ASP.NET 2.0 platform incorporates codified guidance through industry-proven design patterns that provide a solid foundation for building tomorrow's software solutions today. As an added bonus, Excel Services allows developers to participate in the rich SharePoint end user experience. For instance, custom code can hook into the new feature of SharePoint that allows clients to connect any list or document library to Outlook. The integration with Outlook extends to offline scenarios so that clients can remain close to their data even though they aren't tethered to a modem.

In Figure 1-1, observe that the Excel Services components isolate programmatic access to the Excel model into logical layers. For instance, the front end is exposed through Excel Web Access (EWA) and the middle tier is exposed through Excel Web Services (EWS). These layers can then be run on a single machine or across machines in a farm in true tier fashion. This is how the model achieves horizontal scale. For vertical scale, the Excel Services architecture supports multiple CPU configurations and memory resource additions up to the physical limit of the server. In fact, your applications built on the Excel Services platform will provide near linear performance for each processor!

If you pause for a moment to reflect on the architecture shown in Figure 1-1, you should realize that this new technology opens up all sorts of programming possibilities. For instance, the entire range of Office products can now be addressed programmatically through the Excel Services bridge or independently through SOAP clients. And what's more interesting is the fact that all three pieces that make up the Excel Services architecture combine to expose a single point of entry into the Excel calculation engine. The calculation engine will be covered in great detail in Chapter 4.

If you're wondering how this dovetails with SharePoint, consider Figure 1-2, which illustrates the Excel Services architecture.

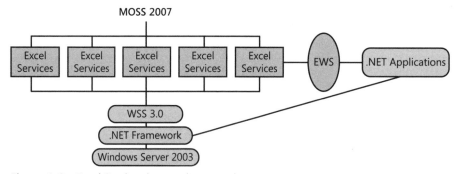

Figure 1-2 Excel Services integration overview.

Observe that Windows SharePoint Services (WSS, rhymes with less) is a key player in the architecture. You'll notice that WSS 3.0 is a separate service. WSS 3.0 is installed independently from MOSS as an operating system service. The separation simply secures a measure of robustness while guaranteeing scalability. Chapter 5, "Windows SharePoint Services 3.0," will explore WSS in a lot more detail.

Windows SharePoint Services

From a business perspective, WSS was designed to offer enterprise-level collaboration services. WSS allows companies to manage and manipulate documents across geographical boundaries and through organizational hierarchical levels. The collaboration can be exposed through thick or thin clients residing locally or across the sea in a way that is user-friendly and focused on the knowledge worker. We won't just talk about these niceties; we'll build them too.

The collaboration is built on a platform that is configurable, easily deployed, and responsive to change. WSS is really a next-generation point-of-convergence layer that caters to real-world demands of software. Whether it is a request from a thick client connected to a platform other than Microsoft Windows or a request through a Web Part located on a dashboard running on Windows, the WSS backbone can flex to service these disparate requests in an efficient manner across the enterprise. That's really what real-world software is about, and WSS is built to handle it gracefully. Chapter 2 will walk you through the process of building applications with this exciting breed of software.

In the next section, we'll start a controlled dive into the bowels of the architecture. Before you can start writing code that targets the Excel Services platform, you need to understand each piece and how the pieces interface with each other. You also need to get a good grasp of what can be done and what should be revisited with a different approach to squeeze performance and functionality out of this new architecture. Then we will write code, lots of it.

Excel Web Access

The Excel Web Access component is the most visible part of Excel Services. EWA renders HTML to the client that is cross-browser compliant. Spreadsheets, PivotTables, and charts render with the same visual fidelity in all browsers. This is fundamentally different from Web applications that are built to target the Office platform. In the past, Web clients built to target the Office platform used an eclectic mix of ActiveX objects and custom objects to render spreadsheets and PivotTables.

Although that approach solved the problem at hand, it was jaundiced and short-sighted because it failed to provide an enterprise-wide solution that allowed disparate clients to see and interact with spreadsheets. One common issue with this approach is that these products added cost and often complicated build and deployment scenarios. Another annoying side-effect is that the use of ActiveX controls imposed browser limitations on the Web clients. Consequently, applications that were based on this technology could run only in Internet Explorer browsers because only these browsers had internal support for ActiveX controls.

The new approach is built on a policy of inclusion. Because all up-level browsers support HTML, DHMTL, and JavaScript, it makes sense for EWA to construct its output in a way that is consumable by all browsers. That way, the developer is not constrained in the type of application that can be built; neither is she limited by the extent of functionality that can be incorporated into such applications. EWA applications can now target the widest possible audience. Chapter 3, "Excel Web Access," will walk you through the process of building and deploying solutions for EWA.

For the most part, the look and feel of the PivotTable or spreadsheet in EWA mirrors the fit and finish of the desktop version. However, some significant inconsistencies in the front-end functionality will take some getting used to. One such inconsistency is the way in which end user data is input into an EWA spreadsheet. The spreadsheet cells are read-only. Data cannot be entered directly into these cells. Instead, data must be entered into controls that are tied to the target cells. Figure 1-3 shows an EWA spreadsheet.

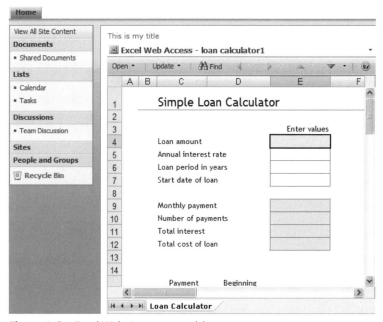

Figure 1-3   Excel Web Access spreadsheet.

To be polite, this approach is rather awkward and certainly looks and feels unnatural when compared to the desktop equivalent. More importantly, time and effort need to be invested in training the user to interact with this new input functionality. Chapter 6, "Advanced Web Parts Programming," will show you a clever way to work around that limitation.

> **Warning**   I do not claim to know the reasons for such a radically different input design. However, it's important to point out that it certainly isn't based on a technical limitation; Google spreadsheets provide the same visual acuity built on HTML, DHTML, and JavaScript, yet end users can enter data into the cells directly.

Another point of departure is that EWA is tightly coupled to Web Parts. ASP.NET Web Parts are controls that provide pockets of functionality on Web pages. These types of functionality are built in by the developer and exposed through well-defined points in the Web Part control. Several code examples to follow in Chapter 3 and Chapter 6 will be geared at improving your level of comfort with Web Parts.

Web Parts also allow application developers to encapsulate functionality behind a user interface that can then be used to improve the user experience and drive functionality on a SharePoint Web page. With Excel Services, you now have the option of developing an application that allows the end user to selectively plug in pieces of functionality on the fly through the use of custom Web Parts.

When developing Excel Services applications, you need to start thinking in terms of providing end user functionality encapsulated in Web Part controls. EWA does not allow spreadsheets, PivotTable controls, or Excel charts to lie bare on a page. It's a bit of a mental side step from ASP.NET development, but there are some benefits to be had through this approach. For one, these Web Parts can be plugged into SharePoint designer pages to provide the same functionality. Another benefit is that Web Parts allow end users to impose personalization themes at the control level so that the user interface can be customized for the end user. This functionality is especially important when designing and building accessible Web pages and applications. Chapter 3 focuses on developing customizable Web Parts. Parts of Chapter 7 will cover accessibility in greater detail.

Excel Web Services

Excel Web Services (EWS) is a bona fide Web service hosted on MOSS 2007. EWS acts to decouple the calculation process from the front end. With this separation of responsibilities, you can now build applications that span operating system boundaries. EWS exposes the feature set of the calculation service and workbook to clients. Clients can focus on the task of displaying the results of the calculation.

EWS can service requests in a scalable manner across the enterprise Web farm in a thread-safe way. The implication here is that the Excel Services infrastructure automatically handles concurrency issues, so there is reduced risk of calculation anomalies. Chapter 4 focuses on the parts of MOSS that allow calculations to scale across a Web farm.

You can access the Excel Web Services either as a regular Web service by calling Web methods through SOAP clients as you normally would any other Web service, or you can access the functionality through a reference to a local assembly using a technique called Direct-Linking. Direct-Linking is typically used for applications that need to run within real-time constraints such as stock trading applications while Web services are used for every other scenario. See the Project Setup Guide for a walk-through on setting a reference locally or adding a Web reference to the Excel Web Services. We reserve a more detailed explanation that explores the technical merit behind these statements for Chapter 2.

Excel Calculation Service Engine

The rubber meets the road in the Excel Calculation Service (ECS) layer. As the name implies, the calculation engine is responsible for servicing calculation requests. Each calculation request is atomic—that is, once a request is received, it is processed as a single transaction. The transaction is pinned to a particular session so that calculation accuracy is guaranteed. The design accommodates distributed computation on high-performance clusters with redundancy software. The architecture has been tuned to provide a near-linear performance increase with each new server added to the farm. The performance increase occurs without penalty to the computational integrity of the calculation engine. In addition, the calculation engine achieves computational fidelity with the Excel desktop version so that you can rest assured that your calculated results, distributed or not, will be Excel accurate.

Aside from the regular duties of loading and calculating workbooks, the Excel Calculation Service also maintains and manages the session state for opened workbooks. Session state operates much like ASP.NET sessions with configurable time-outs and associated events. Chapter 4 will explore the technical parts of this approach in further detail.

The Excel Calculation Service also manages the workbook cache. Opened Excel workbooks are cached according to user sessions. For instance, multiple users sharing the same account credentials are pooled and a single instance of a workbook is used to service these requests. Calculation states, results, and external data also form part of that cached pool managed by the Excel Calculation Service. This behavior is specifically designed to service high concurrency across a farm with the result that performance is improved for the set of pooled users. Chapter 4 will dive deeper into the details of the Excel Calculation Service.

Performance and Scalability Considerations

Excel Services was designed to scale vertically and horizontally. For vertical scaling such as CPU additions, Excel Services automatically adjusts for multiple CPUs. Excel Services includes native support for 64-bit CPU architectures as well. For horizontal scaling, Web application servers can simply be added to the farm and configured using the Central Administration Web application. Each new server addition requires Internet Information Services (IIS).

Functional integrity and calculation fidelity is achieved across an expanding farm due in large part to the Excel load balancer. The load balancer contains a managed library that serves as a proxy component. The ECS proxy automatically handles communication between the Web front end (WFE) and the application service tier on the server farm. The proxy component cannot be programmed through code.

Figure 1-4 shows the administrative console used to configure the load balancer. There are many options that are configurable. However, each option is static—that is, it does not dynamically adjust to load during execution. Administrators have to dial in the settings during use. Figure 1-4 shows the various settings available to the administrator.

MOSS depends on a Microsoft SQL Server database for storage. You will learn how to configure the important parts of the database later on. For now, it's important to realize that no physical upper limits are built into the back-end store. MOSS can service databases ranging in size from megabytes (MBs) on up to terabytes (TBs) and any point in between. The exception to this case is the 4-MB cap placed on the free version of Microsoft SQL Server Express Edition.

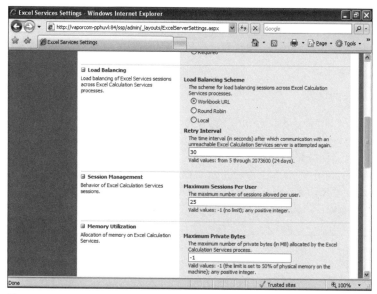

Figure 1-4   Load balancer settings.

Excel Services and SharePoint 2007

SharePoint 2007 didn't magically appear on the scene in 2006—it does, in fact, have a long, rich history. It all started with a product called Site Server, released around 1997, that contained Web content management, personalization, document management, and search services. Site Server morphed into Commerce Server, which was, in turn, replaced with a new product called Digital Dashboard Starter Kit. Digital Dashboard introduced the concept of Web Parts as pluggable bits of functionality that could be added to a Web page.

Digital Dashboard churned through a few revisions and improved its Web portal offering along the way. The feature set of Digital Dashboard merged with a new product called Tahoe and was renamed to "SharePoint Portal Server 2001." Web Part success introduced in the Digital Dashboard continued its evolution into new ASP.NET territory, providing two development code streams for these controls.

Around this time, a product called SharePoint Team Services (STS) that provided Web-based team collaboration was released. STS would morph into Windows SharePoint Services (WSS) available with Microsoft Windows Server 2003. SharePoint Server version 2 was built on top of WSS, and these technologies converged to give birth to MOSS 2007 today.

Through the 10-year evolutionary process, best-of-breed software merged to provide a suite of services, including the following:

- Page and content customization

- Document management and storage

- Notification services

- Search and indexing

This evolutionary path allowed SharePoint to grow and mature into a tool that facilitates collaboration within an organization. This collaboration includes creation, management, and storage of information. Coupled with these exciting features, Excel Services adds a new dimension to collaboration to include Excel workbook integration services. Indeed, much of the functionality available to administrators can be built using the development model exposed by WSS. Chapter 5 will focus on these and other facets of the product.

> **Note**   Here is a short list of the improvements that have been added to Windows SharePoint Services 3.0 over previous versions. Some of these topics are covered extensively in this book: Object Model Enhancements, Extensible Field Types, Site Columns, Content Type Settings, Recycle Bin, RSS Feeds, List Improvements, Workflows, Property Bags, Web Service Enhancements, Change Log, Event Enhancements, Work Items and Timer, Features, and Mobility Functionality.

Before you begin exploring Excel Services programmatically, you need to understand the tight coupling between Excel Services and SharePoint. Excel Services requires SharePoint 2007. However, the Excel Services component is packaged only in the Enterprise edition. Standard edition functionality includes only the following features: Collaboration, Enterprise Content Management, Workflow, My Sites, Profiles and Personalization, and Enterprise Search. Enterprise edition functionality includes the following: Business Data Catalog, Excel Services, Report Center, InfoPath Forms Services, Key Performance Indicator (KPI), Filter Web Parts, and Windows Workflow Foundation.

You should note that although the two packages are cleanly separated, all components are installed on the target machine. The installation key provided with the product simply unlocks a specified package. The key encryption is of sufficient strength to discourage sophisticated hackers from gaining access to unauthorized packages.

If you intend to publish spreadsheets, you must install the Enterprise edition of the Office System or the Professional Plus version. All other versions do not include the ability to publish spreadsheets. In those versions, a published spreadsheet exists in noninteractive mode—that is, the end user cannot input or modify data inside the spreadsheet. Chapter 6 shows a clever approach that allows you to program for interactivity if you do not have the Enterprise or Professional Plus version of the Office System installed. If your programming requirements do not include interactive content, Excel Services may be of little benefit.

Another customer-centric feature is that you can try MOSS 2007 and Excel Services before making a commitment to purchase. The trial period lasts six months, after which certain parts of the software become unusable. The trial version offers the same functionality as the actual product, so you get a real sense of whether or not the software can add value to your enterprise organization. If you decide to keep the product, you purchase it through regular purchasing channels and you receive a key that releases the lock. Software manufacturers that are confident of the capabilities of the software they produce usually offer a trial period, so there's really nothing to lose on your end.

MOSS 2007 Licensing and Terms of Use

An important part of software evaluation deals with licensing configurations and terms of use. Although the product might fulfill every desire, it could be out of reach from a financial perspective for shops that run on a tight budget. It's also important to realize that Excel Services is bundled with MOSS 2007. The two are indivisible; you must purchase the MOSS 2007 Enterprise version to harvest Excel Services functionality.

Another consideration is the fact that licensing extends to the operating system. In that case, Windows Server 2003 has specific licensing regarding the number of concurrent users that can be supported for applications that run on the server.

Another issue to be aware of is that default licensing caters to installations that service intranet applications. For external-facing sites that service unauthenticated users, you must purchase an External Connector license for each Windows 2003 Server that is exposed externally.

Client Access Licenses (CAL) must be purchased for each user on the system. The CALs are for site access. Whether clients require view-only access or not, each client requires a separate CAL. For enterprise-wide consumption, you need an accurate estimate of end users who will be accessing the site. You can do the simple math to see how much the product will cost you based on these estimates.

MOSS 2007 is tightly integrated with either SQL Server 2000 Service Pack 3 (SP3), SQL Server 2005, or SQL Server Embedded Edition. Without exception, all these databases contain end user licensing agreements, some more restrictive than others. It's well worth your while to invest some time and energy in understanding the licensing terms for each of these pieces before making a commitment to Excel Services. You might find that you need to purchase extra products to be able to use Excel Services. The problem is exacerbated by the fact that Excel Services does not allow installers to mix and match packages. For instance, a client can't simply purchase the standard version along with Excel Services since interactivity is not available with that particular combination of products.

The embedded database server that is installed with the standard version is functionally equivalent to full-blown SQL Server where MOSS is concerned. However, there are certain limitations that spoil the fun. Here's a list of limitations in no particular order:

- There is a 4-GB data limit on the database capacity.

- Business Intelligence features are not installed.

- Integration and interoperability functionality are reduced.

- Notification Services are not available.

- There is a reduced manageability feature set.

- There are no tools for scalability and performance tuning.

- The enterprise availability feature set is not available.

If these limitations are unwelcomed, then consider upgrading your database.

About Office Programming

Ever since Office applications gained popularity, developers have tried to leverage the Office platform in custom-built applications. Excel spreadsheets are used heavily in the real world. And although these varied attempts to leverage the Office platform seem fractious in nature, they all target the same underlying Office Component Object Model (COM) platform. The sobering truth is that there might never be a single point of access to Office programmability because each new release is inextricably tied to a particular Office product or Client Access License. For instance, Microsoft Office Web Components (OWC) is tied to licensing, Visual Studio Tools for Office 2003 is tied to Office XP, and Excel Services is firmly moored to MOSS 2007. It's important to focus on who the key players are so that you can make educated choices about developing applications targeting the Office platform.

You might have noticed that the text takes some artistic liberties where Excel Services and Office programmability are concerned. Strictly speaking, it isn't technically correct to claim that Excel Services targets the Office platform. And it is really important to make this clear. Excel Services only allows calling code to manipulate Excel workbooks.

Because Excel workbooks are an integral part of the Office equation and are fairly heavily used, it's safe to assume that Excel Services provides hooks into the Office platform through the Excel Services gateway. As such, the literature in this book will continue to exercise this freedom of association. Also, Chapter 7 will provide examples of Excel Services application code that automates Office components.

Alternatives to Excel Services

Part of the buzz around Excel Services is that there really is nothing like it at the enterprise level for targeting Excel workbooks. The products listed in the next few sections provide a measure of functionality that allows developers to target spreadsheets. But you should understand that these products do not provide the flex and scale of Excel Services–meaning that no single product currently available provides the same depth of functionality as Excel Services.

On the other hand, if you are looking at targeting specific feature sets, such as Excel charts or PivotTables, you'll find ample products that provide that type of functionality. Some third-party products even provide better features and functionality. For instance, charting packages are now sophisticated and specialized, and they typically provide more in terms of raw features than the Excel chart packages bundled within Excel. However, none provide the architectural backbone suitable for developing enterprise applications across the Office suite of products. Bear this in mind while you evaluate and compare Excel Services to the current "competitive" offering.

Office Web Components

Office Web Components was released as an add-in to Office 2000. From that point, the Web application developer world has developed a sort of cult following to this set of components. Even today, consultants continue to recommend its use. Companies continue to implement applications based on OWC despite the fact that Microsoft has discontinued development of these controls. Chapter 6 will walk you through a few examples of integrating these products into Web Parts to overcome some inherent limitations in the Excel Services model. You can find the OWC roadmap at this link: *http://blogs.msdn.com/excel/archive/2006/07/17/668544.aspx.*

To understand why OWC has been such a success, you first have to understand the business need that fueled its creation. Web applications had long lacked the functionality of Excel. OWC provided a way to marry the desktop functionality of Excel to the Web browser experience. OWC opened a sea of possibilities for Web applications. And, to add icing to the cake, OWC could perform double duty by running in Windows applications on the desktop.

However, this flexibility came with a high price. Security was always an issue. OWC suffered some notable security compromises and exploits in part because of the ActiveX platform on which it ran. Microsoft was unable to find an elegant enterprise solution that would close the gaping security hole while justifying continued investment in this technology. It was painfully apparent that if the security issue had to be solved, OWC had to be discontinued in favor of something more secure.

EWA is not a replacement for OWC, but it does provide an elegant enterprise solution to the business need of providing end users with desktop Excel functionality hosted in a browser. As an added bonus, the thorny issue of an Internet Explorer–affined OWC component is a thing of the past; EWA renders completely in non–Internet Explorer browsers with the same visual fidelity found in Excel. The definitive guide to developing with OWC, *The Microsoft Office Web Components Black Book with .NET* (Lulu.com, 2005), is available on Amazon.com.

Excel COM Interop Libraries

Customers have always wanted to use Excel as a server technology. Computing a spreadsheet, calculating a range, or saving changes in a concurrent environment are persistent customer requests. That type of need existed even when Excel was in its infancy. It continues to resonate louder today as companies migrate applications to the Web to dodge the heavy burden of enterprise desktop deployment.

However, the thorn, if there ever was one, is that Excel was designed as a client-side technology. It was never meant to service server-side applications. Forcing a client-side technology to perform server-side duties through clever hacks and shady programming techniques is a recipe for disaster because it overextends the architecture. And there have been some catastrophic disasters that are best left hidden under the software carpet.

Fortunately, Excel Services now provides a calculation engine that is designed to live on the server with Web Service receptacles that reach deep into the client front end, enabling thin, thick, and smart clients to hook into the back end in a scalable fashion.

Visual Studio Tools for Office

Microsoft Visual Studio Tools for Office (VSTO, pronounced "visto") is both an add-on to Visual Studio and a standalone product. As of this writing, the offering is currently in its second revision with a third on its way. The tool suite was designed to allow .NET developers to target Office applications with managed code. VSTO services Windows applications. It was not designed for the Web. However, there is a server component in VSTO that allows documents to be manipulated on the server. VSTO contains several limitations. The most noticeable is that it targets specific versions of Office.

Note that VSTO was not designed from the ground up. Rather, it is built on top of the Office COM libraries and installs as a template that makes VSTO functionality available to Windows applications. Consequently, scalability and performance take a back seat to functionality. For instance, VSTO allows Windows controls to be embedded in the spreadsheet.

There are many more advantages to VSTO that are worth considering; however, the product is designed only for the desktop. Excel Services provides much of this functionality with the added benefit that performance and scalability take the front seat. And Excel Services functionality isn't limited to desktop applications. A suitable resource for VSTO development is my recent book, *Professional VSTO 2005: Visual Studio 2005 Tools for Office* (Wrox, 2006).

Third-Party Components

It should be obvious by now that these ad hoc technologies aimed at providing Office functionality have created a sort of vacuum. It is difficult to choose a suitable product if you are developing a smart client application for the Internet, for instance. For that particular scenario, VSTO might not be a suitable choice because it is tied to a particular Office version.

Another burden is that each VSTO installation requires a specific version of the .NET Framework.

Office Web Components is a suitable choice. However, the end user licensing agreement dictates that these components be used in an intranet environment. To be clear, the exact rules that govern OWC terms of use are sufficiently complex to merit their own book. But the rules can be distilled into a policy that does not include Internet deployment for interactive use.

To address these and other types of needs, third-party controls have been developed to allow developers to target the Office model. These controls are too numerous to mention; however, they all share the same concerns. The industry-proven products are not free, contain their own licensing agreements, and offer varying levels of support.

Business Intelligence Systems

In the last decade or so, Business Intelligence (BI) has evolved to mean much more than data mining. The term encompasses everything from data harvesting across disparate back ends to model-driven analysis of data. Knowledge workers typically employ a variety of tools to make sense of this mass of data. It should come as no surprise that Excel spreadsheets drive the majority of this business in the real world. Consequently, Microsoft has provided leadership in this domain by empowering SharePoint 2007 with a complete suite of BI tools that put knowledge workers in the driver's seat.

SharePoint 2007 bridges the data gap by allowing knowledge workers to connect to disparate back ends, such as SQL Server, SAP, Siebel, spreadsheets, and Web services. The mass of data is untangled and normalized inside a new potent tool called the SharePoint Report Center. Knowledge workers can interrogate the data through Key Performance Indicators (KPI) analysis.

The SharePoint 2007 Reporting Center makes use of Excel Services to display Web Parts and KPI. Data can be harvested across platforms through built-in connection points stored in special Data Connection Libraries (DCLs). The now structured data can be viewed through Pivot-Table reports or displayed prominently on MOSS dashboards in real time.

Installation and Deployment

MOSS 2007 is a resource hog. Its default configuration is to use exactly 50 percent of memory. There's ample justification for its greedy nature because the MOSS platform runs several services, each responsible for a variety of jobs. In addition, SQL Server 2005 also consumes its fair share of resources. The point being made is that this platform requires an abundance of computing resources. For developers concerned with running the software on personal computers for evaluation purposes, you should be aware that there is a noticeable performance penalty being paid to run MOSS 2007.

The performance penalty manifests itself in client-facing applications such as the Central Administration Console and in server-facing functionality such as calculation engine response times. On the other hand, servers that meet the minimum hardware and software requirements run MOSS 2007 efficiently.

You'll need to bear that in mind when you begin to write and deploy applications on your desktop or laptop. It warrants repeating that MOSS 2007 is a platform designed to run on high-end servers with sufficient computing and hardware resources, as outlined in the deployment and setup guide. For an enterprise, Excel Services resource consumption can be configured either upward or downward for improved site performance.

Installation Prerequisites and System Requirements

Excel Services can be installed either as a standalone application or in a server farm environment. For a standalone setup, you need to make sure that the server has the following:

- Dual processor with processor clock speeds at 2.5 GHz or higher
- At least 1 GB of RAM
- Microsoft Windows Server 2003 Service Pack 1 with NTFS
- Microsoft .NET Framework 2.0
- Windows Workflow Foundation (WF) Runtime Components
- Microsoft Internet Information Services 6.0

A standalone configuration is helpful if you need to evaluate the software or reduce the overhead cost of administration. The standalone application installs and configures Windows Internal Database, which is used to power the SharePoint site.

For the server farm environment, you need to meet all the requirements just listed plus have SQL Server 2005 or SQL Server 2000 Service Pack 3.

There are two modes available for MOSS. These modes are configured by the administrator after installation. In evaluation mode, the default model is delegation. Trusted subsystem model is the default for enterprise mode. From a security point of view, delegation mode does not guarantee stronger data protection. In fact, there are instances where delegation mode is less secure. Delegation allows user credentials from the Excel Services front end to flow to the back end. Kerberos is used with delegation to enable credentials to work in a multitier scenario.

Important The Kerberos version 5 protocol is the primary security protocol for authentication within a domain. It uses mutual authentication to verify the identity of both the user and the network services. The system attempts to negotiate authentication over the Kerberos protocol first, but if it is not successful, the NTLM protocol is used. NTLM is based on a challenge-response mechanism for client authentication. NTLM is available in MOSS to facilitate communication with systems that are able to use only NTLM authentication.

Assuming the minimum requirements are met, simply run the SharePoint Products And Technologies Configuration Wizard to configure MOSS. The wizard walks you through the installation and configuration of the database, SharePoint Server Services 3.0, and the SharePoint Central Administration application.

After the wizard has completed, you need to add the SharePoint Central Administration site to the list of trusted sites so that you are not prompted for the user name and password each time you invoke the SharePoint Central Administration application. You can do this through Internet Explorer trusted site settings.

Next, you need to configure MOSS Services. The services can be configured through the SharePoint Central Administration application. The SharePoint Central Administration application also allows you to perform a number of configuration adjustments to include the following functionality:

- Configure e-mail messages
- Create SharePoint sites
- Configure logging and auditing behavior
- Configure antivirus applications

The SharePoint Central Administration application is the core piece in the administration infrastructure. It has been rewritten to provide central management and configuration for MOSS. For instance, administrative changes made to one server in the farm are automatically propagated to the rest of the farm. The automatic synchronization and propagation is handled by two services, Windows SharePoint Services Administration service and Windows SharePoint Services Timer service. The SharePoint Shared Services option allows you to manage most aspects of Excel Services, so you should become very familiar with it.

For the server piece, installation and configuration of IIS enables the Excel Services piece on the WFE to forward requests to the Excel Calculation Service on the application server. The Excel Services component cannot be used if IIS is not present or is configured incorrectly.

Caution   This book is not designed as a SharePoint tutorial. The focus of the book is .NET development with Excel Services. However, where applicable, certain pieces of SharePoint administration might be covered if these pieces enable functionality in Excel Services. A suitable book for SharePoint is *Microsoft Office SharePoint Server Administrator's Companion* (Microsoft Press, 2007).

Excel Services Permissions

Administrative control extends to workbook resources that are being used in the Excel Services application. For instance, you can limit the use of clients to view-only mode for shared workbooks. Or you can restrict client access to open, interact, and calculate workbooks while preventing the end user from viewing the file source or formulas in the workbook. Configuring permissions for all these activities follows the same procedure and forms part of the administrator's responsibility.

As an IT support person or a site administrator, you have no obligation to understand the programming details for the applications that run on Excel Services. However, you need to be able to author and enforce policy that will allow these applications to run and execute underneath an umbrella of security within an enterprise. If you are a developer in an enterprise organization, there should be a dedicated resource specialized in SharePoint administration and configuration so that you needn't be too concerned about these parts.

For small to medium shops where one developer wears several hats, it's absolutely crucial to understand administration and configuration options. To that extent, the various administrative tools and configuration options put you in the driver's seat. These tools are designed with flexibility and ease of use in mind. There's also a healthy dose of documentation to help you get up to speed in the shortest possible time. You will get a feel for configuration as we walk through code examples later.

Installation Walk-Through

The SharePoint Central Administration application is the core piece in the administration infrastructure. It has been rewritten to provide central management and configuration for MOSS. For instance, administrative changes made to one server in the farm are automatically propagated to the rest of the farm.

Caution   MOSS deployment requires an account with local administrative privileges at the domain level. This account will also be used to access configuration database changes when Web pages are being assembled. The account being used as your database account will need permissions to run as a service as well because some critical services will run under this account. For MOSS to install and work correctly, you need to remove those restrictions if your group policy explicitly prevents it.

Let's get started with the installation. Run the setup application to invoke the installation wizard. During the installation process, you need to choose between Basic and Advanced installation options, as shown in Figure 1-5.

About Configuration Options

Figure 1-5 shows the configuration options available during setup.

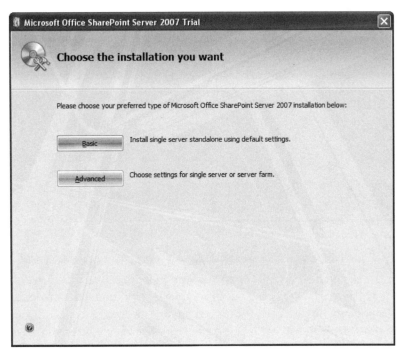

Figure 1-5   Installation choices during setup.

The Basic option installs as a single, standalone server using default settings on the target machine. You are not prompted for any configuration settings or credentials. These default configurations are also used if you repair, upgrade, or select the standalone option from the Advanced installation option. For this option, a special Windows database MSSEE (Microsoft SQL Server Embedded Edition) is installed.

There are no further options to consider after choosing the Basic installation option. You should consider this option if you do not have a licensed version of SQL Server, do not care for account credentials configuration, or are evaluating the software. As of this release, MOSS supports only databases from the SQL Server family of products. Figure 1-6 shows the server type settings during installation.

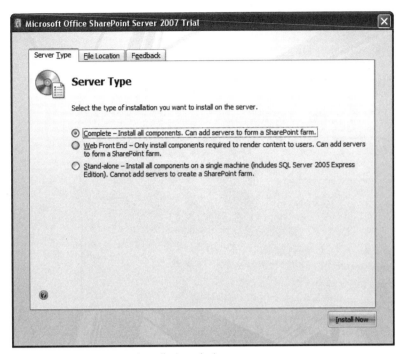

Figure 1-6 Server type installation choices.

The Advanced option allows you to install the components for a single server or for a server farm. There are three options present: Complete, Web Front End, and Stand-Alone. These options are self-explanatory. During installation, you will be prompted for credentials. You should note that even in the case of the Advanced options, the components can run with full functionality against the SQL Server Embedded Edition. The wizard will finalize the installation without further input. If errors are encountered during the installation process, the files are not rolled back. You need to rerun the setup application after diagnosing the problem. A log file is written that provides detailed messages of the error. The error dialog box indicates the path of the log file stored on disk. Figure 1-7 shows an example of a failed configuration.

With the installation of MOSS complete, the installation wizard will immediately launch the SharePoint Products And Technologies (SPPT) Configuration Wizard. The wizard walks you through configuring Windows SharePoint Services 3.0 to complete the installation of MOSS 2007. WSS is the focus of Chapter 5.

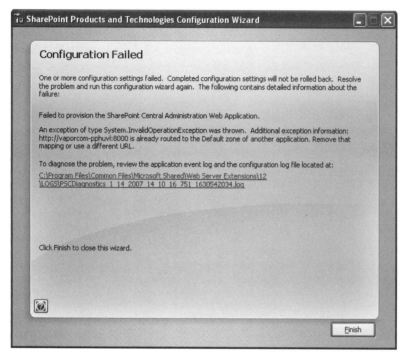

Figure 1-7   Failed configuration dialog box.

About the SharePoint Products And Technologies Configuration Wizard

The SharePoint Products And Technologies Configuration Wizard must run to start SharePoint Central Administration. The wizard performs the following functions:

- Initial configuration
- Identification of missing components
- Configuration validation and repair
- Security reset

The configuration wizard might have to start, stop, or reset the SharePoint Administration service, the SharePoint Timer service, Internet Information Services (IIS), and services from other applications that depend on Windows SharePoint Services and are appropriately registered. You can run the wizard from the Start menu at any time from the Microsoft Office Server menu group.

Part of the wizard install process involves database configuration. During database configuration, you have the option to configure database settings. The fields are self-explanatory. If the database name does not exist, one is created for you. If the database name exists, it must not contain tables; otherwise, an error dialog box will inform you of the problem.

If you are installing the Advanced option (shown in Figure 1-6) but do not have a valid or licensed copy of SQL Server 2000 or SQL Server 2005, you can point the SPPT Configuration Wizard to the SQL Server Embedded Edition by entering the name of the database server as **\##SSEE** (SQL Server Embedded Edition). Be aware though that, as pointed out earlier, a number of limitations are imposed on MSSEE. Figure 1-8 shows the configuration database settings dialog box.

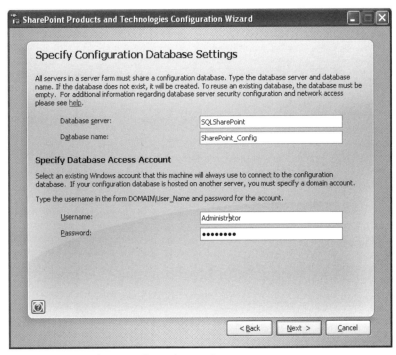

Figure 1-8   Database configuration options.

About the Configuration Database

The configuration database is used to store configuration and site-mapping information for your server farm. There is exactly one configuration database per server farm whether or not the server farm consists of one machine or several machines. If you are creating a new configuration database, provide the name of the database to the configuration wizard. If an existing database is used, it must not contain any tables, stored procedures, or other objects; otherwise, a duplication error will occur. You might also notice that the various database tables contain GUIDs. The naming convention enforces the fact that you should not be tampering with those tables except through the Excel Services object model.

If you are connecting to an existing configuration database, you can click Retrieve Database Names. The configuration databases that exist on the computer running SQL Server will be listed, and you can choose the appropriate configuration database. This option is not available if you elect to create a new database server. If the configuration database is hosted on a different computer, you must provide the credentials for a domain account. A domain account is recommended so that you can scale vertically.

For configuration databases hosted on domain accounts, you need a unique domain user account that you can specify as the Windows SharePoint Services version 3 service account. This user account is used to access the configuration database. The database access account will be used for both initial database configuration and ongoing connections.

The unique user account that you create also acts as the application pool identity for the SharePoint Central Administration application pool. This is the same account under which the Windows SharePoint Services Timer service runs. The SharePoint Products And Technologies Configuration Wizard adds this account to the SQL Server Logins, the SQL Server Database Creator server role, and the SQL Server Security Administrators server role.

After database provisioning is complete, the wizard allows you to perform port configuration. Figure 1-9 shows the Central Administration Web Application page, which allows you to configure a port.

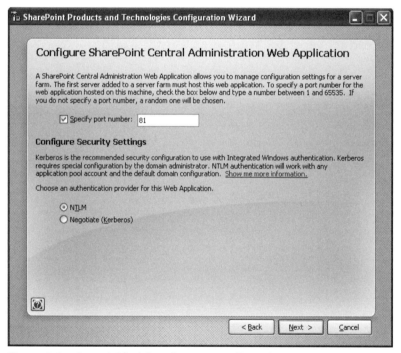

Figure 1-9   Central Administration port configuration.

Database Permissions Configuration

The database access account requires the following permissions:

- Security Administrator
- Database Creator
- Database Owner

You need to manually configure these permissions in SQL Server. The configuration wizard does not perform these configurations.

The account that you specify for database access must have the following minimum permissions:

- Read/write access to the configuration database
- Server-wide permissions in SQL Server
- DBO permissions

For new configuration databases, the database access account must have the following permissions:

- Create Database
- Create Procedure

SharePoint Products and Technologies Configuration

At this point, SPPT runs and configures a predetermined set of tasks, as shown in Figure 1-10.

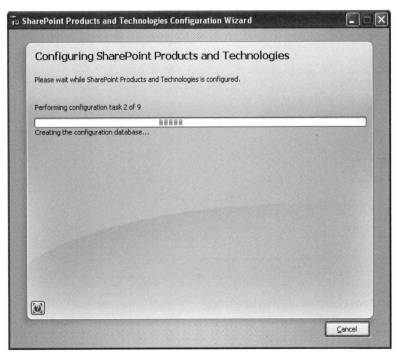

Figure 1-10 Configuration of SharePoint Products and Technologies.

The SharePoint Products And Technologies Configuration Wizard performs a number of functions. It examines the system for legacy SharePoint products, prompts for use of the prescan tool, and exits if it detects legacy components. It configures database access for use with MOSS 2007. The wizard also installs and configures various features and services for use. These services and features include the Excel Calculation Service and document management library. The wizard configures security and provides the hook for the Central Administration Wizard to customize site security and configuration at run time. The wizard also creates sample data for use in Business Intelligence scenarios. As a result of the changes that need to be made on your system, the account running SPPT must be a member of the administrator group.

> **Note**   Before performing an upgrade, you must run the prescan tool. You can run the prescan tool at a command prompt by typing **c:\program files\common files\shared\web server extensions\12\bin\prescan.exe /all**. The scan can take anywhere from a few minutes to several hours, depending on the size of the farm.

When the wizard is finished, one of three possible messages is displayed. The Configuration Complete dialog box indicates that the required configuration tasks have been completed and Central Administration is available and ready for use. The Configuration Successful dialog box indicates that the required configuration tasks have been successfully completed with no errors. If it hasn't, an error dialog box appears informing you that the wizard was not successful.

When setup is finished, your machine contains a single Web application. That Web application contains a single SharePoint site collection that hosts a SharePoint site. You can use the Central Administration utility discussed shortly to create more SharePoint site collections, sites, and Web applications.

For Basic installation, Central Administration is invoked automatically after this dialog box is dismissed. For Advanced installation, a dialog appears confirming the settings that were applied during the configuration process. If you need to rerun the SPPT Configuration Wizard, click Start | Programs | Administrative Tools | SharePoint Products And Technologies (SPPT) Configuration Wizard.

If you choose to uninstall the product by using the Windows Add Or Remove Program option, the SPPT Configuration Wizard is invoked in silent mode. If an error occurs during silent mode, the failure code is returned to SPPT and the Configuration Failed dialog box is displayed. If you exit setup after an error is displayed, the target machine will contain the configuration up to this point—that is, no rollback will be performed.

After installation is complete, the Central Administration (CA) Web application is invoked. The CA allows you to manage configuration settings for a server farm.

Note The CA contains several tabs and links, including the My Site tab. The My Site site is a personal site that individual team members can use to store personal information. It is not shared with other members.

When the Central Administration virtual server and site have been created, they are assigned a random port number between 1023 and 32767. To access the Central Administration site remotely, you must know this port number. You can use the stsadm.exe command-line utility to view or change the administration port number.

The CA Configuration dialog box allows you to configure the security aspects and assigned port for the CA Web application. Although Kerberos is the recommended security setting, it requires special configuration. The Kerberos configuration document for Windows Server 2003 is located at *http://www.microsoft.com/windowsserver2003/technologies/security/kerberos/default.mspx*. In any case, most enterprise installations can safely use NTLM authentication. Figure 1-11 shows the Central Administration home page.

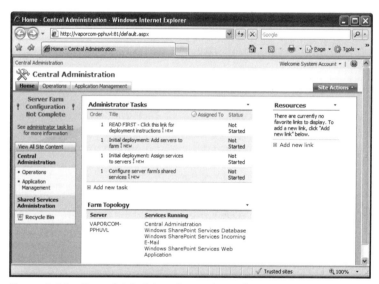

Figure 1-11   Central Administration Web application.

The CA is the main tool for MOSS 2007 configuration. The key parts of the CA are the Central Administration and Shared Services Administration menus on the left; the Home, Operations, and Application Management tabs toward the top; and the Site Actions menu to the far right. These menus allow an administrator to find and configure every service and feature installed on a specific machine or across a farm.

Note This book is not designed as a CA tutorial. Instead, the material is designed to teach you configuration aspects as they apply to the supporting code that you will write from .NET. In any case, the configuration aspects are more than sufficient to provide you with working knowledge about the CA and SharePoint.

Configuration of Excel Services

At this point in the installation, Excel Services is not provisioned on the server. The next few steps involve configuration and provisioning of the Excel Services feature. The configuration options detailed here will use the CA exclusively, so it is important that the CA is running correctly. As an alternative, MOSS provides stsadm.exe, which gives you another way to configure and provision SharePoint.

From the CA home page, you note that there are administrative tasks to be performed upon first use. The main task to be performed is the provisioning of the Shared Service Provider (SSP). The best way to understand the concept of the SSP is through the "grape analogy." Consider a bunch of grapes on a stalk, each drawing nutrients from the main vine. That particular organization lends itself well to the proper distribution of nutrients from the main vine to the grapes attached to the stalk.

Within the context of the MOSS architecture, the grapes are actually portals containing Web sites and subsites, as numerous as the grapes on the stalk. The stalk is the SSP. It is responsible for servicing the needs of the grapes in a manner that will allow the grapes to grow without being starved for resources. Similarly, the SSP provides a set of shared services to the portals and Web sites so that they can service end user requests in an efficient manner. The SSP provides Reporting Services, Personalization Services, Business Data Catalog Services infrastructure, Search Services, and Excel Services. Figure 1-12 shows an illustration of the SharePoint architecture.

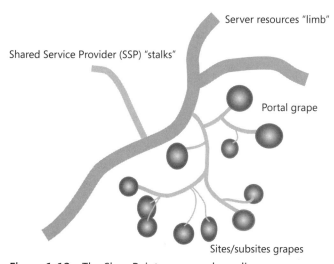

Server resources "limb"

Shared Service Provider (SSP) "stalks"

Portal grape

Sites/subsites grapes

Figure 1-12 The SharePoint grape analogy diagram.

For each vine, several stalks might contain grapes. So too, in the MOSS architecture, several SSPs might exist, each servicing one or more portals. You can set up and configure multiple SSPs if you intend to manage different resources across a farm. Portals serviced by an SSP can provide only these services defined within the SSP, nothing else. A grape or portal can be serviced only by a single SSP. A bunch of grapes or site collections on a particular stalk or SSP consumes resources from that particular SSP. There is no way to physically limit the "nutrients" or network resources servicing the grapes or Web applications. However, you can impose restrictions using privacy policies if you need to. The concept of an SSP works particularly well if you need to govern content and resources for various Web sites within SharePoint. We will return to the grape analogy again in Chapter 5.

> **Tip**   As pointed out earlier, Windows SharePoint Services is an update and revision to SharePoint Team Services 1.0. WSS offers many improvements over SharePoint Team Services 1.0, several of which are detailed in the following sections.

About Provisioning Excel Services

So far, you have created the Central Administration site that governs access to all things SharePoint. The CA is hosted on the first server that is added to the farm. However, administrators don't typically develop and run code, developers do. We need to create and provision a new Web application either on this server or any other server in the farm for the express purpose of supporting the code that we will write for the rest of the chapters. This will be the team site. MOSS supports a large number of team sites, up to the resource limit of the server.

Security best practices recommend that you avoid deploying your applications to the administrative site. You also should not be running this new Web site under administrative privileges. When and if the text breaks with these recommendations, it does so sparingly and only for illustrative purposes.

One more thing to consider is that a link to the CA can be found in Administrative Tools in the Programs menu on Windows Server 2003. However, there is no quick link to the new team site you will create. Because these two sites, Central Administration and Team Site, aren't necessarily hosted on the same machine, you can create your own link to the team site. Or, if you prefer, you can reach the team site through the Shared Service Provider link on the Central Administration menu. This outlines the fundamental difference between the two sites, and it is very important for you to understand the difference between the two.

Let's provide a brief overview of the process before starting so that you have a sense of direction. We first need to create a Web application for the SharePoint site. IIS will direct client requests to this Web application. The Web application will contain the portal sites. Portal sites allow team members and users to log in, use Web Parts, and perform other activities.

Portal sites use resources that are provided by the Shared Service Provider, meaning that we first need to provision an SSP for the Web application and then create the first portal site.

Finally, just as the Central Administration site provides administrative functionality for SharePoint, the Web application that we are creating to hold the portal site also contains an administrative page. This page helps the administrator govern access to the portal. This administrative page is not necessarily related to the Central Administrative page or the account that runs the CA.

This new portal site should not be confused with the My Sites link on each page. The My Sites tab at the top of each page is a link to a special site that provides a personal space for each individual who is authenticated. This site is not accessible by other team members. A link to the My Sites page is available so that you can quickly jump to your personal space from any page in SharePoint. The next few steps walk you through the SSP and Web application provisioning steps.

To provision Excel Services, you need to first configure one or more SSPs. A number of dependent tasks need to be performed before you can provision an SSP. From the CA, select Operations. From the main window, select Services On This Server. Start the Excel Calculation Service. You also need to provision the search service. Click the Start button, and fill in the appropriate items, as shown in Figure 1-13.

Figure 1-13   Search provisioning and configuration.

Confirm that Excel Calculation Service is running by clicking Manage Farm Features on the Operations menu, as shown in Figure 1-14.

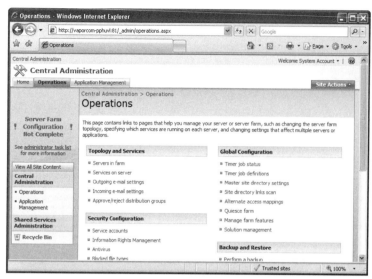

Figure 1-14   Farm session configuration option.

The Status column, shown in Figure 1-15, confirms whether the service is running.

Figure 1-15   Service confirmation.

Perform similar steps to confirm that the search service is running. SSP provisioning requires an active index. The active index is configured from the search service.

Next, click Shared Services Administration to begin provisioning the SSP. Select New on the tab at the top, and walk through the wizard. You need to create a central site and an administration site. The site creation is a straightforward process. Once the SSP is provisioned, click on the link in the left navigation menu.

Examine the options in this window to configure Excel Services for the farm. You might not be familiar with the short session and long session settings. Let's consider those. For efficiency reasons, calls from the front end are handled based on user sessions. These sessions have a time limit associated with them. If a request does not involve access to the spreadsheet, it is considered a short session and the time limit is adjusted downward to save on resources.

Otherwise, the session is adjusted upward based on the assumption that the user is interacting with the spreadsheet and should have a persistent session to the back end. This is the long session. Adjust these settings appropriately.

Troubleshooting   SharePoint Configuration Analyzer is a tool that you can download from the Microsoft Download Center to analyze and report on your Windows SharePoint Services installation and content. SharePoint Configuration Analyzer reports on a wide range of configuration issues, configuration files, and other data. The data is written to a results folder for further analysis or archiving.

About the Trusted File Location

While we are at this point, let's configure the trusted file location. A trusted file location is a secured repository for document storage and retrieval in MOSS 2007. You'll store your spreadsheets here and assign security access rights to these documents. The access rights extend to include the front-end and Web Service manipulation of the document. To configure the trusted file location, select Trusted File Locations from the Excel Services Settings menu. Figure 1-16 shows the Excel Services Settings menu.

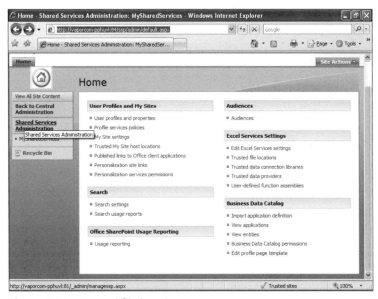

Figure 1-16   Trusted file location.

Use the server name and port information in your browser address bar to define a trusted file location. A good starting point is *%PROGRAMFILES%\common files\microsoft shared\Web server extensions\12\bin*. Click OK to save the information. The code you will write in Chapter 2 will load spreadsheets from this location because it is trusted.

If you are unfamiliar with SharePoint or get lost in the process, it might help to examine the breadcrumb trail at the top of the figures provided in this chapter. Every page on the CA contains a trail. These trails help you to determine where you are in the page hierarchy.

Don't be intimidated by the large number of settings and the different pages that make up the CA. As you progress through the book, you will gain hands-on experience with the various settings and pages. In any case, these various pages and settings are not that complicated, requiring only a moderate amount of effort to become functional in the administration and enterprise provisioning of a site. The CA was designed with ease of use in mind.

Unsupported Features and Limitations

Part of any evaluation process should cover unsupported features. Discovery of unsupported features can stall the adoption process or lead to a sour attitude aimed at the software. You are well aware that sour attitudes can inadvertently poison the enthusiasm of prospective clients. Let's walk through a short list of major unsupported features.

Although it is possible to copy the managed Excel assemblies to Windows XP Professional and compile Excel Services projects successfully, the run-time creation of the Excel Web Access object will fail. Excel Services was conceived to run on a server machine such as Windows Server 2003. Consumer operating systems such as Windows XP and Vista will not run MOSS. However, if you have downloaded and installed the Excel Services templates, you will be able to create projects that compile on any operating system. You will not be able to execute these assemblies, but you will be able to push these assemblies out to the server for deployment. Chapter 3 will talk more about this process.

Excel Services is not designed to author Excel workbooks. To author workbooks, you need to use the desktop version of Excel. Excel Services simply provides access to these authored workbooks and enforces the security constraints baked into the workbooks. Bear this in mind when you evaluate MOSS.

The Central Administration Web application does not provide configurations for the entire MOSS feature set. The complete configuration for the entire MOSS feature set is provided by the stsadm.exe tool. For default installations, the tool is available at *%PROGRAMFILES%\ common files\shared\Web server extensions\12\bin*. The stsadm.exe tool provides command-line administration for SharePoint 2007. If you need to run batch files or scripts, you need to use the stsadm.exe tool. Help for this tool is provided at the command prompt by typing **stsadm.exe /?**. Chapter 2 touches on the points of MOSS that are necessary for deployment and Web Parts.

Excel Services does not support external references in cells. The workaround for this is to implement user-defined functions (UDFs), which are discussed in Chapter 4 and Chapter 7. UDFs can be used to perform a wide variety of tasks, such as calling Web Services, calling external libraries, and so on and so forth.

Finding the Web Application Root

When MOSS is installed, the Internet Information Services application is extended to include Windows SharePoint Services. The extended Web application contains a root that maps to a Uniform Resource Identifier (URI). However, the majority of SharePoint Services functionality is stored in a content database and not in the root site or in the file structure of the Web application. Chapter 5 will discuss this in more detail. For now, note that the root does contain some files to include the *web.config*, user controls, Web Part definition files, and any other resources specific to the Web application.

In some cases, the resulting Web page is therefore a combination of content from the file structure and from the content database with a physical location pointing to *<Drive>:\inet-pub\wwwroot\wss\virtualdirectories\<guid>*. There might be two or more <guid> directories in the virtual directory. One guid represents the Central Administration, and the other represents the default content application. The <guid> provides no easy way to differentiate between the two from the administrator's perspective.

Follow these steps to determine the Web application root directory:

1. At a command prompt, enter **inetmgr**.

2. Expand the Websites node.

3. Right-click the Web application in question.

4. Note the path from the home directory, as shown in Figure 1-17.

This set of steps comes in handy for Web Part deployment, so be sure to familiarize yourself with it.

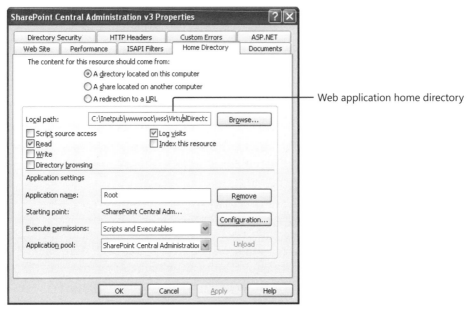

Web application home directory

Figure 1-17   Determining the Web application root from IIS.

Summary

Excel Services is a new technology built and conditioned to interact with Excel spreadsheets. One of the defining points of this new technology is that it is designed to use Office SharePoint Server 2007. The programmable parts of Excel Services are hooked into the .NET Framework so that Web Parts can be created to run on SharePoint.

The decision to use SharePoint as a platform for Excel Services, coupled with the extensibility hooks available through the .NET Framework, means that you need to be at least familiar with the basic principles of SharePoint configuration and management. The chapter presented the key parts that you should be familiar with. In any case, configuration and management can be learned without too much effort. You also need to possess more than a passing knowledge of .NET Framework security and customization concepts to tame this brute. And what a brute it is! Applications written for Excel Services can support large numbers of concurrent connections with internal load-balancing capabilities in clustered environments across a server farm.

Lessons learned from the past strongly influenced Microsoft's decision to use MOSS as a platform for Excel Services. MOSS is mature, configurable, scalable, and secure. The symbiotic relationship means that Excel Services essentially derives these significant benefits without an added burden. All in all, Excel Services is an innovative stride forward built to avoid the missteps of past endeavors. Developing Office applications that are well behaved has become progressively easier. And there's still more progress to be made. With the installation basics out of the way, it's time to write code!

Chapter 2
Excel Web Services

In Chapter 1, "An Introduction to Excel Services," some time was spent examining the Excel Web Services architecture. In this chapter, the focus is more on the technical aspects. The material is designed to strengthen your foundation by taking you through some simple exercises to get your feet wet. Once you are comfortable with the basics, you do some heavy lifting. Along the way, ample doses of theory will be interwoven to complement the practical approach.

An Introduction to Excel Web Services

The Excel Web Services (EWS) service is a server component that provides programmatic access to Excel Services. EWS is implemented as a standard .NET Web service hosted in SharePoint that allows Simple Object Access Protocol (SOAP) clients to discover and invoke Excel Services methods.

EWS decouples the front-end client from the back-end engine. That type of design pattern has proven to be effective time and again. In fact, the design pattern is prevalent in Service Oriented Architectures (SOA). With this decoupled architecture, any SOAP client can hook into the back-end infrastructure.

Tip Excel Web Services exposes most of the functionality of the object model to SOAP clients. Some important functionality related to security is not available through EWS. Chapter 5, "Windows SharePoint Services 3.0," will provide more details.

And you don't need to be a seasoned expert on design patterns either to realize that separating functionality into logical pieces makes for easier design and maintenance. Decoupling opens up a door of possibilities that can only lead to development of more sophisticated applications that meet real-world demands.

Imagine a front end built on a Java platform that calls into Microsoft Office SharePoint Server (MOSS) 2007 via EWS. These are very real-world requirements that are pervasive, especially in financial institutions and the telecom industry. Until now, SharePoint was unable to provide a solution to this problem domain, resulting in developers rolling their own code. Now, with the release of MOSS, businesses have an enterprise solution to an age-old problem.

Installing and Configuring Excel Web Services

Recall that the infrastructure that supports Excel Web Services is available only in the enterprise version of MOSS 2007. To install the enterprise version, see the installation guide for Chapter 1. Assuming that you have the enterprise version installed and ready to go, you first need to configure access to the Excel Web service. EWS installs on the target machine and exposes functionality through the *excelservice.asmx* file located in *<Drive>:\<servername>\ <site>_vti_bin\excelservice.asmx*.

> **More Info**   If you have dabbled with Web services before, you should be familiar with .asmx files and Web Services Description Language (WSDL) documents. WSDL documents simply describe the Web service functionality available to the client. You access the WSDL document by appending the ?WSDL keyword to the end of the Uniform Resource Identifier (URI) where the Web service is located.

There are two ways to access the Web service. You can access it through the URI by passing in the appropriate query string parameters. This approach is ideal for high-level languages and scripting approaches such as PHP, VBScript, or JavaScript. Or you can access the object model directly.

Creating a Simple Excel Web Services SOAP Client Project

One of the better ways to understand EWS is to write code to exercise the model. Let's create a HelloWorld application based on a Microsoft Windows Console Application template from Microsoft Visual Studio. First, you need to create a Visual Studio 2005 console application. Name the project **EWSHello**, as shown in Figure 2-1, which shows a Console Application template.

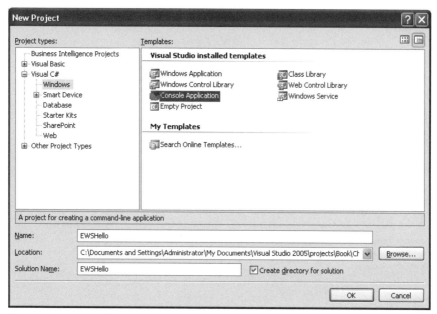

Figure 2-1   Console Application template.

Add a reference to EWS by using Visual Studio, as shown in Figure 2-2, which shows the Add Web Reference dialog box in Visual Studio .NET.

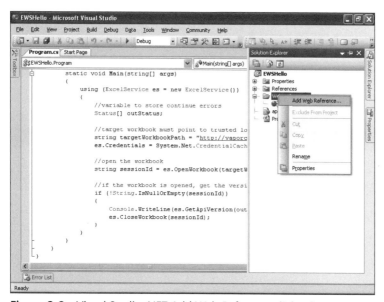

Figure 2-2   Visual Studio .NET Add Web Reference dialog box.

Locate the *ExcelService* method in the right window. In the Add Reference text box, enter the name **ExcelWebservice**.

> **Important**   It's quite possible to find more than one method named *ExcelService*. This can occur if you have installed and uninstalled MOSS a few times. You must select the one that matches the name of the site where you want to access the Web services.

Click Add Reference to dismiss the dialog box. Add code to invoke the Web service. The complete code is provided in Listing 2-1.

Listing 2-1   A HelloWorld Excel Web Services service.

```csharp
C# Snippet
using System;
using EWSHello.ExcelWebservice;
using System.Web.Services.Protocols;

namespace EWSHello
{
    class Program
    {
        static void Main(string[] args)
        {
            ExcelWebservice.ExcelService es = new ExcelService();
            //variable to store continue errors
            Status[] outStatus;
            string sheetName = "Sheet1";
            string targetWorkbookPath = "http://<servername:port>/Shared%20Documents/
              TestBook.xlsx";
            es.Credentials = System.Net.CredentialCache.DefaultNetworkCredentials;
            string sessionId = es.OpenWorkbook(targetWorkbookPath, "en-US",
              "en-US", out outStatus);
            object[] rangeResult1 = es.GetApiVersion(sessionId, sheetName,
              rangeCoordinates, false, out outStatus);
                es.CloseWorkbook(sessionId);
        }
    }
}
```

```vbnet
Visual Basic Snippet
Imports System
Imports EWSHello.ExcelWebservice
Imports System.Web.Services.Protocols
Module EWSHello
    Friend Class Program
        Shared Sub Main()
            Using es As ExcelWebservice.ExcelService = New ExcelService()
                'variable to store continue errors
                Dim outStatus As Status()

                'target workbook must point to trusted location
                Dim targetWorkbookPath As String =
                  "http://<servername:port>/Shared%20Documents/TestBook.xlsx"
                es.Credentials = System.Net.CredentialCache.DefaultNetworkCredentials
```

```
                     'open the workbook
                     Dim sessionId As String
                     sessionId = es.OpenWorkbook(targetWorkbookPath, "en-US",
                        "en-US", outStatus)

                     'if the workbook is opened, get the version of the Webservice
                     If (Not String.IsNullOrEmpty(sessionId)) Then
                         Console.WriteLine(es.GetApiVersion(outStatus))
                         es.CloseWorkbook(sessionId)
                     End If
               End Using
          End Sub
     End Class
End Module
```

A short code walk-through is appropriate. The first line of code creates an object that represents the Web service. If the call fails, an exception is thrown; otherwise, the object *es* holds a reference to the Web service proxy. Next a file path to the workbook is assigned. The path to the document must lead to a trusted location; otherwise, the EWS *OpenWorkbook* method call will fail. Workbooks can be loaded only from trusted locations.

The next line of code in the example populates a *CredentialCache* object. We will describe the *Credentials* object in greater detail later. For now, you should note that credentials are required with SOAP clients for EWS calls to be successful, even though default credentials are used.

Finally, note that the *outStatus* variable holds error information associated with the call. We defer a more detailed discussion of status objects for later in this chapter. For now, we note that the code should at least check the *outStatus* variable to see whether an error occurred. After the plumbing is constructed, the HelloWorld application simply calls the *GetApiVersion* method passing in the *outStatus* variable.

Configuring Workbooks for Programmatic Access

The code, as presented, will not run because a workbook does not exist at the location pointed to by the URI: *http://<servername:port>/Shared%20Documents/TestBook.xlsx*. A workbook will not be created to service the request; Excel Services is not designed to author workbooks. Each workbook must be created and provisioned ahead of time by a knowledge worker or administrator.

Warning   Excel Services is designed to enforce workbook security through the object model and Web service application programming interface (API). Settings applied to a workbook cascade to all callers and SOAP clients locally and remotely. As such, Excel Services cannot be used to circumvent the security that the workbook's creator specified.

Open Office Excel 2007. Save the new spreadsheet to the document library that was configured in Chapter 1. This should be the same path used in the code example just shown. This path, minus the file, points to a trusted location. EWS will be able to load and save any document with an *.xlsx* (normal spreadsheet) or *.xlsb* (spreadsheet with binary data) extension in that location. Documents with any other extension will result in an exception.

Finally, let's confirm that the workbook in the trusted location has the appropriate permissions. Navigate to Central Administration (CA), select your Shared Service Provider (SSP), and choose Trusted File Locations. You should see the new document listed. Verify that the permissions resemble those listed in Figure 2-3. By tweaking these settings, you can control access to the document. EWS enforces these permissions at run time. Figure 2-3 shows the Excel Services trusted file locations.

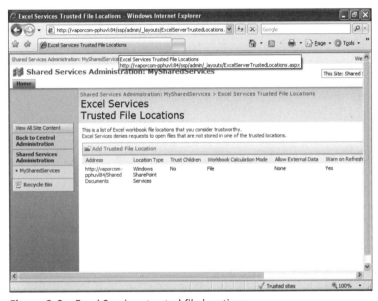

Figure 2-3   Excel Services trusted file locations.

Press F5 to exercise the application. The output in the console window should read "Excel Web Services (12)". The important points to remember are as follows:

- Excel Services can connect only to workbooks that contain valid worksheets.

- Excel Services cannot author spreadsheets or workbooks.

- The workbooks must have an .xlsx or .xlsb extension.

- The workbooks must reside on the MOSS server in the trusted file location with the appropriate permissions.

- The Internet Information Services (IIS) server must have the Office Web Server Services service running.

- Permissions that are applied to the workbook are enforced by EWS at run time.

You'd be surprised to learn that the vast majority of issues can usually be resolved by sticking firmly to the simple rules just outlined.

Guidelines for Developing EWS Applications

Let's have a short discussion about the dangers lurking behind this simple exercise; it's part of the learning process. First, if your custom application is being run on the same machine where the *ExcelService.asmx* file resides, the code approach presented here will be suboptimal at best. The reason for this is that significant overhead is involved in calling a local service through a remote SOAP invocation. Instead, you should link directly to the Web service assembly; it exposes the same functionality except that the call is local. Direct linking is discussed in more detail next.

> **Warning**   By design, a Web application services, at most, two concurrent connections by default. The limit is imposed by RFC 2068 specifications. There's a very good reason for that specification. Because a Web service connects over HTTP, the limit applies to the Web services as well. Web service applications can be called by any SOAP client, so it's quite possible that the upper limit can be exceeded. The following code will ease the restriction:
>
> ```
> <connectionManagement>
>     <add address="*" maxconnection="2">
>     <add address="localhost_ip_address" maxconnection="10">
> </connectionManagement>
> ```
>
> Place the snippet in the *Web.config* file for Web applications or the *application.exe.config* file for other types of applications.

Even with a fairly liberal dose of concurrent connections, EWS applications can still experience performance degradation. The reason for this is largely because long-running requests, such as calculation invocations against a large spreadsheet, can cause connections to remain open for a considerable period of time. During peak load, it's easy to overflow the maximum connection limit. There's no bulletproof way to avoid this situation except to be prudent about long-running calls. Setting a very large limit on the maximum connections is also an unwise strategy because there is an increased risk of resource exhaustion.

Be aware that testing configuration settings—such as the *maxconnection* presented earlier—against localhost might fail to uncover noticeable performance issues. The reason is that localhost does not impose any upper limit on the number of simultaneous connections. However, when the code is deployed to production and a server name other than localhost is used (the actual name of the server for instance), the RFC 2068 specification limitation is enforced. You might then start to experience connection issues and performance degradation under load that you did not experience during the testing phase. The important point to understand here is that the configuration file tweak needs to be tested in an environment that approximates the production environment.

EWS Direct Linking

Recall that we discussed avoiding using the Web service invocation locally. The reason for this recommendation is that .NET applications use a thread pool to handle client requests. A thread pool has a limited number of available threads that service client applications. However, this same thread pool also handles Web service requests. In this scenario, the Web pool is performing double duty, servicing client calls from a SOAP client and servicing EWS calls because the client and the Web service live on the same machine. It's easy to see why the thread pool can be depleted under even moderate amounts of load.

The remedy for this ailment is EWS Direct-Linking. Let's consider a detailed example that mirrors the previous exercise with the exception that a local reference is used instead of a reference to the SOAP Web service. First, create a project called **DirectLink** based on a Windows Console Application template. From the property pages, choose the Add Reference item. Select the Browse tab, and navigate to *<Drive>:\Program Files\Common Files\Shared\Web server extensions\12\ISAPI\Webservice.dll*. The assembly can also be found in the global assembly cache (GAC), as shown in Figure 2-4.

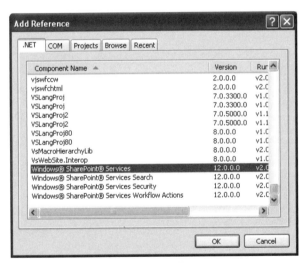

Figure 2-4   Local Web service reference.

Modify the previous code so that it looks like the code in Listing 2-2.

Listing 2-2   Direct-Linking call to a Web service.

```
C# Snippet
using System;
using .Office.Excel.Server.WebServices;
namespace DirectLink
{
    public partial class _Default : System.Web.UI.Page
    {
        protected void Page_Load(object sender, EventArgs e)
```

```
        {
            ExcelService es = new ExcelService();
            //variable to store continue errors
            Status[] outStatus;
            //target workbook must point to trusted location
            string targetWorkbookPath = "http://<servername:port>/Shared%20Documents/
              TestBook.xlsx";
            //open the workbook
            string sessionId = es.OpenWorkbook(targetWorkbookPath,
              "en-US", "en-US", out outStatus);
            //if the workbook is opened, get the version of the Webservice
            if (!String.IsNullOrEmpty(sessionId))
            {
                outStatus = null;
                Console.WriteLine(es.GetApiVersion(out outStatus));
                es.CloseWorkbook(sessionId, out outStatus);
            }
        }
    }
}
```

Visual Basic Snippet

```
Imports System
Imports .Office.Excel.Server.WebServices
Partial Class _Default
    Inherits System.Web.UI.Page
    Protected Sub Page_Load(ByVal sender As Object, ByVal e As EventArgs)
        Dim es As ExcelService = New ExcelService()
        'variable to store continue errors
        Dim outStatus As Status()
        'target workbook must point to trusted location
        Dim targetWorkbookPath As String = "http:// <servername:port>/
          Shared%20Documents/TestBook.xlsx"
        'open the workbook
        Dim sessionId As String = es.OpenWorkbook(targetWorkbookPath,
          "en-US", "en-US", outStatus)
        'if the workbook is opened, get the version of the Webservice
        If (Not String.IsNullOrEmpty(sessionId)) Then
            outStatus = Nothing
            Console.WriteLine(es.GetApiVersion(outStatus))
            es.CloseWorkbook(sessionId, outStatus)
        End If
    End SubEnd Class
```

A couple things should stand out. Starting with the assemblies imported, we no longer need to import the protocols assembly because this is no longer a SOAP client invocation. There is no need to use the *Credentials* object because it is SOAP dependent. You will notice also that the *CloseWorkbook* method now takes an extra object parameter and returns a type of void. We talk more about this parameter in Chapter 4, "Excel Calculation Service."

Finally, you might notice a significant performance boost on the order of a magnitude or more. Bear this in mind when trying to decide whether or not to build an architecture based on Direct-Linking. That sort of boost makes it feasible to write applications that rely on artificial intelligence, such as game programming or financial applications that rely on real-time data analytics.

Guidelines for Developing Direct-Linking Applications

As is usually the case, you need to be aware of some issues in the code. The code presented compiles cleanly, but it will cause an exception when an object of type *ExcelServices* is created. The reason for this is that the code makes the assumption that a Direct-Linking example is being run on the SharePoint server. This assumption is almost always right and presents no major obstacles. However, a further assumption is being made—that is, the code will actually run in a SharePoint context.

The issue we run into here is that the code is created on the SharePoint server but it does not have a SharePoint context associated with it. Because of this, when the *ExcelServices* proxy object is instantiated, the run time will attempt to extract credential information from the SharePoint context to create the *ExcelService* object. The fix for this is to deploy the code to SharePoint either in a Web Part or to the _layout folder, where a valid SharePoint context can be obtained.

Finally, you should exercise the discipline to make use of the *using* construct whenever it is available. For instance, the *ExcelServices* object implements the *IDisposable* interface. The code should rightly employ a *using* construct so that the variable *es* is properly de-allocated at the end of scope.

EWS and Authored Spreadsheets

There is a good reason why the first EWS exercise only called *GetApiVersion*. Without explicitly providing increased permissions, clients can access only the *GetApiVersion* method in the EWS API. To gain extended access to the other methods, you need to configure the relevant permissions using the Shared Services Provider. We talk more about these security aspects in later chapters.

Caution   The URL property of an Excel Web Services proxy generated by Visual Studio points specifically to the Web service, not to any document.

Excel Services development on the .NET platform is about extensibility. .NET developers need to distance themselves from the build-from-scratch mentality that is so pervasive with developer frameworks. The next exercise reinforces these two points. Our programming effort will demonstrate how your .NET skills can be applied to Excel Services development. In addition, we crank up the coding effort a notch or two because you have a good grasp of the basics by now.

Extending the Simple EWS Client

The Office Web site has a few free Excel templates that contain functionality already built in. Conceptually, we pretend that these templates are prepared by our hotshot accountants in the analytics department. Much of your real-world development will follow this path of writing code to target an existing Excel spreadsheet stored in a trusted location, so it is well worth your while to get acquainted with this approach.

Open a browser window to this URI: *http://office.microsoft.com/en-us/templates/ TC062062871032.aspx*. Follow the instructions on the Web page to download and install the spreadsheet template. The template opens in a browser window similar to Figure 2-5, which shows an Excel spreadsheet template provisioned for calculating mortgages.

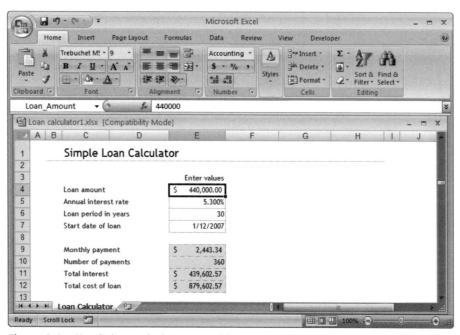

Figure 2-5   Simple loan calculator spreadsheet.

Get a feel for the spreadsheet application by entering some relevant values and viewing the computed results and payment schedules. Review the named ranges, formatting, and formulas that are programmed in. Pay special attention to the responsiveness and usability of the spreadsheet; we intend to focus on these a bit later. Our programming effort will involve extending the spreadsheet to a Windows client that uses EWS to perform the number crunching. We ignore the table containing the schedule of payments. For now, we focus on taking and mastering baby steps. We intend to revisit it after the exercise is complete.

To use the spreadsheet as the backbone for our Windows application, it will need to be placed in the trusted file location. Save the spreadsheet using an HTTP path similar to *http://servername:port/Shared documents/workbook.xlsx*. Review Chapter 1 if you need help storing worksheets to trusted file locations.

Create a new project based on a Windows Forms template. The Windows Forms representation looks like Figure 2-6. The form uses buttons, labels, and text boxes. Figure 2-6 shows a Windows application that is designed to call Excel Services.

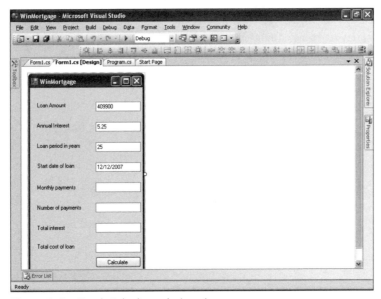

Figure 2-6 SimpleCalculator design view.

When you are done building the user interface, enter the code shown in Listing 2-3 into the *form1.cs* file.

Listing 2-3 Windows client code to connect to a Web service.

```csharp
C# Snippet
using System;
using System.Windows.Forms;
using WinMortgage.SimpleCalculator;
using System.Web.Services.Protocols;

namespace WinMortgage
{
    public partial class Form1 : Form
    {
```

```
        public Form1()
        {
            InitializeComponent();
        }
        static readonly string targetWorkbookPath = "http://<servername:port>/
          Shared Documents/Loan Calculator1.xlsx";

        private void Calculate_Click(object sender, EventArgs e)
        {
            using (SimpleCalculator.ExcelService es =
              new SimpleCalculator.ExcelService())
            {
                //set up the regular plumbing
                Status[] outStatus;
                es.Credentials = System.Net.CredentialCache.DefaultNetworkCredentials;
                string sessionId = es.OpenWorkbook(targetWorkbookPath, "en-US",
                  "en-US", out outStatus);
                if (!String.IsNullOrEmpty(sessionId))
                {
                    //use range terminology
                    es.SetCellA1(sessionId, string.Empty, "Loan_Amount",
                      paymentField.Text);
                    es.SetCellA1(sessionId, string.Empty, "Interest_Rate",
                      annualInterestField.Text);
                    es.SetCellA1(sessionId, string.Empty, "Loan_Years",
                      loanPeriodField.Text);
                    es.SetCellA1(sessionId, string.Empty, "Loan_Start",
                      startDateField.Text);
                    object[] monthlyPayment = es.GetRangeA1(sessionId, string.Empty,
                      "e9", true, out outStatus);
                    object[] numberPayments = es.GetRangeA1(sessionId, string.Empty,
                      "Number_of_Payments", true, out outStatus);
                    object[] totalInterest = es.GetRangeA1(sessionId, string.Empty,
                      "Total_Interest", true, out outStatus);
                    object[] costLoan = es.GetRangeA1(sessionId, string.Empty,
                      "Total_Cost", true, out outStatus);
                    monthlyPaymentsField.Text =
                      ((object[])monthlyPayment[0])[0].ToString();
                    numberPaymentsField.Text =
                      ((object[])numberPayments[0])[0].ToString();
                    totalInterestField.Text =
                      ((object[])totalInterest[0])[0].ToString();
                    totalCostField.Text = ((object[])costLoan[0])[0].ToString();
                }
            }
        }
    }
}
```

Visual Basic Snippet

```
Imports System
Imports WinMortgage.SimpleCalculator
Imports System.Web.Services.Protocols
Public Class Form1
    Private Shared ReadOnly targetWorkbookPath As String = "http:// <servername:port>/
      Shared Documents/Loan Calculator1.xlsx"
```

```
Private Sub Calculate_Click(ByVal sender As System.Object,
    ByVal e As System.EventArgs) Handles Calculate.Click
    Using es As SimpleCalculator.ExcelService = New
        SimpleCalculator.ExcelService()
        'set up the regular plumbing
        Dim outStatus As Status()
        es.Credentials = System.Net.CredentialCache.DefaultNetworkCredentials
            Dim sessionId As String = es.OpenWorkbook(targetWorkbookPath, "en-US",
                "en-US", outStatus)
            If (Not String.IsNullOrEmpty(sessionId)) Then
                'use range terminology
                es.SetCellA1(sessionId, String.Empty, "Loan_Amount",
                    paymentField.Text)
                es.SetCellA1(sessionId, String.Empty, "Interest_Rate",
                    annualInterestField.Text)
                es.SetCellA1(sessionId, String.Empty,  "Loan_Years",
                    loanPeriodField.Text)
                es.SetCellA1(sessionId, String.Empty, "Loan_Start",
                    startDateField.Text)
                Dim monthlyPayment As Object() = es.GetRangeA1(sessionId,
                    String.Empty, "e9", True, outStatus)
                Dim numberPayments As Object() = es.GetRangeA1(sessionId,
                    String.Empty, "Number_of_Payments", True, outStatus)
                Dim totalInterest As Object() = es.GetRangeA1(sessionId,
                    String.Empty, "Total_Interest", True, outStatus)
                Dim costLoan As Object() = es.GetRangeA1(sessionId, String.Empty,
                    "Total_Cost", True, outStatus)

                monthlyPaymentsField.Text = (CType(monthlyPayment(0),
                    Object()))(0).ToString()
                numberPaymentsField.Text = (CType(numberPayments(0),
                    Object()))(0).ToString()
                totalInterestField.Text = (CType(totalInterest(0),
                    Object()))(0).ToString()
                totalCostField.Text = (CType(costLoan(0), Object()))(0).ToString()
            End If
        End Using
    End Sub
End Class
```

From a high-level overview, the code simply invokes the calculation method on the target range. You'll notice that because we are using a named range, we can ignore the *sheetname* parameter. The named ranges are part of the original spreadsheet. The results are placed in a range A12, and the Web service simply queries that range. You should note also that the range address implicitly targets sheet1 of the active spreadsheet. If you wanted to target sheet2, you would need to qualify the range appropriately like so: *Sheet2!E9*. The syntax is case insensitive. Notice too that there is an ugly cast to extract the value out of the jagged array for each item being returned. That is simply unavoidable!

Finally, note that the returned values are formatted with appropriate currency notations that are localized for the current culture. Formatting is activated with the Boolean value of *true* passed in to the *GetRangeA1* method call. Formatting does not extend to cell styles—that is, cell coloring, font attributes, and custom styles are not returned. (See Figure 2-7.)

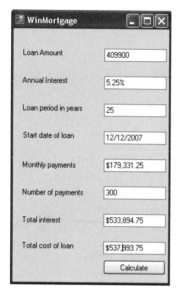

Figure 2-7   Simple loan calculator output.

In our code, we have blissfully indexed into object arrays without a shred of care. That type of code should never be allowed to grace a monitor's screen. Best practices recommend that you test objects both for null and for valid values before indexing into arrays.

Additionally, if you have noticed a bit of a lag, say a second or two, for the results to be returned, there are a few things to keep in mind. EWS needs a warm-up period. The initial call is always a lot slower than subsequent calls. The lag is a result of the setup of various data structures and initial population of cache stores. With subsequent runs, the performance should improve.

Analyzing EWS Behavior

EWS calls to the spreadsheet are blocking calls. By default, the call from the SOAP client waits as long as necessary for the response. If this is not particularly appealing to your design, you can choose to set the *timeout* property on the *ExcelService* proxy object. An exception is thrown if this timeout expires. EWS does offer asynchronous method access, but we will reserve a more detailed examination for Chapter 5. As an aside, it's important to understand that the proxy object is not the EWS; it simply contains information that allows the SOAP client to call methods available in the EWS.

EWS writes to the target range without regard to its contents. If it contains data, it is overwritten without prompting. It's easy to see why this approach is problematic—you stand to lose data in the current session if you are not careful. It would seem that one potential way to avoid this problem is to lock the range so that careless writes to the target will fail with access permissions exceptions.

> **Note**   In the Setup Configuration Wizard phase, MOSS provisioned a database with the naming convention *SharePoint_AdminContent_<guid>*. For flexibility, Excel Calculation Services can also open workbooks from UNC paths and HTTP Web sites as well. Unless you have a particularly good reason for doing so, you should avoid the UNC and HTTP Web site options. The reason is that Windows SharePoint Services 3.0 maintains an access control list (ACL) for database files so that they can be protected from unauthorized access.

Although this option is valid for other programming models, EWS offers no way to lock the range. If this is an application requirement, you can lock the range from a macro embedded in the spreadsheet. You can then trigger the macro by setting a value in an appropriate cell. In fact, this technique can be extended to add all sorts of functionality that is, in turn, triggered by an external client through EWS. This is one compelling reason why the EWS interface is lean. We will return to this scenario in Chapter 7, "Advanced Concepts with Excel Services."

To claim that EWS writes to the target range without regard to its contents is a mild contortion of the truth. There is a special case where EWS does care. If the target range contains a formula, EWS returns a *soapexception* with a message: "The requested operation attempted to overwrite the contents of cells that cannot be edited." There is no way to programmatically clear the contents of the spreadsheet, except through an embedded macro approach, as discussed earlier. You need to exercise a bit of judgment that includes judicious use of exception-handling code to guard against this condition. We talk more about exceptions at the end of this chapter. In addition, you can read about exception handling best practices at *http://msdn.microsoft.com/library/default.asp?url=/library/en-us/cpguide/html/ cpconbestpracticesforhandlingexceptions.asp*.

> **Note**   Excel Services opens workbooks in user sessions. These user sessions can be pooled across users with the same security access. Sessions that are not shared cannot possibly corrupt worksheets in other sessions. The issue is limited to sessions that are shared across a pool. Chapter 4 will provide a working example and more information.

Another welcomed addition is the fact that EWS implicitly understands formatted input and makes the appropriate adjustments automatically before proceeding with a calculation request. As an example, you can enter **0.03** or **3%** in the Windows application and EWS will return the correct answer. Or you can enter **January 3, 2007** in the date field and EWS will format the field to 01/03/2007 before performing the calculation.

If you care to experiment further, you can enter an invalid entry in one of the formatted cells, such as @409,900 for the loan amount. This entry causes an error in the spreadsheet version. In the Windows client, an exception is thrown in the calculation engine that is rewrapped and returned to the SOAP client as an Excel #ERROR. In all cases, the behavior is consistent across the Excel platform because EWS preserves the formatting integrity tied to the cell in the back-end spreadsheet.

What about performance? You might have noticed that the SOAP client call is orders of magnitude slower than the spreadsheet version. There's no magic pill for fixing this. A SOAP client call contains necessary overhead as the call travels across machine boundaries, and that overhead can add up to a performance drain. You should be mindful of this when deciding whether to use Excel Services rather than a simple published spreadsheet approach. For access that must execute within tight time constraints, such as game programming or real-time analytics, you should consider using the Direct-Linking approach instead of the Web service approach.

Binding EWS Data to .NET Controls

Recall that we did not implement the schedule of payments in our Windows client example. You can see the schedule of payments in your own copy of the spreadsheet—it is the table at the bottom of the spreadsheet. Have you given some thought to incorporating the schedule of payments into your Windows application? Arguably, there are a lot of ways to accomplish this. All approaches should focus on retrieving the range and displaying it in a suitable control. Let's review two approaches.

Approach 1: EWS with a *listbox*

This strategy involves enhancing the form to include a *listbox* control. Then you supply the necessary code to move the spreadsheet objects into the *listbox*. Listing 2-4 shows the relevant portion of code.

Listing 2-4   Binding EWS results to a *listbox* control.

```
C# Snippet
object[] schedulePayment = es.GetRangeA1(sessionId, string.Empty, "b15:h375", true,
   out outStatus);
if (schedulePayment.Length > 0)
{
    StringBuilder val = new StringBuilder();
    foreach (object[] rows in schedulePayment)
    {
        val.Length = 0;
        foreach (string columns in rows)
        {
            val.Append(columns).Append("\t");
        }
```

```
        listBox1.Items.Add(val.ToString());
    }
}
```
Visual Basic Snippet
```
Dim schedulePayment As Object() = es.GetRangeA1(sessionId, String.Empty, "b15:h375",
  True, outStatus)
If schedulePayment.Length > 0 Then
    Dim val As StringBuilder = New StringBuilder()
    For Each rows As Object In schedulePayment
        val.Length = 0
        For Each columns As String In rows
            val.Append(columns).Append(Constants.vbTab)
        Next columns
        listBox1.Items.Add(val.ToString())
    Next rows
End If
```

The spreadsheet returns cells in jagged arrays or arrays of arrays. The outer array contains objects representing rows in the spreadsheet. Each object in this row holds another array of objects that, in turn, hold references to the column cells in the spreadsheet. To iterate object arrays, you typically use a double nested loop construct. The "Assigning Values to Ranges" section earlier in the chapter walks you through an exercise on range manipulation with jagged arrays.

The range containing the results is static, so we can hard-code a target of B15:H375 based on our intimate knowledge of the spreadsheet. We then use a *stringbuilder* object to iterate the jagged array, appending a tab delimiter for formatting purposes. The code is fast and efficient but dreadfully ugly when compared to the Excel spreadsheet implementation, as we can see in Figure 2-8, which shows the results of an EWS invocation displayed in a *listbox* control.

What are the advantages of this approach? There are relatively few advantages, if any! In fact, we have actually lost the aesthetic appeal of the spreadsheet because the figures don't line up correctly in the *listbox* version and return junk for some values. That sort of output makes it difficult to work with numbers, especially for accountants. The application has added no supplemental functionality, not to mention it has introduced a noticeable dip in performance.

> **Tip**   Figure 2-8 adds a *listbox* control with a colored background. For accessibility programming, you should always make use of system colors and avoid custom or Web color palettes where possible so that accessible screen changes can cascade down to your control. Chapter 7 will focus more on accessibility programming with Excel Services.

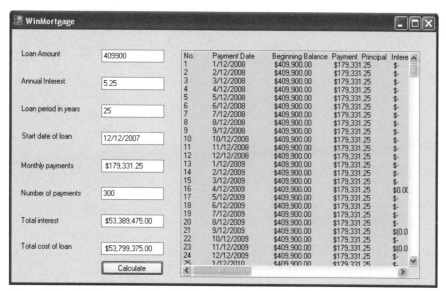

Figure 2-8   EWS results displayed in a *listbox* control.

Approach 2: EWS with a *DataGridView*

Bind a *DataGridView* object to the results of the EWS call. Consider the piece of code in Listing 2-5.

Listing 2-5   Binding EWS results to a *DataGridView* control.

```
C# Snippet
object[] schedulePayment = es.GetRangeA1(sessionId, string.Empty, "b15:h375", true,
  outStatus);
if (schedulePayment.Length > 0)
{
    DataSet ds = new DataSet();
    DataTable myDataTable = new DataTable("Schedule");
    ds.Tables.Add(myDataTable);
    DataRow myDataRow = null;
    DataColumn myDataColumn = null;
    int row = 0;
    while (row < schedulePayment.Length)
    {
        object[] col = schedulePayment[row] as object();
        myDataRow = myDataTable.NewRow();

        int column = 0;
        while (column < col.Length-1)
        {
            if (row == 0 && column == 0)
            {
                int i = 0;
                while (i < col.Length - 1)
                {
                    myDataColumn = new DataColumn();
```

```
                    //typeof(string) will work here as well
                    myDataColumn.DataType = System.Type.GetType("System.String");
                    myDataTable.Columns.Add(myDataColumn);
                    i += 1;
                }
            }
            myDataRow[column] = col[column].ToString();
            column += 1;
        }
        myDataTable.Rows.Add(myDataRow);
        row += 1;
    }

    dataGridView1.DataSource = ds;
    dataGridView1.DataMember = "Schedule";
}
```

Visual Basic Snippet

```
Dim schedulePayment As Object() = es.GetRangeA1(sessionId, String.Empty, "b15:h375",
  True, outStatus)
If schedulePayment.Length > 0 Then
    Dim ds As DataSet = New DataSet()
    Dim myDataTable As DataTable = New DataTable("Schedule")
    ds.Tables.Add(myDataTable)
    Dim myDataRow As DataRow
    Dim myDataColumn As DataColumn

    Dim row As Integer = 0
    Do While row < schedulePayment.Length
        Dim col As Object() = TryCast(schedulePayment(row), Object())
        myDataRow = myDataTable.NewRow()

        Dim column As Integer = 0
        Do While column < col.Length-1
            If row = 0 AndAlso column = 0 Then
                Dim i As Integer = 0
                Do While i < col.Length - 1
                    myDataColumn = New DataColumn()
                    'GetType(String) will work here as well
                    myDataColumn.DataType = System.Type.GetType("System.String")
                    myDataTable.Columns.Add(myDataColumn)
                    i += 1
                Loop
            End If

            myDataRow(column) = col(column).ToString()
            column += 1
        Loop
        myDataTable.Rows.Add(myDataRow)
        row += 1
    Loop

    dataGridView1.DataSource = ds
    dataGridView1.DataMember = "Schedule"
End If
```

The approach is basically the same, with the exception that we are binding to an intermediary data set first. We can extract the contents of the rows with a nested *for* loop. We perform the usual iteration for the outer loop to extract the array of cells that form the rows. Inside each row, we then iterate to extract the contents, building a data row as we go along.

> **Tip**   There's an *if* block inside the inner loop. Its purpose is to build the data columns of the *DataTable*. Ideally, we could have written a separate procedure to build the required columns first. However, this approach centralizes the code and is simple to understand. We only need to add data columns once. This is the reason for the check condition *row == 0 && column == 0*. Once the columns are built, we tack on rows as they are exposed through the looping mechanism.

A Comparison of Both Approaches

You'll notice that the *DataGridView* approach is marginally slower than the *listbox* approach, but it allows us more control for formatting the output. In fact, all the snazzy features of a *DataGridView* object are now available to the application, as shown in Figure 2-9. Compare this figure to Figure 2-8 to see the difference.

WinMortgage					
Loan Amount	409900	Column1	Column2	Column3	Column4
		No.	Payment Date	Beginning Balance	Payment
Annual Interest	5.25	1	1/12/2008	$409,900.00	$179,331.2
		2	2/12/2008	$409,900.00	$179,331.2
Loan period in years	25	3	3/12/2008	$409,900.00	$179,331.2
		4	4/12/2008	$409,900.00	$179,331.2
Start date of loan	12/12/2007	5	5/12/2008	$409,900.00	$179,331.2
		6	6/12/2008	$409,900.00	$179,331.2
Monthly payments	$179,331.25	7	7/12/2008	$409,900.00	$179,331.2
		8	8/12/2008	$409,900.00	$179,331.2
Number of payments	300	9	9/12/2008	$409,900.00	$179,331.2
		10	10/12/2008	$409,900.00	$179,331.2
Total interest	$53,389,475.00	11	11/12/2008	$409,900.00	$179,331.2
		12	12/12/2008	$409,900.00	$179,331.2
Total cost of loan	$53,799,375.00	13	1/12/2009	$409,900.00	$179,331.2
	Calculate				

Figure 2-9   The *DataGridView* implementation.

Aside from adding the dazzle and aesthetic appeal of the *DataGridView* object, we really haven't extended the application. It simply reproduces some of the functionality in the spreadsheet. The spreadsheet can do a whole lot more than our application, and it would take enormous coding effort to even approach what the spreadsheet delivers as default functionality. However, our aim is not to reproduce; rather, it is to extend. Always bear this in mind.

One extensible feature is to provide a paging infrastructure that remembers calculated schedules. The user can then navigate through these results much like the use of recordsets in ActiveX Data Object (ADO) days. The spreadsheet application doesn't even understand this concept. Yet it is a good feature, especially for what-if scenarios. Consider a mortgage calculator where you are plugging in rates. With the spreadsheet version, you need to make a note of each rate reading as you go along. With our new approach, you simply need to page through the historical results. The code approach for our new extensible model is shown in Listing 2-6.

Listing 2-6   Adding paging to the *DataGridView* control.

```csharp
C# Snippet
private void Next_Click(object sender, EventArgs e)
{
    if ((currentCount + 1) < listSchedules.Count)
    {
        dataGridView1.DataSource = listSchedules[++currentCount];
        dataGridView1.DataMember = "Schedule";
    }
}
private void Previous_Click(object sender, EventArgs e)
{
    if (currentCount > 0)
    {
        dataGridView1.DataSource = listSchedules[--currentCount];
        dataGridView1.DataMember = "Schedule";
    }
}
private void Start_Click(object sender, EventArgs e)
{
    if (currentCount > 0)
    {
        dataGridView1.DataSource = listSchedules[0];
        dataGridView1.DataMember = "Schedule";
        currentCount = 0;
    }
}
private void End_Click(object sender, EventArgs e)
{
    if (currentCount < listSchedules.Count)
    {
        int count = listSchedules.Count;
        dataGridView1.DataSource = listSchedules[listSchedules.Count - 1];
        dataGridView1.DataMember = "Schedule";
        currentCount = listSchedules.Count - 1;
    }
}
```

Visual Basic Snippet
```vb
Private Sub Next_Click(ByVal sender As Object, ByVal e As EventArgs)
If (currentCount + 1) < listSchedules.Count Then
    currentCount += 1
    dataGridView1.DataSource = listSchedules(currentCount)
    dataGridView1.DataMember = "Schedule"
End If
End Sub

Private Sub Previous_Click(ByVal sender As Object, ByVal e As EventArgs)
If currentCount > 0 Then
    currentCount += 1
    dataGridView1.DataSource = listSchedules(currentCount)
    dataGridView1.DataMember = "Schedule"
End If
End Sub

Private Sub Start_Click(ByVal sender As Object, ByVal e As EventArgs)
If currentCount > 0 Then
    dataGridView1.DataSource = listSchedules(0)
    dataGridView1.DataMember = "Schedule"
    currentCount = 0
End If
End Sub

Private Sub End_Click(ByVal sender As Object, ByVal e As EventArgs)
If currentCount < listSchedules.Count Then
    Dim count As Integer = listSchedules.Count
    dataGridView1.DataSource = listSchedules(listSchedules.Count - 1)
    dataGridView1.DataMember = "Schedule"
    currentCount = listSchedules.Count - 1
End If
End Sub
```

In addition, you need to add the declarations shown in Listing 2-7 inside the class so that the methods can have access to these objects.

Listing 2-7   Declarations for a generic list object.

C# Snippet
```csharp
System.Collections.Generic.List<DataSet> listSchedules = new List<DataSet>(10);
int currentCount = -1;
```
Visual Basic Snippet
```vb
Dim listSchedules As System.Collections.Generic.List(Of DataSet) =
  New List(Of DataSet)(10)
Dim currentCount As Integer = -1
```

Update the *currentCount* variable each time you retrieve data from EWS. The code is shown in Listing 2-8. It needs to be placed inside the *calculation_click* event handler.

Listing 2-8   Implementing a synchronized counter.

C# Snippet
```
//existing code in the calculation_click routine
dataGridView1.DataSource = ds;
dataGridView1.DataMember = "Schedule";
//new code added here to update our current count and store the current calculation
listSchedules.Add[ds];
currentCount++;
```

Visual Basic Snippet
```
'existing code in the calculation_click routine
dataGridView1.DataSource = ds
dataGridView1.DataMember = "Schedule"
'new code added here to update our current count and store the current calculation
listSchedules.Add(ds)
currentCount += 1
```

The variable *currentCount* tells us the current calculation that is being examined. The *current-Count* approach forces the code to index a particular set of data based on the current record. Without this approach, the Previous and Next buttons would function much like an Internet browser application. Figure 2-10 shows what the application looks like.

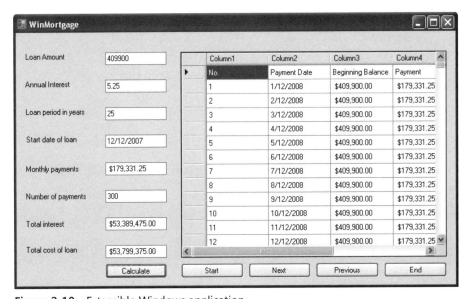

Figure 2-10   Extensible Windows application.

I'm sure you'll agree that our Windows application extends the published worksheet by providing functionality that is not available to published spreadsheets in Excel Services. We have built an application that preserves calculated history. Among other things, history can be used to beef up analytics or to provide deeper context for what-if scenarios.

You'll note that our application caches values. Caching provides a significant performance boost, surpassing the performance of the published spreadsheet. There's also no physical limit to the number of calculations we can store. Although a seasoned Excel guru could probably write a large wave of hack code to reproduce that type of functionality, the intensive effort would not be a cost-effective solution for enterprise organizations.

And, in terms of functionality, that's just the tip of the iceberg. There's a lot more extensibility that can be added. And that's the whole point of wooing .NET developers into the SharePoint realm. It's certainly not to reproduce worksheet functionality; rather, it is to build sophisticated applications firmly rooted in the Excel platform. As an additional exercise, you can implement the necessary code to purge the cache and store the input values along with the schedule payments.

Assigning Values to Ranges

As a supplement to what you have learned so far, let's consider a few lines of code that will exercise your knowledge of range manipulation. The exercise will also serve to increase your comfort level with ranges.

You can assign a contiguous block of data directly to a range on the spreadsheet using the *SetRangeA1* method. It's a bit tricky, so let's consider naming the contiguous blocks with names that approximate their functionality. Consider the code shown in Listing 2-9.

Listing 2-9   Assigning a range object.

```
C# Snippet
object[] rows = new object[7];
int columns = 0;
while (columns < rows.Length)
{
    rows[columns] = new object[15];
    columns += 1;
}
Visual Basic Snippet
Dim rows As Object() = New Object(6){}
Dim columns As Integer = 0
Do While columns < rows.Length
    rows(columns) = New Object(14){}
    columns += 1
Loop
```

This *for* loop sets up a contiguous block of cells that is exactly 15 rows long and 7 columns wide. This block of cells will hold the data we are trying to write to the spreadsheet. You can use the code in Listing 2-10 to add values to this contiguous block.

Listing 2-10   Assigning a range object using a *for* loop.

```
C# Snippet
foreach(object[] myRow in rows)
{
    for(int i = 0; i < myRow.Length; i++)
    {
        myRow[i] = i.ToString();
    }
}
Visual Basic Snippet
For Each myRow As Object In rows
    Dim i As Integer = 0
    Do While i < myRow.Length
        myRow(i) = i.ToString()
        i += 1
    Loop
Next myRow
```

After the code executes, each cell contains some data. You can assign this contiguous block of cells to a similar sized block of cells on the spreadsheet in one line of code. However, you need to make sure that the area on the spreadsheet is sized and shaped exactly like the 15 by 7 contiguous block of cells and that the destination range is unlocked and writable. If the origination and destination cells don't match exactly, or the range is locked, an exception is thrown. Note, too, that the contiguous block of cells can contain anywhere from 1 cell, or A1:A1, to 16 billion cells, or 1 million by 16,000.

If you open a spreadsheet and assign a 15 by 7 contiguous block starting at A1, your destination target should be G15, as shown in Figure 2-11.

The Big Grid Statistics

The limits of Excel have expanded in every conceivable way. Here is a short list of the improvements in the program known as *the Big Grid*:

- The total number of available columns: 16,384

- The total number of available rows: 1,048,576

- Number of unique colors allowed in a single workbook: 4.3 billion

- Number of cell format conditions: No limit

- Number of levels of sorting: 64

- Number of items shown in the AutoFilter drop-down list: 10,000

- The total number of characters that can display in a cell: 32,000

- The number of printable characters per cell: 32,000

- The total number of unique cell styles in a workbook: 64,000

- The maximum length of formulas: 8,000

- The number of levels of nesting in formulas: 64

- Maximum number of arguments to a function: 255

- Maximum number of items found by "Find All": 2 billion

- Number of rows allowed in a PivotTable: 1 million

- Number of columns allowed in a PivotTable: 16,000

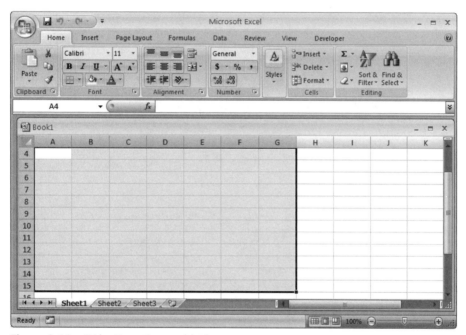

Figure 2-11   15 by 7 contiguous block.

EWS is not particularly concerned with the starting block; the overriding concern is that the block is sized proportionately. You'll be able to assign your contiguous block to any point on the spreadsheet as long as there is a contiguous block of cells that are 15 by 7 cells wide. Listing 2-11 shows the code needed to copy the block.

Listing 2-11 Assigning a contiguous block of data.

```csharp
C# Snippet
Status[] outStatus;
RangeCoordinates rangeCoordinates = new RangeCoordinates();
string sheetName = "Sheet1";
string targetWorkbookPath = "http://<servername:port>/
  Shared%20Documents/TestBook2.xlsx";
es.Credentials = System.Net.CredentialCache.DefaultNetworkCredentials;
string sessionId = es.OpenWorkbook(targetWorkbookPath,
  "en-US", "en-US", out outStatus);
//only proceed on a valid session
if (!String.IsNullOrEmpty(sessionId))
{
    object[] rows = new object[7];
    for (int columns = 0; columns < rows.Length; columns++)
    {
        rows[columns] = new object[15];
    }

    foreach(object[] myRow in rows)
    {
        for(int i = 0; i < myRow.Length; i++)
        {
            myRow[i] = i.ToString();
        }
    }

    es.SetRangeA1(sessionId,"","a1:g15",rows);
}
```

```vbnet
Visual Basic Snippet
Dim outStatus As Status()
Dim rangeCoordinates As RangeCoordinates = New RangeCoordinates()
Dim sheetName As String = "Sheet1"
Dim targetWorkbookPath As String = "http://<servername:port>/
  Shared%20Documents/TestBook2.xlsx"
es.Credentials = System.Net.CredentialCache.DefaultNetworkCredentials
Dim sessionId As String = es.OpenWorkbook(targetWorkbookPath, "en-US", "en-US",
  outStatus)
'only proceed on a valid session
If (Not String.IsNullOrEmpty(sessionId)) Then
    Dim rows As Object() = New Object(6){}
    Dim columns As Integer = 0
    Do While columns < rows.Length
        rows(columns) = New Object(14){}
        columns += 1
    Loop
    For Each myRow As Object In rows
        Dim i As Integer = 0
        Do While i < myRow.Length
            myRow(i) = i.ToString()
            i += 1
        Loop
    Next myRow
    es.SetRangeA1(sessionId,"","a1:o7",rows)
End If
```

If you experiment with the target range by sizing it differently from the originating contiguous block of cells, the code will generate an exception. Additionally, if you distort the contents of the originating block by replacing this line of code

```
rows[columns] = new object[15]
```

with these lines:

```
rows[columns] = new object[15]
rows[columns] = columns.ToString()
```

and commenting out the *foreach* loop, you get the exact same exception. At times, debugging these ambiguous exceptions can be tedious.

> **Warning**   Excel Services does not allow addressing of noncontiguous blocks from EWS code. If you need to do this, you have to use a Spreadsheet macro. Additionally, Excel Services does not allow you to assign a formula to a cell programmatically. In fact, if any cell in the target range contains a formula, an exception is thrown and none of the contiguous cells are updated.

About Range Coordinates

In the past few examples, we learned to manipulate cells and also to use named ranges. The majority of the code you write will be focused on manipulating ranges. Excel Services does allow you to manipulate ranges without using named range notation. However, the preferred approach is to use named range notation. In any case, direct cell access is exposed through the *GetRange* method call.

Range coordinates provide an alternative to "A1" notation and enable Excel ranges to be specified using direct integer indexing. Range coordinates include top row, left column, height, and width properties that define the bounds of the target range. A range includes at least one or more cells. Listing 2-12 provides an example of direct cell access.

Listing 2-12   Range coordinate manipulation.

```
C# Snippet
RangeCoordinates rangeCoordinates = new RangeCoordinates();
rangeCoordinates.Column = 2;
rangeCoordinates.Row = 3;
rangeCoordinates.Height = 12;
rangeCoordinates.Width = 13;
object[] rangeResult1 = xlservice.GetRange(sessionId, sheetName, rangeCoordinates,
  false, out outStatus);
```

```
Visual Basic Snippet
RangeCoordinates rangeCoordinates = new RangeCoordinates()
rangeCoordinates.Column = 2
rangeCoordinates.Row = 3
rangeCoordinates.Height = 12
rangeCoordinates.Width = 13
object[] rangeResult1 = xlservice.GetRange(sessionId, sheetName, rangeCoordinates,
    false, out outStatus);
```

As you can see, the *GetRange* method call behaves no differently than the *GetRangeA1* call except that it takes a range coordinate parameter. The *RangeCoordinates* object being passed in must contain the target row and column. This is an absolute cell reference exactly equivalent to row/column notation. The height and width properties define the size of the block in the originating cell. For instance, if you are copying a single cell, the height and width should be equal to 1. If you are copying a rectangular block of cells 2 columns wide and 10 rows in height, the height should be set to 10 and the width should be set to 2. The remainder of the code works exactly the same as for range notation because the return value for the *GetRange* and *GetRangeA1* style methods are equivalent.

Programming for Web Service Exceptions

The Excel Services architecture presents a unique challenge for .NET when framed within the context of exceptions. In the .NET world, exceptions are defined as a violation of an assumption. As an example, consider a method that accepts two integer parameters and divides the first by the second. The implicit assumption here is that the second parameter must not be equal to zero because the mathematical result of the operation cannot be stored in a variable.

In .NET, there is no way to alert the caller to assumptions made by the method as in C++, for instance. In this case, proper exception management techniques dictate that the method promptly throw an exception if the second parameter is equal to zero because the implicit assumption has been violated. This is the trivial case.

Now consider the nontrivial case. A SOAP client invokes a calculation in the spreadsheet, but one of the arguments is invalid. .NET exception architecture dictates that an exception be thrown. However, in some cases, this draconian policy needs to be tempered—that is, the method might still be able to run to completion. How should this case be handled?

Stop and Continue Alerts

Excel Services introduces the concept of alerts. If the method call cannot finish successfully, an exception is thrown. This is a *stop alert*. If the method can complete successfully but an error occurred during the servicing of the request, an error object is returned to indicate to the SOAP client that there was an issue with the request. This is a *continue alert*.

Alerts aren't sent to the SOAP client directly. Instead, they are wrapped in a serializable SOAP exception object. Two important fields, the *Actor* and *Code* properties of the *SoapException* object, are automatically set by the framework before the *SoapException* object is transmitted back to the SOAP client. The *Actor* property usually holds the URI to the XML Web service. The *Code* property contains an *XmlQualifiedName* that specifies the SOAP fault code that occurred.

> **Tip**   In SharePoint Team Services 1.0, alerts were called *Web subscriptions*, but the functionality has not changed significantly.

The *Code* property specifies the type of error that occurred. The type of error is described using a limited number of predefined error codes specified by the SOAP protocol. If you need to provide user-defined error codes tailored to your application, you should use the *subcode* element of the *SoapException* object.

Unfortunately, the *subcode* property is exposed only in Visual Studio 2005. It does not exist in previous versions. Additionally, the *subcode* property is ignored when the SOAP protocol version 1.1 is used to communicate with an XML Web service. If your exception-handling code examines the *subcode* property, it would be prudent to first test to see whether *subcode* contains a value before blindly using it.

Listing 2-13 adds exception-handling code.

Listing 2-13   Exception-handling code for EWS invocations.

```csharp
C# Snippet
private static void NotifyUserOfError(Status[] errorObject)
{
    foreach (Status err in errorObject)
    {
        switch (err.Severity)
        {
            //stop on fatal errors, alert the user on non-fatal errors
            case "Error":
                Console.WriteLine(err.Message);
                Console.ReadLine();
                return;
            case "Warning":
            case "Information":
                Console.WriteLine(err.Message);
                break;
            default:
                break;
        }
    }
}
try
{
    //sanity check in main
```

```csharp
    if (outStatus != null && outStatus.Length > 0)
    {
        NotifyUserOfError(outStatus);
    }
}
catch (SoapException e)
{
    StringBuilder errString = new StringBuilder();
    errString.Append(System.Environment.NewLine).Append("Fault Namespace: ")
        .Append(e.Code.Namespace);
    errString.Append(System.Environment.NewLine).Append("Fault Name: ")
        .Append(e.Code.Name);
    errString.Append(System.Environment.NewLine).Append("SOAP Actor that threw
        Exception: ").Append(e.Actor);
    errString.Append(System.Environment.NewLine).Append("Error Message: ")
        .Append(e.Message);
    Console.WriteLine("A SOAP Exception Occurred {0}", errString.ToString());
}
```

Visual Basic Snippet

```vb
Private Shared Sub NotifyUserOfError(ByVal errorObject As Status())
    For Each err As Status In errorObject
        Select Case err.Severity
            'stop on fatal errors, alert the user on non-fatal errors
            Case "Error"
                Console.WriteLine(err.Message)
                Console.ReadLine()
                Return
            Case "Warning"
            Case "Information"
                Console.WriteLine(err.Message)
            Case Else
        End Select
    Next err
End Sub

Try
'sanity check in main
If Not outStatus Is Nothing AndAlso outStatus.Length > 0 Then
    NotifyUserOfError(outStatus)
End If
Catch e As SoapException
    Dim errString As StringBuilder = New StringBuilder()
    errString.Append(System.Environment.NewLine).Append("Fault Namespace: ").
        Append(e.Code.Namespace)
    errString.Append(System.Environment.NewLine).Append("Fault Name: ").
        Append(e.Code.Name)
    errString.Append(System.Environment.NewLine).Append("SOAP Actor that threw
        Exception: ").Append(e.Actor)
    errString.Append(System.Environment.NewLine).Append("Error Message: ").
        Append(e.Message)
    Console.WriteLine("A SOAP Exception Occurred {0}", errString.ToString())
End Try
```

The code imports *System.Web.Services.Protocol*. The assembly is used because it exposes the classes that define the protocols used to transmit data to SOAP clients. The *SoapException* class is a part of this hierarchy. Turn your attention to the *try* block. If an exception occurs during code execution inside this block, the exception will be caught in the *catch* block. The bulk of code in the *catch* block is concerned with extracting the various parts of the exception detail and formatting it for end user consumption.

> **Warning**   The code presented here is shortened for brevity. It contains a method and a *try/catch* block of code. The *try/catch* block of code is usually placed in the main method of an application. The method can be placed anywhere within the class scope.

Now focus on the method *NotifyUserOfError*. Within the *try* block presented earlier, the code tests the returned value, examining it for a continue error. If a continue error has occurred, the *errorObject* variable of type *Status* stores the contents of the error. The bulk of the code is concerned with extracting the details of the continue error by examining the *severity* property.

Table 2-1 outlines the three properties available in the *Status* object.

Table 2-1   Status Object Properties

Property	Description
Message	The *Message* property holds a string that describes the current exception. The message is not localized and should not be shown to clients.
Name	This property retrieves the status message code.
Severity	This property retrieves the severity of the message.

In addition to using error codes, the spreadsheet object also returns error information in the cell or range using a style similar to the desktop version of Excel. These Excel error codes are mapped directly to an enumeration of type *CellErrorEnum.ExcelWebService.CellError*.

> **Best Practices**   The Web service class implements the *IDisposable* interface. Best practices recommends making use of the *using* construct, which is available in both C# and Microsoft Visual Basic, to take care of releasing the unmanaged resources tied to the EWS invocation. There is no requirement to call the *closeworkbook* method if you use the *using* construct. The Direct-Linking proxy *Webservice* object is purely managed code and does not implement the *IDisposable* interface.

You can probe the error object to find out the exact cause of the continue alert. To trigger this behavior, you can refer back to the Windows mortgage application and enter an invalid value in one of the fields. The enumeration does not encapsulate all spreadsheet values, just the important ones. For now, you should note that the *cellerror* object is set when either *GetRange* or *GetCell* is used. For a *GetRange* call, the code approach to retrieving the *cellerror* object remains the same.

Web Services in SharePoint

Most administrators I know guard production servers with a jealous zeal. They claim it's a job mandate! However, this zeal often becomes a barrier to forward movement, at least from a developer's perspective. For instance, a developer can bang out a spiffy new application in a wave of late night coding. But she can't simply deploy the application to production! For obvious reasons, things don't work that way and they shouldn't either.

However, that sort of reasoning has a ring of counterproductivity to it when viewed from a dollars and sense perspective. The more time that is spent in the wheel spin between testing and refactoring is more time that is essentially handed off to the competitor. At the enterprise level, reduced time to market helps to increase revenue. What is needed is a way to access the resources of the server with reduced risk of instability to the server resources.

MOSS solves these problems by exposing a suite of Web services that are already deployed and ready for use on the server. The Web services that are available on MOSS include methods for accessing site content, managing lists, and customizing data on the SharePoint site. There are approximately 20 Web services available on a default installation of MOSS 2007. You can browse these Web services using Visual Studio.

When you select Web Service On The Local Machine in the Visual Studio 2005 Add Web Reference dialog box, Visual Studio iterates the *C:\Program Files\Common Files\Microsoft Shared\web server extensions\12\isapi* directory compiling a list of files with an .asmx extension. Next, Visual Studio iterates the Internet Information Services Web sites, compiling a list of Web sites that are available on the Web server. For each Web site, Visual Studio adds the list of .asmx files.

At any point in time, you can change the name of the Web service file name. For instance, you can simply rename the *alerts.asmx* file to *AdventureworksNotification.asmx* in the *C:\Program Files\Common Files\Microsoft Shared\web server extensions\12\isapi* directory and re-open the Add Web Reference dialog box to see the updated changes. You can also remove Web services by deleting the file or renaming the extension to hide the availability of these services. Finally, you can add your own .asmx file to this directory to implement your custom Web service. If your custom Web service contains an assembly, place it in the bin folder of the Web application. I'll provide more details about this process in Chapter 7.

Summary

This chapter walked through the Excel Web Services machinery built into Excel Services. Hopefully, it helped set some expectations about the platform. The platform is designed to facilitate distributed computing. Distributed computing holds tremendous promise, especially as applications evolve toward an SOA.

For the .NET developer, the role has morphed into one of support and extensibility. The .NET developer now needs to be able to write applications that supplement SharePoint functionality. Part of that new job description involves integration with desktop applications so that SharePoint applications can extend into new domains.

From a technical perspective, programming for EWS is dominated by range manipulation. And you've had plenty of practice with the *GetCell/GetCellA1* and *GetRange/GetRangeA1* constructs. You've also learned how to probe jagged arrays with loop code to extract cell contents, binding the results efficiently to user-interface controls in a Windows Forms application. Although the code construct to probe jagged arrays is untidy at best, jagged arrays are the most convenient and flexible data structure available that can hold spreadsheet data. Blame the .NET Framework for the unsightly code.

You might also have noticed that the last few sections were particularly heavy on exception management. The reason for this is that exception management is a very real-world design requirement both for organically grown code and for offshore development.

Chapter 3
Excel Web Access

The Microsoft Office Excel Web Access (EWA) component is one of the primary interfaces for Excel Services and consists of Web Parts. EWA forms part of the Excel Web front end (WFE) and allows .NET applications to hook into Microsoft Windows SharePoint Services. This chapter will focus on building Web Parts from Microsoft Visual Studio 2005 and installing them on Microsoft Office SharePoint Server (MOSS) 2007 so that they can be used in SharePoint applications. You'll get a feel for configuration and integration as well. The material will also examine some of the new templates that ease the burden of Web Part creation and deployment. You can find more information about Web Parts at *http://msdn2.microsoft.com/en-us/library/ms379628(VS.80).aspx.*

An Introduction to Excel Web Access

Chapter 1, "An Introduction to Excel Services," introduced Excel Web Access (EWA). EWA services the need to write applications that render in Web browsers. EWA outputs HTML and JavaScript that can be consumed by any Web browser. However, a short list of inconsistencies crop up on different browsers. These inconsistencies are mainly driven by the extent of DHTML support. In any case, common up-level Web browsers should have no trouble displaying the output from Excel Services.

EWA is built on the concept of Web Parts. Web Parts are Web control containers that expose functionality to the client page. EWA Web Parts are built on ASP.NET Web Parts, meaning that the base class for the Web Parts control is the *System.Web.UI.WebControls.WebParts.WebPart* class. This approach is a departure from previous versions of SharePoint, and it highlights the tighter coupling between ASP.NET and SharePoint 2007.

The Web Parts that you build as an ASP.NET developer from Visual Studio .NET will be deployed to a SharePoint server. Administrators and end users will then be able to add your Web Part to their pages. When the Web Part is invoked, the code that you wrote will be executed in the SharePoint Web page. The Web Part that is being executed exists within the executing context of SharePoint. The architecture implies that a Web Part has implicit access to SharePoint page-level resources, such as session and view-state intrinsics.

A SharePoint Web page is simply an ASP.NET Web page that is dynamically compiled at request time and might or might not include content stored in a SharePoint content database. We will explain exactly what this means later in the chapter. For now, note that after the page has been created, the Web Part code is invoked. The Web Part also contains .NET Framework code because it was built using the .NET platform. Therefore, a Web Part that is being run on a SharePoint Web page allows .NET code to interact with a Web page on the SharePoint site.

Earlier, we mentioned briefly that dynamically compiled pages can source data from a content database. There are certain advantages to storing a page in a content database as opposed to disk. Some of these benefits include transactional updates of documents and document metadata, consistent backups of documents and document metadata, a programmable storage layer, and deadlock detection and resolution. If you think about it, you should realize that this architecture is aimed at satisfying the need to scale to large numbers of users. You should also be pleased to learn that the architecture handles low to moderate loads comfortably as well.

Programming with Excel Services Web Parts

SharePoint comes stocked with a number of Web Parts, as shown in Figure 3-1. Figure 3-1 shows a sampling of Web Parts that can be added to a Web page in SharePoint.

If these Web Parts don't suit your need, you can build your own custom Web Parts. Custom Web Parts can perform any function that the developer empowers them to fulfill. For instance, custom Web Parts can draw charts, exchange data, provide search functionality, or read files. Later chapters will show examples of each of these functions. In addition, several vendor-supplied Web Parts can be downloaded or purchased for use. The Office Web site also offers Web Parts that can perform analysis services and other tasks.

Before blindly setting out to write Web Parts, you first need to figure out the range of functionality that is built in. If these Web Parts don't suit your fancy and you can't customize their behavior, you will need to build your own. The rest of the chapter is dedicated to expanding your knowledge in that direction.

Let's get started with a HelloWorld Web Part. The Web Part simply writes some text—specifically, "Hello world"—to the client. We then deploy the assembly to a SharePoint server. After the assembly has been deployed, you add the Web Part to a page on the SharePoint site so that the piece of text can be displayed. You perform this sequence of steps every time a Web Part is authored or updated. By default, you can't simply build the Web Part and refresh the Web page like you do in ASP.NET.

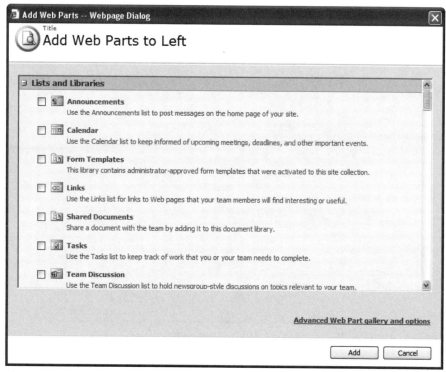

Figure 3-1   SharePoint default Web Parts.

In the next few sections, we break up the sequence of steps so that you can learn each piece and gain appreciation for how it all fits together. Separating each step into its own topic also allows you to refer back to individual sections if you run into trouble later on.

Manual Creation of Web Parts

As an ASP.NET developer, you might be disappointed to learn that Visual Studio .NET does not ship with a development environment that allows developers to create Web Parts that can be deployed to SharePoint. It also does not have integrated development environment (IDE) design-time support for Web Part creation. The implication here is that you cannot drag and drop controls on a design surface to create SharePoint Web Parts. You have to construct the Web Part by hand.

The exercise to build Web Parts in this fashion is similar to classic ASP programming. The manual process involves building Web Parts from Web Control Libraries. There are workarounds to getting the designer up and working. Parts of this chapter and Chapter 6, "Advanced Web Parts Programming," will outline those approaches. However, for now, let's focus on the basics.

Open Visual Studio if it is not already opened, and create a new project based on a Class Library template, as shown in Figure 3-2. Name the project **HelloWorldWebPart**.

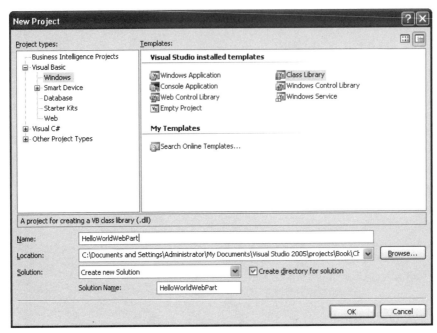

Figure 3-2   Web Part based on a Class Library template.

In the HelloWorldWebPart code file, enter the code shown in Listing 3-1.

Listing 3-1   The HelloWorld Web Part.

```
C# Snippet
using System;
using System.Web.UI;
using System.Web.UI.WebControls.WebParts;

namespace HelloWorldWebPart
{
    public class HelloWorldWebPart : WebPart
    {
        protected override void Render(HtmlTextWriter writer)
        {
            writer.Write("Hello world");
        }
    }
}
```

Visual Basic Snippet

```
Imports System
Imports System.Web.UI
Imports System.Web.UI.WebControls.WebParts

Namespace HelloWorldWebPart
    Public Class HelloWorldWebPart
        Inherits WebPart
        Protected Overrides Sub Render(ByVal writer As HtmlTextWriter)
```

```
            writer.Write("Hello world")
        End Sub
    End Class
End Namespace
```

The code compiles with a reference to *System.Web*. There's not a whole lot going on in there to be excited about. The class inherits from the Web Part class and overrides the *Render* method. Although you can inherit from a SharePoint Web Part class, you should prefer the ASP.NET class instead because the SharePoint Web Part is present for backward compatibility. We talk more about specific functionality that is unique to Web Parts based on the SharePoint Web class in Chapter 7, "Advanced Concepts with Excel Services." The *Render* method makes a *System.Web.UI.HtmlTtextWriter* object available. Its responsibility is to serve as a container for moving data to the client for display.

Signing Web Part Assemblies

You then need to sign the assembly. Signing an assembly, or strongly naming it, allows the .NET Framework to execute the assembly with full trust. The reason for this requirement is evident. Code running on the SharePoint site has access to the object model—discussed in Chapter 5, "Windows SharePoint Services 3.0"—which can perform privileged functions such as document library creation, data management, and a wide spectrum of other administrative functions. The strong name requirement acts as a first-level gate that confirms the intent of code being deployed on the site. You can read more about code signing at this link: *http://msdn2.microsoft.com/en-us/library/xc31ft41.aspx*.

Also, you need to understand that these types of assemblies are designed to be delivered over the Internet through the browser to be installed and executed on the local machine. Signing these types of assemblies provides an explicit guarantee that the code has not been tampered with since it was signed by the author. Code signing does not make any other implicit or explicit guarantees.

Open the property pages for the project, as shown in Figure 3-3. Figure 3-3 shows the Signing tab in Visual Studio .NET.

After you have signed the assembly, retrieve the details of the public token. See the next section, "Retrieving Signing Details," if you do not know how to do this. You can also choose to sign the assembly from the Visual Studio .NET command prompt. Here is an example:

```
Sn.exe -k myTempKey.snk
```

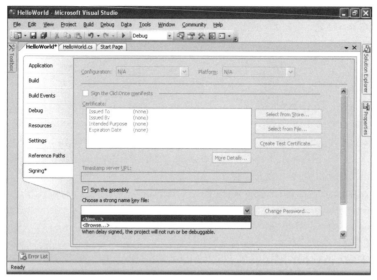

Figure 3-3 Signing your assembly.

> **Note** After you sign the assembly, your assembly runs with full trust from a Code Access Security (CAS) policy perspective. You can also restrict these assemblies by tweaking CAS policy so that they run with partial trust. Chapter 7 will walk you through the details. After you sign your assembly, other assemblies that need to call methods or create types from your assembly must either be strongly named themselves or be decorated with the *AllowPartialTrustedCallers* (APTC) attribute.

Retrieving Signing Details Open a Visual Studio 2005 command prompt window, and type **sn.exe –t** [*full path*]\ **HelloWorldSharePoint.dll**. Copy the public key token that is returned from the output window. Listing 3-2 provides a complete example.

Listing 3-2 Output after running **sn.exe –t**.

```
C:\Program Files\Visual Studio 8\VC>sn -T "C:\
Documents and Settings\Alvin\My Documents\Visual Studio 2005\
Projects\HelloWorldWebPart\HelloWorldWebPart\bin\Debug\
helloworldwebpart.dll"

 (R) .NET Framework Strong Name Utility  Version 2.0.50727.42
Copyright (c) Corporation.  All rights reserved.

Public key token is 4847df5260465341
```

The *.snk* file must be located in the same directory with the *.dll*; otherwise, an error will occur.

***web.config* Modification**   Open the *web.config* file for the Web site where you intend to
deploy the Web Part. Add the code shown in Listing 3-3 to the *web.config* file.

Listing 3-3   *web.config* file modification.

```
<SafeControl Assembly="Enter your Assembly Name Here",
 Version=1.0.0.0, Culture=neutral,
 PublicKeyToken="Enter your public key token here"
 Namespace="Enter your name space here"
 TypeName="Enter your type name here" Safe="True" />
```

The namespace and type name can be obtained by examining the code file for the project.
They correspond to the namespace and the name of the class. To retrieve the version and culture, navigate to the bin\debug folder and examine the properties of the assembly. Alternatively, you can click the Assembly Information button of the Application tab on the property
pages to view the Assembly Information dialog box, which is shown in Figure 3-4.

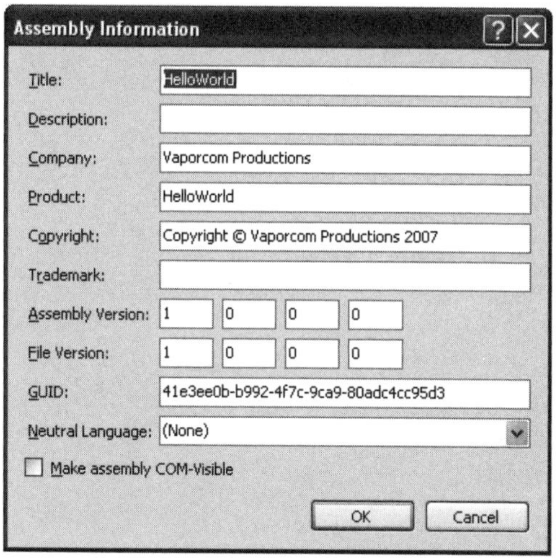

Figure 3-4   Assembly Information dialog box.

Listing 3-4 provides a complete example of the *web.config* file entry.

Listing 3-4   Actual modification in *web.config*.

```
<SafeControl Assembly="HelloWorldWebPart",
 Version=1.0.0.0, Culture=neutral,
 PublicKeyToken=4847df5260465341
 Namespace="HelloWorldWebPart"
 TypeName=" HelloWorldWebPart" Safe="True" />
```

That's it. The next section demonstrates how to create Web Parts using the Visual Studio Extensions add-in.

Creating Web Parts Projects via Visual Studio Templates

Visual Studio contains an add-in that enables developers to build Web Parts that can be deployed on SharePoint sites. The add-in takes care of much of the internal plumbing required to move a Web Parts project from Visual Studio to the SharePoint repository. If you have not done so by now, download and install the Visual Studio Extensions for SharePoint 2007 from MSDN (*http://www.microsoft.com/downloads/details.aspx?familyid=5D61409E-1FA3-48CF-8023-E8F38E709BA6&displaylang=en*).

The Visual Studio Extensions contain Visual Studio project templates, Visual Studio Item templates, and a SharePoint solution generator. We examine only the Web Part template here. Working examples of the other templates are provided in Chapter 7. Here is a summary of these items:

Visual Studio 2005 Project Templates Templates that allow developers to build Web Parts. Four templates are available: Web Part, Team Site Definition, Blank Site Definition, and List Definition.

Visual Studio 2005 Item Templates Items that can be added to an existing project. Four Item templates are available: Custom Field, List Definition, Content Type, and Module.

SharePoint Solution Generator A standalone program that builds a site definition project from an existing SharePoint site.

Assuming you have downloaded and installed the Visual Studio Extensions, select New | Project from the Visual Studio File menu. Select SharePoint from the Project Types pane on the left side of the page. From the Templates pane on the right side of the page, select the Web Part template. Name the project **HelloWorldWebPart**. Click OK to proceed. Figure 3-5 shows a project being created using the new add-in.

The HelloWorldSharePoint project should resemble Figure 3-5. Figure 3-6 shows the Solution Explorer view for a project created using the new Visual Studio templates for SharePoint.

Notice that the default class automatically inherits from *System.Web.UI.WebControls.WebParts.WebPart*. In addition, there is a stub *Render* function, also shown in Figure 3-6, that is commented out. Uncomment the last line, and change the text from "Output HTML" to **"Hello world"**. Then build the application.

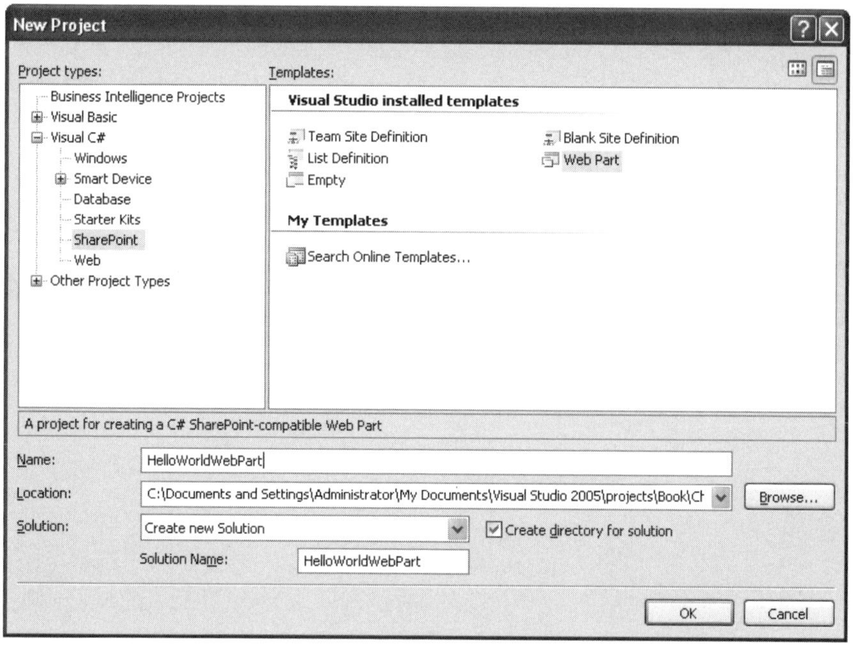

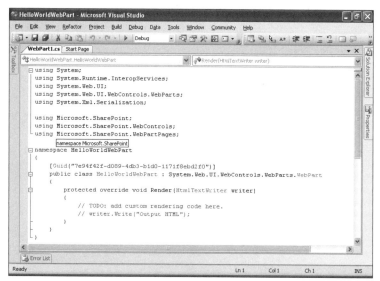

Figure 3-5   Visual Studio Extensions for SharePoint.

Figure 3-6   HelloWorldSharePoint project.

Now take a closer look at the Solution Explorer window. Click on the Properties tab. Notice that the Properties folder contains a *temporary.snk* file. This is the key file that is used to sign the assembly. That information was part of the Signing tab you saw in Figure 3-3. You learned about signing in the "Signing Web Part Assemblies" section earlier. The extension also adds a reference to the *Microsoft.SharePoint* managed assembly and adds three references to classes inside the SharePoint assembly. You can see those references at the top of the code file.

Before you can deploy the application, you need to configure a deployment path to the SharePoint server. Figure 3-7 shows the Properties option that leads to the property pages.

Figure 3-7 HelloWorldSharePoint property objects.

From the property pages, select the Debug tab in the left column. Figure 3-8 shows the Debug tab in Visual Studio.

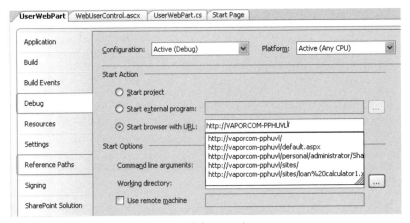

Figure 3-8 HelloWorldSharePoint debug options.

In the text box next to the Start Browser With URL option, add the path to your server—for instance **http://<*servername*:port>**—as shown in Figure 3-8. This is the portal site where you intend to deploy the Web Part. If you do not modify this path and the default path does not point to your portal site, the F5 command will fail with an error message. Another tab that you should focus on is the SharePoint Solution tab shown in Figure 3-9.

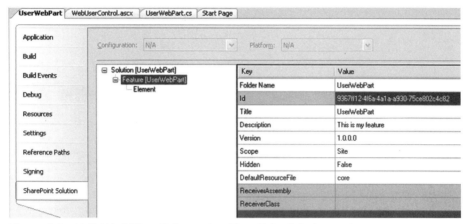

Figure 3-9   HelloWorldSharePoint project SharePoint Solution options.

The details you enter into the fields on the SharePoint Solution tab provide information to the end user about your Web Part. The descriptions you enter here show up when your Web Part appears in the Web Part Gallery.

Deploying Web Parts

Web Parts can be deployed either manually or through an automatic installation process. Let's consider the manual process first. All installation processes use the *stsadm.exe* tool to install the required files to the SharePoint server. Assuming your solution is named HelloWorldWeb-Part, follow these steps to deploy your application to SharePoint.

Manual Installation Walk-Through   Open a command prompt to your solution directory, and set the PATH variable to the stsadm executable. You need to set up some variables that ease the manual process, as shown by the code in Listing 3-5.

Listing 3-5   Variable declaration for *SPAdminTool*.

```
set SPAdminTool=%CommonProgramFiles%\Shared\web server extensions\12\BIN\stsadm.exe
set Task=install
set PackageFile=%~dp0HelloWorldWebPart.wsp
set PackageName= HelloWorldWebPart.wsp
set TargetUrl=http://<servername:port>
```

The *SPAdminTool* variable allows you to invoke stsadm from the current directory; otherwise, you need to use a fully qualified file path to stsadm. The other variables are self-explanatory.

Next, add the solution package to the SharePoint server. To do this, open the command prompt window and type in the following:

```
"%SPAdminTool%" -o addsolution -filename "%PackageFile%"
```

Deploy the solution to SharePoint by typing in the following:

```
    "%SPAdminTool%" -o deploysolution -name
"%PackageName%" -local -allowGacDeployment -url %TargetUrl%
```

Finally, activate the SharePoint Web Part so that it shows up in the Web Part Gallery by typing the following line at the command prompt:

```
    "%SPAdminTool%" -o activatefeature -id
f13d7cc3-fd1b-43cd-80a2-cf107522cbe2 -url %TargetUrl%
```

That's it for the manual process. The steps performed here are equivalent to the steps we performed in the manual deployment step, so you should have a firm understanding of the process. The manual process comes in handy when Web Parts start to misbehave and interfere with the execution of a page on the portal site. For instance, a malfunctioning Web Part can cause the page to fail to load. In some cases, you will need to fix the page by unloading the culprit Web Part using the manual process.

Automatic Installation Walk-Through   In the usual case, the developer copies the required files to a network file share on SharePoint and the administrator installs the Web Part to SharePoint. If the developer has administrative privileges on SharePoint, the developer can use the Visual Studio Extensions add-in to deploy the Web Part to SharePoint. The act of deploying a Web Part makes the Web Part available to a SharePoint—that is, it will show up in the Web Part Gallery. An end user needs to add the Web Part to a SharePoint page for it to run. If this is your first walk on the SharePoint side, you need to remember that SharePoint development in .NET is a three-part dance of development, deployment, and user addition.

To use the Visual Studio Extensions add-in, simply press F5. F5 deploys the assembly to the SharePoint server. It does not execute the assembly as would be the case for normal ASP.NET development. The action invokes a *setup.bat* file in the \bin\debug directory that copies the relevant files onto the server and installs the solution file (WSP) containing the code for the Web Part in the root of the Web site.

In some cases, the installation might fail. You can manually force an installation by navigating to the \bin\debug directory of your project from a command prompt. Run **setup /uninstall** to uninstall the application followed by **setup /install** to re-install the application. You should use this option sparingly. If further issues remain, it might help to open the *setup.bat* file in a text editor to figure out the exact line causing the error. The content of the *setup.bat* file is similar to the content you created for the manual installation process.

Deployment Through CAB Files   To confirm that your Web Part is correctly installed, follow these steps. From the portal home page, select Edit Page from the Site Actions link. Click Add Web Part. Figure 3-10 shows a SharePoint Web page in edit mode.

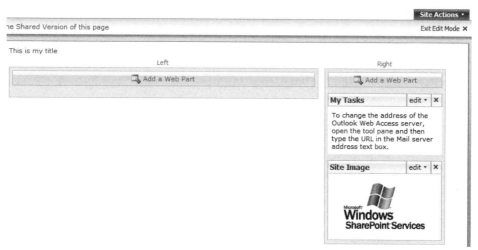

Figure 3-10   Web Part confirmation process.

Click Advanced Web Part Gallery And Options. You can find this option by clicking the Add Web Part button in SharePoint. Click Server Gallery. Your Web Part will show up in the list. If you do not see your Web Part, uninstall the Web Part and re-install it.

Uninstalling Web Parts from SharePoint   If your Web Part does not show up, you need to redo the installation steps. It's always advisable to first remove all files through the uninstall process before installing. If you have created a .cab file, you can use a single command to remove the package from SharePoint:

```
stsadm -o deletewppack -name HelloWorldWebPart.cab -url <http://servername:port>
```

If you do not have a .cab file, you can use the following set of commands to invoke the uninstall procedure. Define a set of variables if they have not already been defined.

```
set SPAdminTool=%CommonProgramFiles%\Shared\web server extensions\12\BIN\stsadm.exe
set Task=install
set PackageFile=%~dp0HelloWorldWebPart.wsp
set PackageName= HelloWorldWebPart.wsp
set TargetUrl=http://<servername:port>
```

To use the Deactivate feature for HelloWorldWebPart, type the following text into a command line:

```
"%SPAdminTool%" -o deactivatefeature -id
f13d7cc3-fd1b-43cd-80a2-cf107522cbe2 -url %TargetUrl%
```

To use the Uninstall feature for HelloWorldWebPart, type the following text into a command line:

```
"%SPAdminTool%" -o uninstallfeature -id f13d7cc3-fd1b-43cd-80a2-cf107522cbe2 -force
```

To use the Retract solution for HelloWorldWebPart, type the following text into a command line:

```
"%SPAdminTool%" -o retractsolution -name "%PackageName%" -local -url %TargetUrl%
```

To use the Delete solution for HelloWorldWebPart from SharePoint, type the following text into a command line:

```
"%SPAdminTool%" -o deletesolution -name "%PackageName%"
```

In case you are wondering, SharePoint differentiates between installations and activations of Web Parts. You need to perform both operations to remove the solution from the SharePoint server.

In some cases, malformed Web Parts can cause the Web site to malfunction. For instance, the Web site might refuse to start. One good approach to solving these types of issues is to uninstall custom Web Parts via the link in the error page until the site starts working correctly again. As a note to advanced users, in addition to using batch file automation, you can build an executable using the object model that will perform these steps. (See Chapter 5.)

Modifying Web Parts from SharePoint

As a developer, you need to know that Web Parts you develop for SharePoint can be customized by the end user or administrator. This is the default behavior. The next section will guide you through developing Web Parts that allow you to hook into the SharePoint Web Part customization theme. For now, let's briefly walk through the steps an end user would use to customize a Web Part.

Click Modify Shared Web Part on the edit menu for your Web Part, as shown in Figure 3-11. Figure 3-11 shows a Web Part's modification property being invoked.

Figure 3-11   SharePoint Web Part modification.

Three default categories—Appearance, Layout, and Advanced—occupy the Web Part menu. Each category presents different attributes that can be tweaked to adjust the appearance and layout of the control on the Web page. Figure 3-12 shows the tool pane in Visual Studio .NET.

Figure 3-12   Tool pane editor.

As a developer, you need to learn how to hook into these customizations to enable a feature-rich Web Part control. An example will be provided later in the chapter.

Debugging Web Parts in Visual Studio

Malformed Web Parts or other Web Part run-time anomalies that are not caught can cause the Web page to fail to load. It's comforting to know that the powerful Visual Studio debugger is available to developers in much the same way as it is for .NET applications. Web Parts debugging is dependent on having a working ASP.NET debugger, so you need to make sure that you can at least set and hit a breakpoint in a regular ASP.NET application.

Consider Figure 3-13. This page is produced because an ill-behaved Web Part could not be loaded.

In most cases, SharePoint exception handling code will catch the error and display the error page. You can use the link on the error page to find the Web Part and close it. (See Figure 3-14.) Alternatively, you can uninstall the Web Part using the techniques described previously.

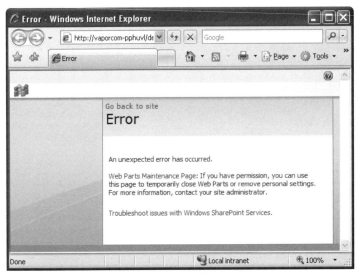

Figure 3-13   Error page for an unhandled exception.

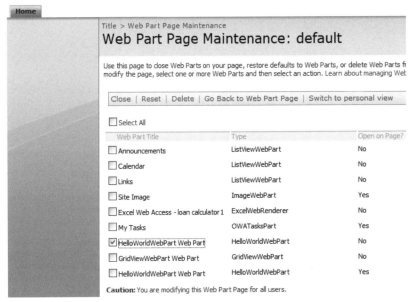

Figure 3-14   Web Part page maintenance.

To debug a Web Part in Visual Studio .NET using the new Visual Studio Extensions for SharePoint, you need to attach the debugger to an executing process. The process of attaching the debugger is straightforward.

Let's consider a concrete example for an errant Web Part called DynamicDgWebPart. When the Web Part is added to the page, it causes the page to crash. To debug the Web Part, open Visual Studio and select Attach To Process from the Debug menu, as shown in Figure 3-15.

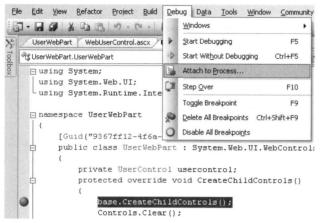

Figure 3-15   Snapshot of the Visual Studio debugger.

In the Available Process list, find the *w3wp.exe* worker process and double-click it to attach the debugger to the ASP.NET worker process, as shown in Figure 3-16. Then simply refresh the error page in SharePoint. The debugger will break on the breakpoint if that breakpoint occurs before the actual error that caused the page failure.

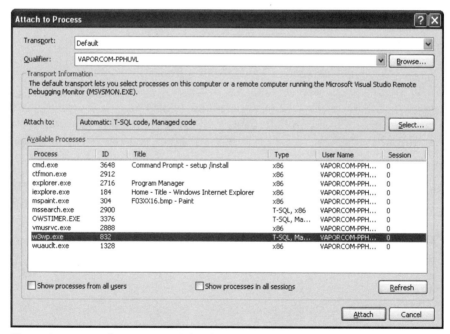

Figure 3-16   Attach To Process dialog box in Visual Studio .NET.

In some cases, the issue that is causing the page to fail to load occurs long before user code is called. In those cases, the debugger is of little assistance. You need to view as much error information as possible from the stack trace that is dumped to the error page—also known as the yellow screen of death.

The SharePoint page configuration does not dump a full stack trace by default. You need to turn on that functionality. To do so, navigate to the *web.config* file for the error page being displayed. Review Chapter 1 to find out how to determine the Web application for a particular site. Make the modification to the *web.config* file that is shown in Listing 3-6.

Listing 3-6 *web.config* safe control modification.

```
<SharePoint>
    <SafeMode MaxControls="200" CallStack="true"
DirectFileDependencies="10" TotalFileDependencies="50"
AllowPageLevelTrace="true">
        <PageParserPaths>
        </PageParserPaths>
    </SafeMode>
```

Reset Internet Information Services (IIS), and refresh the Web page. A stack trace will appear if the exception occurs again. Remember to undo the changes you made to the code after debugging is complete. Stack traces in production aren't only an eyesore, they present serious security issues as well.

Responding to Events in Web Parts

Web Parts are key building blocks for SharePoint software development. The next example walks you through the process of building a Web Part with an embedded control that is able to respond to end user events. The example is based on a *DataGrid* control that loads data from the SQL Server AdventureWorks database and allows the end user to sort columns. You can find the AdventureWorks database at this link: *http://www.microsoft.com/downloads/details.aspx?familyid=e719ecf7-9f46-4312-af89-6ad8702e4e6e&displaylang=en*.

Use the Class Library template in Visual Studio to create a library named **WebPartGrid**. You need to import the namespaces shown in Listing 3-7.

Listing 3-7 Web Part namespace declaration.

```
System
System.Web
System.Web.UI
System.Web.UI.WebControls
System.Web.UI.WebControls.WebParts
System.Data
System.Data.SqlClient
Microsoft.SharePoint
Microsoft.SharePoint.WebControls
Microsoft.SharePoint.WebPartPages
```

Next, let's create a *DataGrid* object. Inside the class, add a *CreateControls* method. These namespaces are located in the *System.Web*, *System.Drawing*, and Windows SharePoint Services libraries. Listing 3-8 illustrates the process.

Listing 3-8   Web Part *CreateChildControls* method.

```
C# Snippet
protected override void CreateChildControls()
{
    itemsAvailable = new DataGrid();

    itemsAvailable.HeaderStyle.BackColor = System.Drawing.Color.SlateGray;
    itemsAvailable.HeaderStyle.Font.Bold = true;
    itemsAvailable.AllowSorting = true;
    itemsAvailable.AllowPaging = true;
    itemsAvailable.HeaderStyle.HorizontalAlign = HorizontalAlign.Center;
    itemsAvailable.AlternatingItemStyle.BackColor = System.Drawing.Color.Gainsboro;
    itemsAvailable.SortCommand +=
        new DataGridSortCommandEventHandler(itemsAvailable_SortCommand);
    itemsAvailable.PageIndexChanged +=
        new DataGridPageChangedEventHandler(itemsAvailable_PageIndexChanged);
    itemsAvailable.DataSource = GetData();
    itemsAvailable.DataBind();

    Controls.Add(itemsAvailable);
}
```
```
Visual Basic Snippet
Protected Overrides Sub CreateChildControls()
    itemsAvailable = New DataGrid()

    itemsAvailable.HeaderStyle.BackColor = System.Drawing.Color.SlateGray
    itemsAvailable.HeaderStyle.Font.Bold = True
    itemsAvailable.AllowSorting = True
    itemsAvailable.AllowPaging = True
    itemsAvailable.HeaderStyle.HorizontalAlign = HorizontalAlign.Center
    itemsAvailable.AlternatingItemStyle.BackColor = System.Drawing.Color.Gainsboro

    AddHandler itemsAvailable.SortCommand, AddressOf itemsAvailable_SortCommand
    AddHandler itemsAvailable.PageIndexChanged, AddressOf
        itemsAvailable_PageIndexChanged
    itemsAvailable.DataSource = GetData()
    itemsAvailable.DataBind()

    Controls.Add(itemsAvailable)
End Sub
```

The *CreateChildControls* method is called by the ASP.NET page framework to notify server controls that use composition-based implementation to create any child controls they contain in preparation for rendering. *CreateChildControls* is called immediately before a control is rendered, and it is responsible for populating the child controls that might be part of the page. The code places the *DataGrid* in this method because it is a child control of the form and needs to be initialized before the Web Part is rendered. The *DataGrid* is then added to the controls collection so that it can participate in the render process later.

Examine the snippet of code shown in Listing 3-9.

Listing 3-9   Web Part *Render* method.

```
C# Snippet
protected override void Render(HtmlTextWriter output)
{
    this.EnsureChildControls();
    this.itemsAvailable.RenderControl(output);
}
```

```
Visual Basic Snippet
Protected Overrides Sub Render(ByVal output As HtmlTextWriter)
    Me.EnsureChildControls()
    Me.itemsAvailable.RenderControl(output)
End Sub
```

Code that makes use of the *CreateChildControls* method requires a call to the *EnsureChild-Controls* method. The *RenderControl* method of the *DataGrid* is used to format the output for the client. At this point, the *DataGrid* renders on the client if it contains data.

The code to load data into the *DataGrid* follows the standard pattern, which is presented in Listing 3-10 for your benefit.

Listing 3-10   Code to load data from SQL Server.

```
C# Snippet
protected DataSet GetData()
{
    string sqlString = "SELECT AddressID, AddressLine1, AddressLine2, City,
      StateProvinceID, PostalCode FROM Person.Address";
    string connectionString = @"Data Source=<servername>\SQLSVR2005;
    Initial Catalog='C:\PROGRAM FILES\MICROSOFT SQL SERVER\MSSQL.1\MSSQL\DATA\
      ADVENTUREWORKS_DATA.MDF';Integrated Security=True";

    using (System.Data.SqlClient.SqlConnection mySQLConnect =
      new SqlConnection(connectionString))
    {
        mySQLConnect.Open();
        SqlCommand myCmd = new SqlCommand(sqlString, mySQLConnect);
        System.Data.SqlClient.SqlDataAdapter myAdapter = new SqlDataAdapter(myCmd);
        DataSet ds = new DataSet();

        myAdapter.Fill(ds, "ItemsTable");

        return ds;
    }
}
```

Visual Basic Snippet

```
Protected Function GetData() As DataSet
    Dim sqlString As String = "SELECT AddressID, AddressLine1, AddressLine2, City,
      StateProvinceID, PostalCode FROM Person.Address"
    Dim connectionString As String = "Data Source=<servername>\SQLSVR2005;
      Initial Catalog='C:\PROGRAM FILES\MICROSOFT SQL SERVER\
      MSSQL.1\MSSQL\DATA\ADVENTUREWORKS_DATA.MDF';Integrated Security=True"

    Using mySQLConnect As System.Data.SqlClient.SqlConnection =
      New SqlConnection(connectionString)
        mySQLConnect.Open()
        Dim myCmd As SqlCommand = New SqlCommand(sqlString, mySQLConnect)
        Dim myAdapter As System.Data.SqlClient.SqlDataAdapter =
          New SqlDataAdapter(myCmd)
        Dim ds As DataSet = New DataSet()

        myAdapter.Fill(ds, "ItemsTable")

        Return ds
    End Using
End Function
```

The code queries the AdventureWorks database for data specified by the query. For illustrative purposes, the query and connection string sit inside the *GetData* method. In production code, this would certainly not be the case. A data set is returned if the query is successful.

Build and deploy the Web Part using the approach outlined earlier in the "Deploying Web Parts" section. From your site collection, find the Web Part and add it to the page. Your application's output should resemble Figure 3-17.

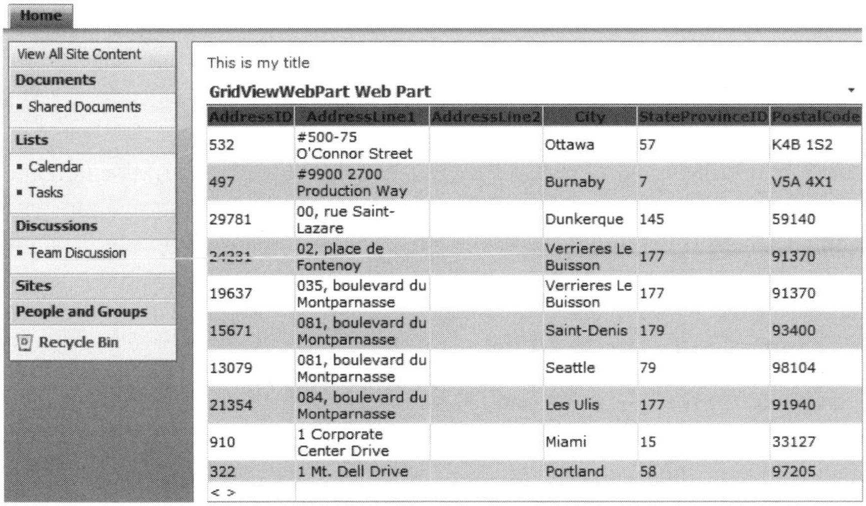

Figure 3-17   GridViewWebPart with data.

The effort wasn't entirely painful, but there isn't much real-world functionality baked in. Let's add the sorting functionality. Although sorting is implemented by default in the *GridView*, the *DataGrid* lacks that feature. Listing 3-11 shows the code needed, starting with the *PreRender* method of the page.

Listing 3-11   Page sorting through the *PreRender* method.

```csharp
C# Snippet
protected override void OnPreRender(EventArgs e)
{
    DataSet ds = GetData();
    DataView dv = ds.Tables[0].DefaultView;

    if (ViewState["SortExpression"] != null && ViewState["SortDirection"] != null)
    {
        dv.Sort = ViewState["SortExpression"] + " " + ViewState["SortDirection"];
    }
    itemsAvailable.DataSource = dv;
    itemsAvailable.DataBind();

    base.OnPreRender(e);
}
```

```vb
Visual Basic Snippet
Protected Overrides Sub OnPreRender(ByVal e As EventArgs)
    Dim ds As DataSet = GetData()
    Dim dv As DataView = ds.Tables(0).DefaultView

    If Not ViewState("SortExpression") Is Nothing AndAlso Not
      ViewState("SortDirection") Is Nothing Then
        dv.Sort = ViewState("SortExpression") & " " & ViewState("SortDirection")
    End If
    itemsAvailable.DataSource = dv
    itemsAvailable.DataBind()

    MyBase.OnPreRender(e)
End Sub
```

The sort functionality requires that the control remember the last sort direction and sort expression. However, because the *DataGrid* itself offers no place to store these items, we use *ViewState*. The idea is to retrieve the stored values of the last sort performed and invert the functionality on the appropriate column. Finally, we bubble the event to the parent control by calling *MyBase.OnPreRender*. This type of code is not SharePoint specific; rather, it relates to ASP.NET and you should be quite familiar with it.

Finally, we add the sort command handler shown in Listing 3-12.

Listing 3-12   Sort command handler.

C# Snippet

```
void itemsAvailable_SortCommand(object source, DataGridSortCommandEventArgs e)
{
    string SortExpression = (string)ViewState["SortExpression"];
    string SortDirection = (string)ViewState["SortDirection"];

    if (SortExpression != e.SortExpression)
    {
        SortExpression = e.SortExpression;
        SortDirection = "asc";
    }
    else
    {
        if (SortDirection == "asc")
            SortDirection = "desc";
        else
            SortDirection = "asc";
    }

    ViewState["SortExpression"] = SortExpression;
    ViewState["SortDirection"] = SortDirection;
}
```

Visual Basic Snippet

```
Private Sub itemsAvailable_SortCommand(ByVal source As Object,
ByVal e As DataGridSortCommandEventArgs)
    Dim SortExpression As String = CStr(ViewState("SortExpression"))
    Dim SortDirection As String = CStr(ViewState("SortDirection"))

    If SortExpression <> e.SortExpression Then
        SortExpression = e.SortExpression
        SortDirection = "asc"
    Else
        If SortDirection = "asc" Then
            SortDirection = "desc"
        Else
            SortDirection = "asc"
        End If
    End If

    ViewState("SortExpression") = SortExpression
    ViewState("SortDirection") = SortDirection
End Sub
```

Essentially, when the sort event fires, we need to remember the column and the type of sort that was performed so that future sorts can occur in the correct order.

The last bit of code, shown in Listing 3-13, wires the event to its handler.

Listing 3-13 Wiring the *Sort* event.

C# Snippet
```csharp
itemsAvailable.SortCommand +=
new DataGridSortCommandEventHandler(itemsAvailable_SortCommand);
```
Visual Basic Snippet
```vb
AddHandler itemsAvailable.SortCommand, AddressOf itemsAvailable_SortCommand
```

Displaying Workbooks in Web Parts

One of the most important functions of Excel Services is that it allows a Web Part to display a workbook. The next example will examine the scenario where a workbook is loaded in a Web Part and displayed in SharePoint.

To load a workbook in a SharePoint Web Part, open the portal and select Edit Page from the Site Actions menu. Click on Add New Web Part. Select the Excel Web Part. Click on Click Here To Open The Tool Pane to open the tool pane. You can also open the tool pane for any Web Part by clicking the Edit button in the Web Part zone and selecting Modify Shared Web Part. Enter the path to a valid workbook in the Excel Web Access tool pane. Figure 3-18 shows Excel Web Access with a loaded spreadsheet.

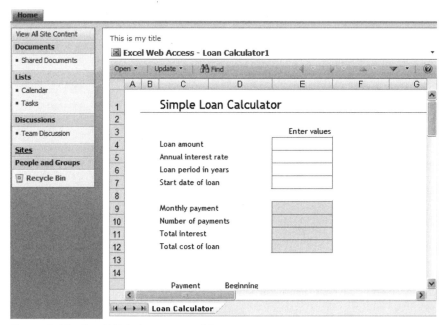

Figure 3-18 Excel Web Access spreadsheet.

Unfortunately, the code to programmatically display a Web Part in SharePoint is a bit more involved. We revisit the issue in Chapter 5 because it involves hooking into the Windows SharePoint Services model, as well as adding certain security configurations to get the Excel Web Part to display correctly.

In any case, any control displayed in a Web Part provides certain default configuration settings that can be applied by the end user. The configuration settings reside in the tool pane container. By default, the tool pane consists of five categories, each containing various properties that can be applied to the Web Part.

As you grow more confident in building Web Parts, you might begin to wonder about influencing the behavior of the properties in the tool pane. In fact, business requirements might even dictate that you customize the tool pane. In any case, we provide the full details of the code in Chapter 5. For now, we need to realize that building Web Parts with the options presented so far is arduous, time-consuming, and error prone. The next section outlines a way forward that requires less effort.

Web Parts and User Controls

To be absolutely blunt, developing cool Web Parts with arcane classic ASP approaches as the code showed earlier is a bit uncivilized. More significantly, the process is error prone because you cannot immediately see the results of your labor unless you deploy your Web Part to SharePoint and load it into a page. The lack of a tangible design surface on which to model and shape your programming ideas eats aggressively into your development time. There must be a better way!

Fortunately, it's rather easy to incorporate a designer into your Web Part project by using ASP.NET user controls. You might recall that user controls are server controls that contain encapsulated logic. User controls have .ascx extensions and run embedded in ASP.NET pages much like Web Parts. Because they have a lot in common with Web Parts (for example, they implement the *IWebPart* interface), it is possible to use the User Control designer to develop a user control that can be embedded in a SharePoint page as a Web Part. That's a fairly cheap way to gain designer support for creating SharePoint Web Parts in Visual Studio.

Create a project based on a user control template. You need to choose New | Web Site from the Visual Studio toolbar menu. Name the Web site **UserWebPart**. In the solution manager, add a new item of type User Control.

By default, the *UserWebPart* control opens in source view. Select Design to invoke the Visual Studio designer, and drag and drop a *GridView* component on the designer. Configure the *DataSource* property of the *GridView* object to point to a table in SQL Server like you normally would when developing ASP.NET applications. If you prefer, you can edit the .ascx file as well.

In our example, *GridView* is connected to the AdventureWorks database pointed at the Address table. At this time, you can choose to format *GridView* as appropriate. For grins, we have added paging and sorting and enabled the client-side callback mechanism as well as edit functionality. We have also spruced up the view by adding formatting via Auto Format. This is all done from the designer by pointing and clicking. We haven't written any code.

The user control should resemble Figure 3-19.

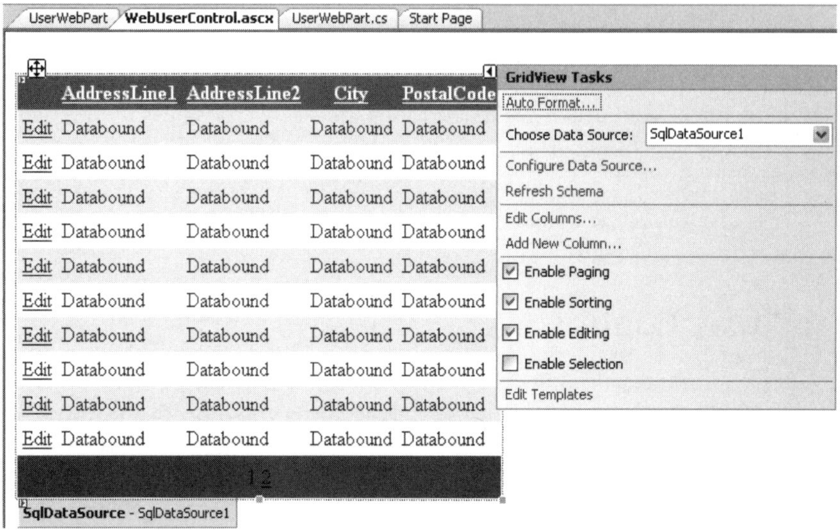

Figure 3-19 Design view of *GridView*.

To confirm that we have a working user control, embed the control in a Web Form and run the application. You can get a feel for presentation and functionality. This is no different from regular ASP.NET development, which is why the text glosses over the details.

All that is needed now is to create the actual Web Part as we have done in the past. Instead of building controls by hand, we only need to create a single user control in the body of the *Render* method and load the contents of the .ascx file. If the load routine is successful, it will render a fully functional grid—complete with editing, paging, and sorting functionality—into the Web Part. Note that we can load as many user controls as we need; there is no set limit. From the point of view of the Web Part, it acts as a host to the user control.

Listing 3-14 shows the complete code for the Web Part. Notice that it has shrunk considerably because the business logic has been encapsulated in the user control. And this is a best practice!

Listing 3-14   Web Part user control code.

C# Snippet

```csharp
using System;
using System.Web.UI;
using System.Runtime.InteropServices;

namespace UserWebPart
{
    [Guid("9367ff12-4f6a-4a1a-a930-75ce802c4c82")]
    public class UserWebPart : System.Web.UI.WebControls.WebParts.WebPart
    {
        private UserControl usercontrol;
        protected override void CreateChildControls()
        {
            base.CreateChildControls();
            Controls.Clear();

            usercontrol = (UserControl) Page.LoadControl(@"/usercontrols/
              webusercontrol.ascx");

            Controls.Add(usercontrol);
        }
        protected override void Render(HtmlTextWriter writer)
        {
            EnsureChildControls();
            usercontrol.RenderControl(writer);
        }
    }
}
```

Visual Basic Snippet

```vb
Imports System
Imports System.Web.UI
Imports System.Runtime.InteropServices

Namespace UserWebPart
    <Guid("9367ff12-4f6a-4a1a-a930-75ce802c4c82")> _
    Public Class UserWebPart
        Inherits System.Web.UI.WebControls.WebParts.WebPart
        Private usercontrol As UserControl
        Protected Overrides Sub CreateChildControls()
            MyBase.CreateChildControls()
            Controls.Clear()

            usercontrol = CType(Page.LoadControl("/usercontrols/webusercontrol.ascx"),
              UserControl)

            Controls.Add(usercontrol)
        End Sub
        Protected Overrides Sub Render(ByVal writer As HtmlTextWriter)
            EnsureChildControls()
            usercontrol.RenderControl(writer)
        End Sub
    End Class
End Namespace
```

There are three parts to this code. One part, *CreateChildControls*, loads the user controls. Another part, the *Render* method, renders the control. The third part is an ugly GUID above the class. We will examine its reason for being in Chapter 7; it does have a purpose. Notice the *LoadControl* call inside *CreateChildControls*. It is responsible for loading the user control from a file on disk located in a directory called usercontrols. There's nothing special about this directory, and the name is arbitrarily chosen. We simply need to create the directory and copy over the .ascx file that was built in the earlier part of the exercise. Once the code executes, the run time will find the user control and load it into the Web Part. You do not need to configure any special permissions for this folder.

Take it for a spin. You will find that the user control is fully functional and that it is able to sort, page, and perform the functions that were programmed in earlier. Notice that the *GridView* object embedded in the Web Part automatically sorts and pages without the postback flash à la AJAX. There's a strong hint in there somewhere that more is possible along that avenue, but we defer a more detailed discussion to Chapter 6. So, finally, you can add a few lines of code to a Web Part and incorporate the world of ASP.NET via user controls into SharePoint.

And in case you missed the signpost in the middle of the road, you should realize that you can swap, adjust, or modify the user controls live while the Web site is running. The new control will simply be loaded on the next pass. There's no price too high for that type of functionality.

Guidelines for Developing User Controls for SharePoint

A few new things are worth mentioning. Every time you modify the user control, you need to manually copy the files to the usercontrol directory. It really isn't a high price to pay, and there is a certain giddy feeling of knowing that you can, through user controls, unleash the ASP.NET productivity monster onto MOSS 2007. The more creative among you can easily modify the *setup.bat* file to copy the files to the directory or provide a build event using MSBuild to do the dirty work.

If you actually ran the application code presented earlier, you would soon find that it throws the following ugly exception:

This control does not allow connection strings with the following keywords: 'Integrated Security', 'Trusted_Connection'.

It is complaining rather loudly about the Windows Authentication portion of the connection string. Recall that the earlier example actually had the connection string embedded in the code. The sleight of hand trick allowed us to focus on the example of building and populating a *GridView* without polluting it with security exceptions.

As it turns out, controls or assemblies loaded from outside the global assembly cache (GAC) are not trusted by default. This rule applies directly to us because we are loading a user control from an untrusted folder. One solution is to simply place the assembly in the GAC using the approach outlined in Chapter 2, "Excel Web Services." That strategy is without merit in this case because .ascx files are not assemblies, contain a user interface piece and, therefore, cannot easily be stored in the GAC.

Another approach is to raise the trust level of the Web Part from the *web.config* file. Consider the following approach:

```
<trust level="Full" originUrl="" />
```

That approach is a punishable offense because it increases the attack surface for malicious code. Although it will work, the potential for damage borders on unacceptable.

The best approach is to make a change to the configuration file of the Web site. Find the *tag-Mapping* attribute in the *web.config* file for the Web site, and replace it with the line of text shown in Listing 3-15.

Listing 3-15   Code to work around the security exception.

```
<tagMapping>
  <clear/>
</tagMapping>
```

Tip   The *tagMapping* element defines a collection of tag types that are remapped to other tag types at compile time. This remapping causes the mapped type to be used in place of the original tag type for all pages and controls in the ASP.NET application that are within the scope of the configuration file. The *tagMapping* attribute is new for .NET 2.0.

Timesheet Application

Consider a request by a client to build a timesheet application. Let's use the example of a small consulting firm that has five consultants who work in the field on a daily basis. These consultants update their timesheet at project completion with billable hours. The accountants in the accounting department keep track of the billable hours by using a spreadsheet. The accountants are accustomed to running reports and macros to extract relevant metrics at the end of the month.

The consultants note that the single spreadsheet version shared among team members often leads to accidents and versioning issues. These accidents and out-of-sync spreadsheets cost the company money through inaccurate reporting.

There are many approaches to writing an application that will service the company's needs. We already have all the fundamentals to put this application together. Let's walk through a few scenarios to see whether we can agree on the best design for updating the system. First, we can write either a Web application or a smart client. The smart client has particular appeal because it is connection-aware. This works out particularly well for field workers who don't always have access to the Internet. If these aren't major issues, an ASP.NET client will do nicely because it hides the burden of installation. The ASP.NET client can connect to a spreadsheet hosted on MOSS that stores the data. We can use Excel Web Services for the connection logic. Let's proceed with an ASP.NET application.

To build the application, you create a new Web Part project, as shown in Figure 3-20. Name the project Accounter. Figure 3-20 shows a Web Part made up of text boxes, labels, and a button.

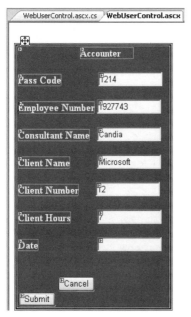

Figure 3-20   Interface for the Accounter application.

Aside from the coding aspects, the spreadsheet needs to be provisioned for each consultant. Provisioning the spreadsheet involves providing the consultant with a pass-code number and a sheet with the consultant's name in the workbook. The sheet for the junior consultant Candia is shown in Figure 3-20.

In the prepared spreadsheet, a hidden column in Excel is used to store the numeric password. Each column in the spreadsheet represents a client and the billable hours attached to the client. As the consultants perform audits in the field, data is entered into the next adjacent column, as shown in Figure 3-21. Excel supports one million rows and 16,000 columns, so there's a fair chance you'll run out of work before exceeding the column limit. The accountants are free to embed macros, formulas, or whatever is necessary to facilitate data extraction. The spreadsheet prepared by the accountant resembles Figure 3-21.

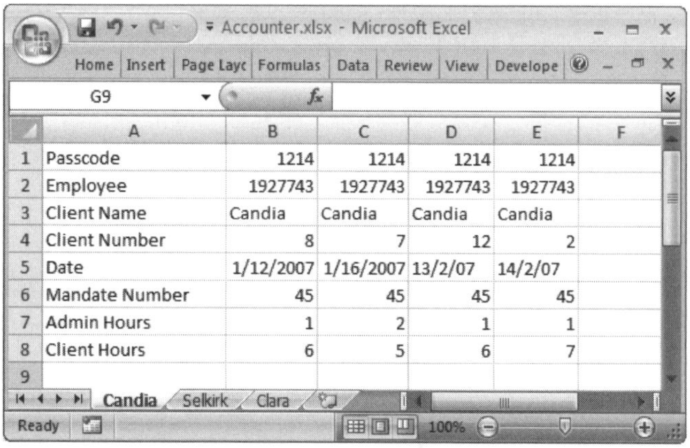

	A	B	C	D	E	F
1	Passcode	1214	1214	1214	1214	
2	Employee	1927743	1927743	1927743	1927743	
3	Client Name	Candia	Candia	Candia	Candia	
4	Client Number	8	7	12	2	
5	Date	1/12/2007	1/16/2007	13/2/07	14/2/07	
6	Mandate Number	45	45	45	45	
7	Admin Hours	1	2	1	1	
8	Client Hours	6	5	6	7	
9						

Figure 3-21 Excel spreadsheet representation of completed Accounter application.

The accountant in charge of the application simply needs to add one sheet per consultant, named appropriately. In addition, the accountant needs to create named ranges in column A. The application that you write will fill columns B, C, D, and so on for each worksheet in the workbook. The accountant saves the spreadsheet in a trusted file location so that EWS can service the spreadsheet. At any point in time, the spreadsheet can be updated, swapped, or calculated for reporting metrics without affecting the user because workbooks are opened in user sessions.

When you are done building the user interface, let's walk through the approach. We provide the relevant code snippets along with the explanation. The driving event for the application code is the Submit button. Submit calls the *SaveClientData* method. The main structure of the *SaveClientData* method call looks like the code shown in Listing 3-16.

Listing 3-16 Accounter application logic.

C# Snippet

```
//save the user input into the spreadsheet session
LoadInputDataIntoSpreadsheet(es, programCode, programCode, sessionId, sheetName);

//write the values in the user session to the workbook in the trusted location
SaveWorkBook(es, targetWorkbookPath);

//clear the form
ClearForm();
```

Visual Basic Snippet

```
'save the user input into the spreadsheet session
LoadInputDataIntoSpreadsheet(es, programCode, programCode, sessionId, sheetName)
'write the values in the user session to the workbook in the trusted location
SaveWorkBook(es, targetWorkbookPath)
'clear the form
ClearForm()
```

Let's begin with the simple method calls. *ClearForm* is a simple routine to clear the form after it is submitted. (See Listing 3-17.)

Listing 3-17 Routine to notify client that data saves are pending.

```csharp
C# Snippet
private void ShowUnsavedClientData(DataItem di)
{
    ConsultantPasscodeField.Text = string.Empty;
    ConsultantNameField.Text    = di.EmployeeName;
    ConsultantNumberField.Text  = di.EmployeeNumber.ToString();
    ClientHoursField.Text       = di.ClientHours.ToString();
    ClientNameField.Text        = di.ClientName;
    ClientNumberField.Text      = di.ClientNumber.ToString();
    DateField.Text              = di.CurrentDate.ToString();
    statusBar.Items[0].Text     = "Click submit to save this data, Cancel to clear.";
    statusBar.Items[0].BackColor= Color.Yellow;
}
```

```vb
Visual Basic Snippet
Private Sub ShowUnsavedClientData(ByVal di As DataItem)
    ConsultantPasscodeField.Text = string.Empty
    ConsultantNameField.Text = di.EmployeeName
    ConsultantNumberField.Text = di.EmployeeNumber.ToString()
    ClientHoursField.Text = di.ClientHours.ToString()
    ClientNameField.Text = di.ClientName
    ClientNumberField.Text = di.ClientNumber.ToString()
    DateField.Text = di.CurrentDate.ToString()
    statusBar.Items(0).Text = "Click submit to save this data, Cancel to clear."
    statusBar.Items(0).BackColor= Color.Yellow
End Sub
```

There isn't much to explain here. This routine will be invoked by a call to *ClearForm* when we submit the form successfully. Another simple method is *LoadInputDataIntoSpreadsheet*, shown in Listing 3-18.

Listing 3-18 Code to load input data into the spreadsheet.

```csharp
C# Snippet
public void LoadInputDataIntoSpreadsheet(ExcelService es,
string sheetname, string programCode, string sessionId, string sheetName)
{
    //valid client, so begin processing
    es.SetCellA1(sessionId, sheetName, programCode + 5.ToString(),
      ClientNumberField.Text.Trim());
    es.SetCellA1(sessionId, sheetName, programCode + 6.ToString(),
      ClientNameField.Text.Trim());

    es.SetCellA1(sessionId, sheetName, programCode + 7.ToString(),
      ClientHoursField.Text.Trim());
    es.SetCellA1(sessionId, sheetName, programCode + 9.ToString(),
      DateField.Text.Trim());
}
```

Visual Basic Snippet

```vb
Public Sub LoadInputDataIntoSpreadsheet(ByVal es As ExcelService, ByVal
sheetname As String,
ByVal programCode As String, ByVal sessionId As String,
ByVal sheetName_Renamed As String)
    'valid client, so begin processing
    es.SetCellA1(sessionId, sheetName, programCode & 5.ToString(),
      ClientNumberField.Text.Trim())
    es.SetCellA1(sessionId, sheetName, programCode & 6.ToString(),
      ClientNameField.Text.Trim())

    es.SetCellA1(sessionId, sheetName, programCode & 7.ToString(),
      ClientHoursField.Text.Trim())
    es.SetCellA1(sessionId, sheetName, programCode & 9.ToString(),
      DateField.Text.Trim())
End Sub
```

This method is responsible for moving the end user input values into the spreadsheet. The *programCode* variable holds the next empty column—for instance, B, C, D, E, and so on. The logic concatenates a numeric position to the address to form a valid range. As an example, the first line of code sets the cell reference to B5. On the next iteration, the reference is set to C5, and so on.

The *SaveWorkbook* method call is responsible for writing the in-memory values of the workbook to the actual workbook in the trusted location, as we can see in Listing 3-19.

Listing 3-19 Code to save a workbook session to disk.

C# Snippet

```csharp
//this routine persists the workbook to the sharepoint document library
void SaveWorkBook(ExcelService es, string targetWorkbookPath)
{
    Status[] status;
    // Open the workbook, then call GetWorkbook and close the session.
    string sessionId = es.OpenWorkbook(targetWorkbookPath, _lang, _lang, out status);

    // Get a full snapshot of the workbook.
    byte[] workbook = es.GetWorkbook(sessionId, WorkbookType.FullWorkbook,
      out status);

    // Close workbook. This also closes the session.
    es.CloseWorkbook(sessionId);

    // Write the resulting Excel file to stdout, as a binary stream.
    FileStream fs = new FileStream(@"E:\Accounter\Accounter.xlsx", FileMode.Create);
    //strictly speaking a binary writer isn't required here
    BinaryWriter binaryWriter = new BinaryWriter(fs);
    binaryWriter.Write(workbook);
    binaryWriter.Close();
}
```

Visual Basic Snippet

```vb
'this routine persists the workbook to the sharepoint document library
Private Sub SaveWorkBook(ByVal es As ExcelService, ByVal targetWorkbookPath As String)
    Dim status As Status()
    ' Open the workbook, then call GetWorkbook
    ' and close the session.
    Dim sessionId As String = es.OpenWorkbook(targetWorkbookPath, _lang, _lang,
      status)

    ' Get a full snapshot of the workbook.
    Dim workbook As Byte() = es.GetWorkbook(sessionId, WorkbookType.FullWorkbook,
      status)

    ' Close workbook. This also closes the session.
    es.CloseWorkbook(sessionId)

    ' Write the resulting Excel file to stdout, as a binary stream.
    Dim fs As FileStream = New FileStream("E:\Accounter\Accounter.xlsx",
      FileMode.Create)
    'strictly speaking a binary writer isn't required here
    Dim binaryWriter As BinaryWriter = New BinaryWriter(fs)
    binaryWriter.Write(workbook)
    binaryWriter.Close()
End Sub
```

We gloss over this piece of code because Chapter 4, "Excel Calculation Service," offers a more detailed analysis. For now, we note that the code grabs the in-memory snapshot of the workbook and uses the .NET API to write the file to disk.

Before this code can run without issues, some plumbing needs to be set up. Let's discuss this process in detail. The plumbing is the heart of the application. It opens the worksheet using the end user's name as the worksheet value. See the code in Listing 3-20.

Listing 3-20   Code showing the logic behind the save data functionality.

C# Snippet

```csharp
public void SaveClientData()
{
    using (ExcelWebService.ExcelService es = new ExcelService())
    {
        string sheetName = ConsultantNameField.Text;
        Status[] outStatus;
        //open the workbook
        string sessionId = OpenWorkbook(es, sheetName);

        //workbook cannot be opened, so inform the user of the issue
        //most likely, an accountant has locked the range for end-of-month reporting
        if (String.IsNullOrEmpty(sessionId))
        {
            statusBar.Items[0].Text = "Unable to save data. Please wait a while
              before trying again";
```

```
                    statusBar.Items[0].BackColor = Color.Red;
                    throw new ApplicationException("The workbook cannot be opened, please
                        try again later");
                }

            //use the consultant's name to retrieve the provisioned data
            object[] rangeResult = es.GetRangeA1(sessionId, sheetName, "a1:a11",
                false, out outStatus);

            string employeePassCode = GetPassCode(rangeResult);
            string programCode = GetProgramCode(rangeResult);
            if(programCode.trim() != string.Empty)
            {
                //authenticate the user
            }
            else
            {
                statusBar.Text = "You are not authorized to access this application.";
                statusBar.BackColor = Color.Red;
            }
        }
}
```

Visual Basic Snippet

```
Public Sub SaveClientData()
    Using es As ExcelWebService.ExcelService = New ExcelService()
        Dim sheetName As String = ConsultantNameField.Text
        Dim outStatus As Status()
        'open the workbook
        Dim sessionId As String = OpenWorkbook(es, sheetName)

        'workbook cannot be opened, so inform the user of the issue
        'most likely, an accountant has locked the range for end-of-month reporting
        If String.IsNullOrEmpty(sessionId) Then
            statusBar.Items(0).Text = "Unable to save data. Please wait a while before
                trying again"
            statusBar.Items(0).BackColor = Color.Red
            Throw New ApplicationException("The workbook cannot be opened, please try
                again later")
        End If

        'use the consultant's name to retrieve the provisioned data
        Dim rangeResult As Object() = es.GetRangeA1(sessionId, sheetName, "a1:a11",
            False, outStatus)

        Dim employeePassCode As String = GetPassCode(rangeResult)
        Dim programCode As String = GetProgramCode(rangeResult)
        If programCode.trim() <> String.Empty Then
            'authenticate the user
        Else
            statusBar.Text = "You are not authorized to access this application."
            statusBar.BackColor = Color.Red
        End If
    End Using
End Sub
```

The method first creates a Web service proxy object within a *using* block. The *using* block guarantees resource de-allocation to avoid memory leaks. Then the consultant's name is used to find and open the workbook through the *OpenWorkbook* method. A valid session ID is returned if the call is successful. The session identifier is a long encrypted string similar to the following:

```
"64.dcb16eaf-ec49-4f54-a2f4-... -03-00-02T02:00:00:0000#-0060"
```

Because the programmer has intimate knowledge of the back-end spreadsheet, she can set a range such as A1:A11. This corresponds to the values entered by the accountant when the spreadsheet was provisioned for a particular consultant. We'll use that range to extract a special pass-code value and a program code value. Obviously, we need to hide rows 1 and 2 because these contain sensitive data. The visibility does not affect program logic. And we can use Excel workbook security to prevent users from turning the visibility back on.

The pass-code value entered by the accountant in the workbook simply provides another level of authentication. The code can check the consultant's name and pass code that were entered in the front-end application against the values in the spreadsheet for a match, taking action as appropriate.

The *programCode* variable is initially empty when the spreadsheet is first provisioned. Recall that the *programCode* variable represents the next column that is available for writing. The *programCode* feature prevents code from overwriting ranges that have already been written to. When the code has updated the spreadsheet with values from the Windows client on the first time through, the value is updated from an initially empty value to C. Column A contains data that was provisioned by the accountant, and column B contains data that was just written when the value of *programCode* was empty. This indicates to the calling code that column C is available for storing values the next time a write is required. On the next pass through, *programCode* will be updated from C to D, and so on. Columns will be filled in sequential fashion.

The method to extract the *programCode* and *employeePassCode* are logically structured the same way. A loop iterates the results of the *GetRangeA1* method, and an appropriate index is used into the object array. Listing 3-21 shows the code for the *GetProgramCode* method.

Listing 3-21   Code to extract the program logic from the EWS jagged array object.

```
C# Snippet
//get the passcode from the input jagged array
string GetProgramCode(object[] input)
{
    string retVal = string.Empty;
    if (input != null && input.Length > 0)
    {
        object[] range = (object[])input[0];
        if (range != null && range.Length > 0)
```

```
        retVal = range[0].ToString();
    }


    return retVal;
}
```
Visual Basic Snippet
```
'get the passcode from the input jagged array
Private Function GetProgramCode(ByVal input As Object()) As String
    Dim retVal As String = String.Empty
    If Not input Is Nothing AndAlso input.Length > 0 Then
        Dim range As Object() = CType(input(0), Object())
        If Not range Is Nothing AndAlso range.Length > 0 Then
            retVal = range(0).ToString()
        End If
    End If


    Return retVal
End Function
```

Another nifty feature that we have added focuses on saving results if exceptions occur. If updates through EWS fail, the application intelligently serializes the data to disk so that application data is not lost. At application startup, the code then checks to see whether there is any serialized data that needs to be saved. Listing 3-22 shows the startup code.

Listing 3-22   Code that runs at startup to deserialize data and prompt user.

C# Snippet
```
private void Page_Load(object sender, EventArgs e)
{
    DataItem di = DeSerialize();
    if (di != null && di.ContainsData)
    {
        statusBar.Text = "You have unsaved data from " +
          di.CurrentDate.ToShortDateString();
        ShowUnsavedClientData(di);
    }
}
```
Visual Basic Snippet
```
Private Sub Page_Load(ByVal sender As Object, ByVal e As EventArgs)
    Dim di As DataItem = DeSerialize()
    If Not di Is Nothing AndAlso di.ContainsData Then
        statusBar.Text = "You have unsaved data from " &
          di.CurrentDate.ToShortDateString()
        ShowUnsavedClientData(di)
    End If
End Sub
```

The serialization and deserialization routines are stock implementations that grab data from the serialized object and store it in the associated text box field. The code is provided in

Listing 3-23, but the details of the process are glossed over because it relates entirely to .NET programming.

Listing 3-23 Serialization and deserialization routines.

```csharp
C# Snippet
public void Serialize(DataItem di)
{
    if (!String.IsNullOrEmpty(ConsultantNameField.Text))
    {
        using (FileStream fs = new FileStream(ConsultantNameField.Text.Trim(),
          FileMode.Create))
        {
            BinaryFormatter bf = new BinaryFormatter();
            bf.Serialize(fs, di);
        }
    }
}
public DataItem DeSerialize()
{
    if (!String.IsNullOrEmpty(ConsultantNameField.Text))
    {
        try
        {
            using (FileStream fs = new FileStream(ConsultantNameField.Text.Trim(),
              FileMode.Open))
            {
                BinaryFormatter bf = new BinaryFormatter();

                return (DataItem)bf.Deserialize(fs);
            }
        }
        catch (FileNotFoundException)
        {//perform some logging here
        }
    }
    return null;
}
```

```vb
Visual Basic Snippet
Public Sub Serialize(ByVal di As DataItem)
    If (Not String.IsNullOrEmpty(ConsultantNameField.Text)) Then
        Using fs As FileStream = New FileStream(ConsultantNameField.Text.Trim(),
          FileMode.Create)
            Dim bf As BinaryFormatter = New BinaryFormatter()
            bf.Serialize(fs, di)
        End Using
    End If
End Sub
Public Function DeSerialize() As DataItem
    If (Not String.IsNullOrEmpty(ConsultantNameField.Text)) Then
        Try
            Using fs As FileStream = New FileStream(ConsultantNameField.Text.Trim(),
              FileMode.Open)
                Dim bf As BinaryFormatter = New BinaryFormatter()
```

```
                Return CType(bf.Deserialize(fs), DataItem)
            End Using
        Catch e1 As FileNotFoundException
            'perform some logging here
        End Try
    End If
    Return Nothing
End Function
```

The *Serialize* method uses the binary formatter to serialize the object. The *DeSerialize* method performs the reverse. The remainder of the code is concerned with niceties that allow application messages to be displayed neatly in the status bar object at the bottom of the form. Figure 3-22 shows the application at run time.

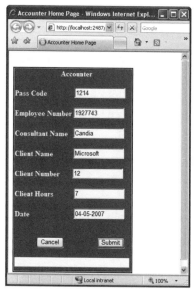

Figure 3-22   Accounter application at run time.

Guidelines for Developing Windows Clients That Target Excel Services

As usual, there are a couple of nuances that you need to be aware of, so let's discuss those. An accountant using MOSS 2007 could simply create a new spreadsheet, provision it for the consultants, and use the Publish feature in Excel 2007 to publish the spreadsheet on the server. The accountant could then provide access to the consultants through a URI. Your services weren't actually needed at all!

This leads us to a much larger question: What is the value of a .NET developer in MOSS applications? To answer that question, you need to learn to think differently. Recall that we focused on extensibility earlier on. A spreadsheet published to MOSS can accommodate only spreadsheet functionality. However, a .NET application hooked into MOSS through EWS can integrate Windows functionality into spreadsheets, thereby extending the spreadsheet capabilities considerably.

Another important point worth mentioning is that budget-conscious shops might purchase MOSS 2007 but elect to stay with their current Office system, such as Office XP or Office 2003. Only Office Enterprise or Professional Plus versions offer the ability to publish spreadsheets.

One important advantage of this application is that it is connection aware. A published spreadsheet will lose user data if the connection is dropped. The published spreadsheet is also limited to sites that guarantee an Internet connection. This can be an issue for consultants working in the field or traveling on the road. In that regard, the customized application extends the usability of the spreadsheet application. The guiding rule here is that if the application requires integration or extra functionality not built into an Excel spreadsheet, it is a good candidate for integration with a .NET client. Otherwise, it isn't and you should be content to allow an accountant to proceed without your help.

Speaking of exceptions, the observant among you might have noticed that the Accounter application contained a vicious bug in the way the *programCode* variable is updated. The next column is a combination of a letter and a number. However, after 26 letters, Excel uses a double-letter naming convention. Because our application does not take this into account, the code will eventually fail. The bug fix as well as the implementation of the *programCode* logic is left as an exercise to the reader.

Summary

This chapter presented the foundation of Web Parts. You learned to build and deploy Web Parts. There are several methods for building Web Parts. The manual approach involves a lot of legwork to create appropriate types and to sign the assembly. The deployment process is equally arduous. However, the manual process has a certain knack for imparting life-long lessons that pay dividends when automated processes go haywire.

To ease the task of writing and deploying Web Parts, Microsoft has released new SharePoint template add-ins. These templates help simplify the programming effort and bring the added advantage of the powerful Visual Studio debugger to SharePoint. Although there are many tools that can help you write Web Parts—such as the new SharePoint 2007 designer, which is simply a rebranded version of Microsoft Office FrontPage—Visual Studio is the recommended tool for developers.

The vigilant among you might have noticed that this chapter glossed over a lot of the internal details of the SharePoint infrastructure. This oversight will be rectified when Chapter 5 nosedives into the bowels of Windows SharePoint Services. For now, you have a good practical overview of developing working solutions in SharePoint. Chapter 6 will build on this platform by diving deep into advanced functionality. The reasons why things work the way they do will be explained in Chapter 5.

Finally, this chapter signed for and delivered the goods that ASP.NET programmers have been patiently waiting for. Using user controls, we have a relatively painless way to build fully functional Web Parts that approach the productivity of the Visual Studio .NET design environment. We can combine this approach with the event code that we learned earlier and take advantage of the design-time capabilities of server controls. You can extend this technique to work with any server control.

This final step completes the puzzle and prepares us to vault beyond the ordinary into advanced programming techniques that push against the boundaries of application functionality. You'll get to experience this from a front row seat in Chapter 6 and Chapter 7.

Chapter 4

Excel Calculation Service

The heart and soul of Excel Services is Excel Calculation Service (ECS). It provides direct access to the calculation engine that powers Microsoft Office Excel. Excel Calculation Service is used to load workbooks, perform calculations, invoke external functions, and refresh data contained in workbooks.

The types that encapsulate the Excel Calculation Service live in the *Micorosoft.Office.Excel. Server* namespace. ECS is intended to be used as a server-side spreadsheet calculation engine. You can access this engine from any type of client by using Excel Web Services (EWS) in your client application to communicate with Excel Calculation Service.

An Introduction to Excel Calculation Service

The design philosophy that drives the Excel architecture is impressive indeed. Microsoft Office SharePoint Server (MOSS) 2007 can scale to support thousands of Web sites across an enterprise farm. Excel Services, part of the Business Intelligence offering in SharePoint, is designed and tested to support the upper limit of this load in a SharePoint farm. The load is distributed across the farm by the ECS proxy. The ECS proxy is invisible to both the user and developer, but it plays an integral role in routing calculation requests to the calculation engine.

The calculation engine manages a cache and security configurations so that the requests are serviced within configurable time constraints without the data being compromised. An administrator can also tweak the tolerance limits and configure the responsiveness of the calculation engine to adjust for load. We show how to perform these tweaks later in the chapter.

The calculation engine can source data from spreadsheets on the farm and from external sources via embedded connections. *Embedded connections* refer to connection information that is part of the workbook.

Excel Calculation Service breaks new ground because it inherently handles concurrency issues. This means that various members of a team of accountants working in a legal department can collaborate on the same spreadsheet without worrying about versioning issues or concurrency limitations. This is simply not possible with current spreadsheet-based applications.

To handle these concurrent requests, ECS services each calculation request on a separate thread across the Web farm—a technique called *multithreaded computation*. ECS then internally implements the correct synchronization behavior to guarantee computational fidelity for the calculation results. The engine automatically adjusts for chained formulas in a spreadsheet, calculation priority, and calculation and recalculation dependencies.

The guarantee is honored in part because each calculation invocation is atomic in nature, meaning that a single computation request by a user will not be broken down into subatomic parts. The computation request will be serviced by a single thread as a single unit of calculation. You can find more information on the internals of the calculation engine at this link: *http://msdn2.microsoft.com/en-us/library/aa730921.aspx*.

The architecture also uses *sticky sessions* so that a subsequent request from the same user is directed to the same Web server in the farm. Sticky sessions help to eliminate the issues that are caused with requests that require state information on a particular server in the farm.

Using our example of accountants provided earlier, if each accountant were to submit a calculation request at the same moment, the ECS proxy receiving the calculation request would forward each computation request to the calculation engine using separate threads. If these computation requests involved shared resources such as read/writes to a common cell, the calculation engine would employ the proper synchronization primitives at the cell level to prevent race conditions and data corruption. This is handled automatically so that the programmer does not incur the burden of synchronization. You are unlikely to find this architecture in any other product this side of the known universe! Let's take a closer look at the Excel Services application programming interface (API).

Excel Services API

The Excel Services API is conceptually simple, as the graphical representation in this section shows. The illustration succinctly describes the API and the extent of functionality available.

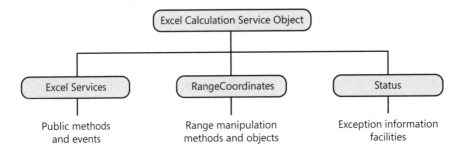

The three core objects—Excel Services, *RangeCoordinates*, and Status—shown in the illustration provide the bulk of functionality.

Excel Services   The Excel Services object can be accessed locally through direct linking or remotely through a SOAP client. Both approaches are outlined in Chapter 2, "Excel Web Services."

RangeCoordinates   For spreadsheet access, the major player is the *RangeCoordinates* object. This object controls access to the cells in the spreadsheet. A cell is an atomic, addressable part of a spreadsheet range. Cells can be either addressed directly or addressed through named ranges.

Status   Because access to the spreadsheet data can result in errors, the status object is available to provide detailed information about the call. Typically, a combination of these three objects provides enterprise-level spreadsheet functionality.

Excel Sessions

It's fundamentally important to understand that Excel Services cannot author Excel workbooks. This behavior is by design and has been influenced by Sarbanes-Oxley regulations enacted by the U.S. government. The regulations are aimed at increasing a corporation's accountability with regard to its data access and storage and reducing the potential for fraud.

As a general note, the auditing ability and control provides functionality out of the box that virtually any company could benefit from. Chapter 6, "Advanced Web Parts Programming," will discuss the auditing capabilities baked into the product in more detail.

As pointed out earlier, Excel Services opens workbooks in user sessions that are stored in memory. Let's take a closer look at the session process. Just before an Excel workbook is opened from Excel Services, the workbook residing in the trusted location is read into memory and a session is opened based on that in-memory workbook stream.

Planning   It's important to note that a workbook doesn't necessarily have to reside in a trusted location in MOSS 2007. However, it must reside in a trusted location if it is to be loaded by Excel Services. Workbooks residing in nontrusted locations can be opened using Microsoft Excel. These sessions do not benefit from the Excel Services machinery.

For performance reasons, an individual session can be pooled so that its contents can be shared among users with the same security attributes who service the same workbook. Let's consider an example for clarification. If the accountants discussed earlier belong to the same department and share the same security privileges (that is, they belong to the same domain, are assigned to the same service account, and have the same user permissions configured in Excel Services), they can automatically collaborate on the same workbook.

If a single user in that pool of accountants does not share the same security privileges, that particular user receives a separate copy of the workbook and she cannot collaborate on the shared workbook that the other accountants are using. The isolation enforces security by allowing only those with the necessary authorization to share data, a concept occasionally referred to as *information sheltering*. This is handled for you automatically, based on Roles, Membership, and Permission sets configured by the administrator when MOSS 2007 is provisioned. You do not have to write any code.

Caution   The trusted file location—or any trusted location for that matter—does not exist on disk. These locations exist in the content database, where access can be controlled and security restrictions can be enforced. You should not directly manipulate tables in the content database. It's important to note that, as a developer, nothing stops you from opening a connection to the content database and writing or reading data. You already have the required information (via the GUID discussed in Chapter 1, "An Introduction to Excel Services") to figure out the appropriate database, connection string, and tables. However, you should resist this urge because you can affect the scalability of the SharePoint product as a whole, not to mention that there is no product support for this approach. However, if you care to understand how the machinery operates, you should certainly examine these databases and tables.

Excel Services manages sessions using unique session identifiers. Session IDs are only unique to a session in the farm—that is, they are not globally unique identifiers (GUIDs). Session IDs are also used to maintain sticky session information as well. Recall that this was discussed earlier with regard to computation fidelity.

An Excel Services session caches the workbook, calculation states, and results. The session is torn down with a call to the *CloseWorkbook* method or when the session times out. Crashes or hiccups in the server that affect Excel Services result in orphaned sessions in memory. These orphans are torn down only after the active session expires. There is no way to access an orphaned session because a request to the workbook opens a new user session with a new session identifier. This underscores the importance of the *using* construct to ensure that the workbook is closed when scope is exited.

Important   While the *using* construct is the recommended practice for closing workbooks, this book discusses the asynchronous close scenario, where the workbook should be closed inside a *finally* block instead.

By navigating to Shared Services Administration: [*SharedServicesProvider*], *Excel Services Trusted File Locations*, *Trusted File Location*, you can fine-tune session settings, as shown in Figure 4-1.

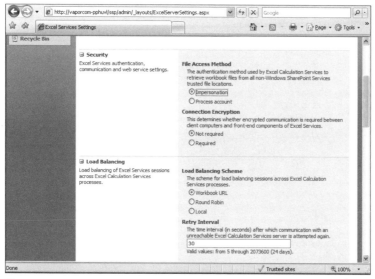

Figure 4-1   User session settings in Microsoft Office SharePointServer 2007.

Saving Workbook Data

The text has pointed out that workbooks are opened in user sessions that are managed by the calculation engine. The implication here is that a server hiccup (a crash, reboot, IIS reset, and so forth) can cause the session to be lost. ASP.NET suffers from the same disease! On one hand, the architecture benefits from a significant performance boost of at least an order of magnitude or more when compared to file-based sessions. On the other hand, there is an ugliness surrounding lost sessions that is discouraging. Fortunately, the burden is not overwhelming if you simply need to save a workbook. Let's have a look, starting with some code in Listing 4-1.

Listing 4-1   Programmatically saving a workbook.

```
C# Snippet
using (Snapshot.ExcelService es = new ExcelService())
{
    Status[] outStatus;
    RangeCoordinates rangeCoordinates = new RangeCoordinates();
    string sheetName = "Sheet1";
    string targetWorkbookPath = "http://<servername:port>/Shared%20Documents/
      Snapshots.xlsx";
    es.Credentials = System.Net.CredentialCache.DefaultNetworkCredentials;
    string sessionId = es.OpenWorkbook(targetWorkbookPath, "en-US", "en-US", out
      outStatus);

    //only proceed on a valid session
    if (!String.IsNullOrEmpty(sessionId))
    {
        outStatus = es.SetCellA1(sessionId, sheetName, "a1", "hello world");
```

```
        byte[] workbook = es.GetWorkbook(sessionId,
          WorkbookType.PublishedItemsSnapshot, out outStatus);

        // Write the resulting Excel file to stdout
        FileStream fs = new FileStream(@"c:\Export\Snapshot.xlsx", FileMode.Create);
        BinaryWriter binaryWriter = new BinaryWriter(fs);
        binaryWriter.Write(workbook);
        binaryWriter.Close();
    }
}
```

Visual Basic Snippet

```
Imports SaveWorkBook.Snapshot
Imports System.IO

Module Module1
    Sub Main()
        Using es As Snapshot.ExcelService = New ExcelService()
            Dim outStatus As Status()
            Dim rangeCoordinates As RangeCoordinates = New RangeCoordinates()
            Dim sheetName As String = "Sheet1"
            Dim targetWorkbookPath As String = "http://<servername:port>/
              Shared%20Documents/Snapshots.xlsx"
            es.Credentials = System.Net.CredentialCache.DefaultNetworkCredentials
            Dim sessionId As String = es.OpenWorkbook(targetWorkbookPath,
              "en-US", "en-US", outStatus)

            'only proceed on a valid session
            If (Not String.IsNullOrEmpty(sessionId)) Then
                outStatus = es.SetCellA1(sessionId, sheetName, "a1", "hello world")
                Dim workbook As Byte() = es.GetWorkbook(sessionId,
                  WorkbookType.PublishedItemsSnapshot, outStatus)
                ' Write the resulting Excel file to stdout
                Dim fs As FileStream = New FileStream("c:\Export\Snapshot2.xlsx",
                  FileMode.Create)
                Dim binaryWriter As BinaryWriter = New BinaryWriter(fs)
                binaryWriter.Write(workbook)
                binaryWriter.Close()
            End If
        End Using
    End Sub
End Module
```

By now, you should be familiar with the code, so we can skip the mundane aspects of it and focus on the new parts. To save a workbook, you must first get a snapshot of the user session of the workbook. This is accomplished through a call to the *GetWorkbook* method. The call returns a byte array representing the current data in the workbook in the user session. The byte array includes any data and objects that might be embedded in the spreadsheet.

Next, we use the .NET API to write the byte array to a file on disk. Note that we can manipulate the contents of the file using the .NET API if we so desired. One important point to remember is that you can't simply write the workbook file to the trusted file location because the trusted file location actually resides in the content database. The difference here is that the file you write to disk cannot then be loaded by EWS because it does not reside in a trusted location. In Chapter 5, "Windows SharePoint Services 3.0," you will learn to write code to move documents like these into the trusted file location in a way that is fully supported by Microsoft Product Support. That type of programming latitude really addresses real-world requirements for application integration.

There's one tasty morsel that we can feast on in the code. Consider the call to the *GetWorkbook* method. Its second argument is an enumeration of type *WorkbookType*. The enumeration actually controls the type of data that is returned to the SOAP client. Table 4-1 shows workbook enumeration values.

Table 4-1   **Workbook Enumeration Values**

Member Name	Description
FullSnapshot	Returns a snapshot of the entire file
FullWorkbook	Returns the entire workbook
PublishedItemsSnapshot	Returns a snapshot containing the published sheets or objects in the file

The SOAP client must have the necessary privileges to invoke certain calls, as discussed in Chapter 2. Let's provide some more detail here. The *GetApiVersion* method call is the only call that can be made without explicit permissions. Every other method call requires *view* permissions in WSS 3.0 or *read* permissions for the workbook.

A *FullWorkbook* request actually returns embedded data and formulas in the workbook. This type of call requires that a caller have *open* permissions for the workbook or *read* permission for a file share. The call fails if the SOAP client does not have the required permissions. In contrast, the *PublishedItemsSnapshot* can retrieve portions of the Excel file that a spreadsheet author selects as viewable even though the SOAP client does not have view permissions on the workbook. The reason is that the *Workbook* enumeration forces the workbook to return only updated data. The formulas and embedded connections, if they exist in the workbook, are not returned. This is the same view that you see when a worksheet is published via Excel.

In every case, Excel Services performs a full calculation, including updating external data sources before data is returned. You can expect performance degradation if a call to *GetWorkbook* services a worksheet with external data connections. We examine external connections later in this chapter.

Excel Services Credentials

If you have been following diligently, you might be wondering how Excel Services determines access rights to the workbook resource. We have glossed over the credentials object in the past, but it deserves a closer look because it offers much more flexibility. Credentials are required before any Excel Web Services (EWS) methods can be called successfully. In the past, we have established system credentials for the current security context in which the application is running by passing in *System.Net.CredentialCache.DefaultNetworkCredentials*. This authenticates the user running the code by passing her default credentials to the Web service from the system credential cache.

The SOAP client can, if it has the relevant information, create any credentials and pass it to EWS. If these credentials match an existing account, the access rights that are provisioned for that account are conferred on the SOAP client. Assuming that the SOAP client has access to the relevant account information—say, the name and password of an account with administrator privileges—the credentials can be created according to the code in Listing 4-2.

Listing 4-2   Creating a credentials object.

```
C# Snippet
ExcelService es = new ExcelService();
System.Net.NetworkCredentials customPermissions = new
System.Net.NetworkCredential( "login_name","login_password", "Domain");
es.Credentials = customPermissions;
```

```
Visual Basic Snippet
Dim es As ExcelService = New ExcelService()
Dim customPermissions As System.Net.NetworkCredentials = New
System.Net.NetworkCredential("login_name","login_password", "Domain")
es.Credentials = customPermissions
```

Using this simple mechanism, EWS can make requests on behalf of any user account. There are a few things to note. The *NetworkCredential* class is actually a .NET type that is responsible for supplying credentials in password-based authentication schemes. One caveat of this simple mechanism is that it does not have support for SSL client authentication.

However, it does not mean that EWS does not support SSL. SSL is supported between the client application and the Excel Services API, and between the Excel Services API and ECS. To enable SSL, configure your SharePoint site to accept SSL connections from the Central Administration site. Then install an appropriate certificate as you normally would for applications that support SSL certificates. After these steps have been completed, you can make requests to the Excel Services API using the HTTPS protocol.

Tip   A short list of known issues that affect Excel Services is located at *http://msdn2. microsoft.com/en-us/library/ms501525.aspx*. You should spend some time familiarizing yourself with this list.

Closing Excel Services Sessions

Several snippets of code in this book have used the *CloseWorkbook* method, and some have even left it out completely within *using* constructs. Best practices recommends always using the *using* construct when it is available. Where the text departs from this convention, it is only to maintain clarity in the examples. The *CloseWorkbook* method tears down the current session and releases any resources that have been allocated. It takes a valid session ID as a parameter and returns a status object that you can examine to determine whether there was a problem. An exception is thrown if the session identifier is invalid or the workbook could not be closed. The method call is not that appealing.

In contrast, the *CloseWorkbookAsync* method is a bit more interesting. First, it does not throw an exception on an invalid argument like its synchronous counterpart—a rather odd design decision when you consider that .NET 2.0 allows child threads to funnel exceptions back to the main thread. In fact, it appears that there is no way to tell whether or not the call actually succeeded because the *userState* object parameter that is part of the method's signature is never set in the current execution scope. (I'll discuss this topic in more detail later.) Second, the *CloseWorkbookAsync* method does fire an event to indicate that the closing of the workbook was completed. Let's examine the code in Listing 4-3.

Listing 4-3   Closing workbooks asynchronously.

```csharp
C# Snippet
using System;
using AsyncCloseWorkbook.AsyncCloseWorkbook;
using System.Web.Services.Protocols;

namespace AsyncCloseWorkbook
{
    class Program
    {
        static void Main(string[] args)
        {
            using (AsyncCloseWorkbook.ExcelService es = new ExcelService())
            {
                Status[] outStatus;
                RangeCoordinates rangeCoordinates = new RangeCoordinates();
                string sheetName = "Sheet1";
                string targetWorkbookPath = "http://<servername:port>/
                  Shared%20Documents/Book1.xlsx";
                es.Credentials = System.Net.CredentialCache.DefaultNetworkCredentials;
                string sessionId = es.OpenWorkbook(targetWorkbookPath,"en-US",
                  "en-US", out outStatus);

                //only proceed on a valid session
                if (!String.IsNullOrEmpty(sessionId))
                {
                    outStatus = es.SetCellA1(sessionId, sheetName, "a1", "hello
                      world");
                    //close workbook asynchronously
                    object[] userState = null;
                    es.CloseWorkbookCompleted += new
                      CloseWorkbookCompletedEventHandler(es_CloseWorkbookCompleted);
                    es.CloseWorkbookAsync("my name", userState);
                }
            }
        }
    }
```

```
            static void es_CloseWorkbookCompleted(object sender,
              CloseWorkbookCompletedEventArgs e)
            {
                Console.WriteLine("Workbook closed successfully.");
            }
        }
}
```

Visual Basic Snippet

```
Imports System
Imports AsyncCloseWorkbook.AsyncCloseWorkbook
Imports System.Web.Services.Protocols
Imports System.Text

Module Module1
    Sub Main()
        Using es As AsyncCloseWorkbook.ExcelService = New ExcelService()
            Dim outStatus As Status()
            Dim rangeCoordinates As RangeCoordinates = New RangeCoordinates()
            Dim sheetName As String = "Sheet1"
            Dim targetWorkbookPath As String = "http://<servername:port>/
              Shared%20Documents/ExcelWorkbook.xlsx"
            es.Credentials = System.Net.CredentialCache.DefaultNetworkCredentials
            Dim sessionId As String = es.OpenWorkbook(targetWorkbookPath, "en-US",
              "en-US", outStatus)
            'only proceed on a valid session
            If (Not String.IsNullOrEmpty(sessionId)) Then
                outStatus = es.SetCellA1(sessionId, sheetName, "a1", "hello world")
                'close workbook asynchronously
                Dim userState As Object() = Nothing
                AddHandler es.CloseWorkbookCompleted, AddressOf
                  es_CloseWorkbookCompleted
                es.CloseWorkbookAsync("my name", userState)
            End If
        End Using
    End Sub

    Private Sub es_CloseWorkbookCompleted(ByVal sender As Object, ByVal e As
      CloseWorkbookCompletedEventArgs)
        Console.WriteLine("Workbook closed successfully.")
    End Sub
End Module
```

The bare-bones code performs some plumbing to open a worksheet and update the range—you are already familiar with that part. The most important parts of the code occur toward the end, where an event handler is wired up to the *CloseWorkbookCompleted* event. When the workbook is closed, the event triggers our handler and we can take appropriate action. In this case, we simply print a suitable message to the console.

But how can a SOAP client know whether or not the asynchronous call actually succeeded without a continue error? If you think about it for a moment, you should realize that after the call to close the workbook has returned, the SOAP client is not notified of the asynchronous close, at least not in the current execution scope. The asynchronous close is a *fire-and-forget* call that occurs on a separate thread.

When the request is made to close a workbook, the main thread continues executing. The child thread receiving the request sets about fulfilling the request. As you can clearly see, there is some hocus-pocus going on underneath the hood because, at some point, the child thread must notify the main thread whether or not an exception has occurred.

For now, you should only note that the exception information is propagated back to the main thread using the internal framework plumbing. Calling code simply needs to add the appropriate logic to extract the error details. We talk more about this in a bit. For further reading, see this link: *http://msdn2.microsoft.com/en-us/library/aa628472.aspx*. Listing 4-4 shows our modification to the asynchronous call to close the workbook.

Listing 4-4   Handling close events.

```
C# Snippet
static void es_CloseWorkbookCompleted(object sender,
CloseWorkbookCompletedEventArgs e)
{
    if (e.Error != null)
    {
        StringBuilder err = new StringBuilder();
        Exception ex = e.Error;
        err.Append(" Full Error Message: ").Append(ex.Message);
        err.Append(ex.StackTrace);
        Console.WriteLine(err.ToString());
    }
}
```
```
Visual Basic Snippet
Shared Sub es_CloseWorkbookCompleted(ByVal sender As Object, ByVal e As
   CloseWorkbookCompletedEventArgs)
    If Not e.Error Is Nothing Then
        Dim err As StringBuilder = New StringBuilder()
        Dim ex As Exception = e.Error
        err.Append(" Full Error Message: ").Append(ex.Message)
        err.Append(ex.StackTrace)
        Console.WriteLine(err.ToString())
    End If
End Sub
```

The preceding code simply examines the *Error* property of the *CloseWorkbookCompletedEvent-Args* parameter to see whether an error occurred. If there is an error, the code graciously extracts an exception object from the error property and performs some rudimentary formatting to display the message. It's comforting to know that, at least in this case, if an exception occurred in the request to close the workbook, the exception handler would fire—which would indicate to us that a problem occurred.

> **Caution** If you are calling the Web service via a local reference and register interest in handling the *CloseWorkbookCompleted* event, you should not implement a *using* construct. The *using* construct calls the *dispose* call when the scope is exited. However, the event handler *CloseWorkbookCompleted* occurs outside of the *using* scope. There is a small chance that the object might be disposed of after the event fires (because there is no longer a valid root, meaning that the object is eligible for garbage collection) but before the event handler actually executes. That situation can manifest itself under heavy load if a workbook takes a considerable amount of time to close. In any case, there are very few circumstances where a SOAP client should use direct linking to the MOSS server. See Chapter 1 for an explanation.

In our urge to cover the basics, we have glossed over a hidden gem. Let's go treasure hunting! You need to be aware that quite a bit of indirection is going on deep inside the framework during asynchronous invocations because context objects implicitly transition from one thread to another. The downside to all this is that the call context of the main thread is irretrievably lost.

Put another way, if this code were in production and you needed to log details of the asynchronous call that failed, you would be left wanting. You can't easily determine user-session information—such as the corresponding session identifier or the end user that was inconvenienced—because that information is part of the main thread context.

Fortunately, the asynchronous method's second parameter accepts an appropriately named *userState* object that you can use to record the calling thread's context. You can then use this object to log the appropriate information when the *CloseWorkbookCompleted* event fires. Consider the piece of code shown in Listing 4-5.

Listing 4-5 Extracting error information.

```csharp
C# Snippet
class ErrorInfo
{
    private string _userName;
    private DateTime _dateNow;
    private string _sessionID;
    private string _workSheet;

    public ErrorInfo(string name, string session, DateTime currentDate, string
      userName)
    {
        _userName = userName;
        _sessionID = session;
        _workSheet = name;
        _dateNow = currentDate;
    }

    public void WebPrintDetails(HttpContext output, Exception ex)
    {
        if (output == null)
            throw new ArgumentNullException("HttpContext is null");
```

```
            output.Response.Write("<script>alert('");
            output.Response.Write("\tUser Specific Info");
            output.Response.Write("\\n\t==========\\n");
            output.Response.Write("\\nDate:\t");
            output.Response.Write(_dateNow);
            output.Response.Write("\\nUser:\t");
            output.Response.Write(_userName);
            output.Response.Write("\\nSession:\t");
            output.Response.Write(_sessionID.Substring(0, 10));
            output.Response.Write("\\nWorksheet:\t");
            output.Response.Write(_workSheet);
            output.Response.Write("\\nError Message:\t");
            output.Response.Write(ex.Message);
            output.Response.Write("')</script>");
    }
}
```

Visual Basic Snippet

```
Friend Class ErrorInfo
    Private _userName As String
    Private _dateNow As DateTime
    Private _sessionID As String
    Private _workSheet As String

    Public Sub New(ByVal name As String, ByVal session As String, ByVal currentDate As _
      DateTime, ByVal userName As String)
        _userName = userName
        _sessionID = session
        _workSheet = name
        _dateNow = currentDate
    End Sub

    Public Sub WebPrintDetails(ByVal output As HttpContext, ByVal ex As Exception)
        If output Is Nothing Then
            Throw New ArgumentNullException("HttpContext is null")
        End If

        output.Response.Write("<script>alert('")
        output.Response.Write(Constants.vbTab & "User Specific Info")
        output.Response.Write("\n" & Constants.vbTab & "==========\n")
        output.Response.Write("\nDate:" & Constants.vbTab)
        output.Response.Write(_dateNow)
        output.Response.Write("\nUser:" & Constants.vbTab)
        output.Response.Write(_userName)
        output.Response.Write("\nSession:" & Constants.vbTab)
        output.Response.Write(_sessionID.Substring(0, 10))
        output.Response.Write("\nWorksheet:" & Constants.vbTab)
        output.Response.Write(_workSheet)
        output.Response.Write("\nError Message:" & Constants.vbTab)
        output.Response.Write(ex.Message)
        output.Response.Write("')</script>")
    End Sub
End Class
```

First, we create a class to store the call context of the main thread. The class is smart enough to print out the context's relevant properties to the client through the *WebPrintDetails* method. We simply pass in that class to the asynchronous call as shown in Listing 4-6.

Listing 4-6   Forcing exceptions to occur in asynchronous code.

C# Snippet
```
//close workbook asynchronously
ErrorInfo ei = new ErrorInfo(sheetName, sessionId, DateTime.Now,
  System.Net.CredentialCache.DefaultNetworkCredentials.UserName);
es.CloseWorkbookCompleted += new
  CloseWorkbookCompletedEventHandler(es_CloseWorkbookCompleted);
es.CloseWorkbookAsync("my name", ei);
```

Visual Basic Snippet
```
'close workbook asynchronously
Dim ei As ErrorInfo = New ErrorInfo(sheetName, sessionId, DateTime.Now,
  System.Net.CredentialCache.DefaultNetworkCredentials.UserName)
AddHandler es.CloseWorkbookCompleted, AddressOf es_CloseWorkbookCompleted
es.CloseWorkbookAsync("my name", ei)
```

The only thing of interest here is that we pass in the call context and intentionally poison the EWS *OpenWorkbook* method call by passing an invalid session *"my name"*, which is guaranteed to cause an exception. This is something you would never do in practice, but it's done here just for the sake of illustration. Listing 4-7 shows the event handler call.

Listing 4-7   Event handler for the asynchronous close event.

C# Snippet
```
static void es_CloseWorkbookCompleted(object sender,
CloseWorkbookCompletedEventArgs e)
{
    HttpContext output = HttpContext.Current;

    if (e.Error != null)
    {
        ErrorInfo ei = e.UserState as ErrorInfo;
        System.Text.StringBuilder err = new System.Text.StringBuilder();
        Exception ex = e.Error;
        err.Append(" Full Error Message: ").Append(ex.Message);
        err.Append(ex.StackTrace);
        ei.WebPrintDetails(output, e.Error);
    }
}
```

Visual Basic Snippet
```
Shared Sub es_CloseWorkbookCompleted(ByVal sender As Object, ByVal e As
  CloseWorkbookCompletedEventArgs)
    Dim output As HttpContext = HttpContext.Current

    If Not e.Error Is Nothing Then
        Dim ei As ErrorInfo = TryCast(e.UserState, ErrorInfo)
        Dim err As System.Text.StringBuilder = New System.Text.StringBuilder()
```

```
            Dim ex As Exception = e.Error
            err.Append(" Full Error Message: ").Append(ex.Message)
            err.Append(ex.StackTrace)
            ei.WebPrintDetails(output, e.Error)
        End If
    End Sub
```

If this code were placed in a project based on an ASP.NET Web site template, it would promptly generate an invalid operation exception. To avoid that situation, you need to decorate the page with the *async* directive set to *true*. The async directive automatically flows the impersonation, culture, and *HttpContext.Current* content to the *CloseWorkbookCompleted* event handler. The automatic flow allows the *HttpContext* output variable in the event handler to contain valid data.

That's a pretty clever piece of functionality included in ASP.NET 2.0. However, it comes at a price. The page, even though it's asynchronous in nature, must now explicitly block until the event handler has executed. There are serious performance consequences associated with hung pages that hold on to resources such as session variables. Figure 4-2 shows us the error message that was triggered with the invalid session.

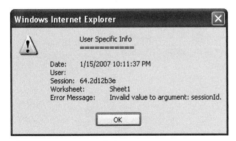

Figure 4-2   Error info program output.

Note that there might or might not be a name printed out in the *ErrorInfo* object. It depends on whether or not you have enabled anonymous access to EWS in Internet Information Services (IIS). In this particular case, *anonymous* is enabled, so the caller credentials are not funneled to EWS. In an intranet scenario, you most likely would be using Windows authentication with anonymous access disabled and the name would be displayed correctly. Figure 4-3 shows the SharePoint Anonymous User Policy configuration page.

From a technical perspective, the *userState* object transitions from the main thread to a thread from the thread pool that has been assigned the task of completing the asynchronous close request. .NET automatically handles the data marshalling so that you only need to be concerned with the data retrieval in the event handler as shown in the code. The variable is of type *object*, so there is a lot of flexibility. The price for this flexibility is that the code does not benefit from compile-time type enforcement. Once the event has completed, the thread pool thread unwinds from the application domain and is no longer accessible.

.NET gurus will note that the thread context problems discussed here can also be remedied by using Anonymous methods. You should consider using Anonymous methods if there is no substantial data to be passed to the calling thread. Otherwise, the *userState* object illustrated here is preferable.

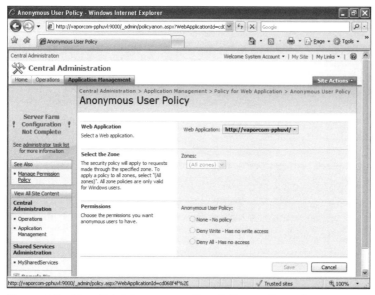

Figure 4-3   SharePoint Anonymous User Policy configuration page.

Trusted Locations

Trusted locations are data stores within SharePoint where data can be stored securely. So far, examples have focused on the trusted file location. This location is used to store workbooks that need to be opened from EWS. Trusted locations are closely associated with document libraries. As the name implies, *document libraries* are containers for storing documents. Spreadsheets stored in SharePoint document libraries can be versioned, secured, and audited by administrators before being published. In addition to the trusted file location, SharePoint exposes the Trusted Data Connection libraries and the Trusted Data Providers.

Data Connection Libraries

A Data Connection Library (DCL) is a list of connection-specific information prepared by an administrator that allows worksheets to query data from external sources. DCLs are not manipulated programmatically; instead, they are mainly used by knowledge workers to retrieve data from sources external to the spreadsheet. DCLs contain user-friendly names to help the knowledge worker determine the correct connection to use.

DCLs are discoverable. A knowledge worker can find these connections and use them to connect to data sources from the client. DCLs can automatically propagate changes to connection information to the client. Finally, DCLs run under the umbrella of security provided by Windows SharePoint Services (WSS). The security configurations for DCLs are as follows:

None   This is the default. Connections to external data sources are disabled.

Trusted Data Connection Libraries Only   Only a DCL can govern connections to external data sources.

Trusted Data Connection Libraries And Embedded   The option allows external data connections to be established by connection strings embedded in workbooks.

Figure 4-4 shows the configuration page for the Trusted Data Connection library.

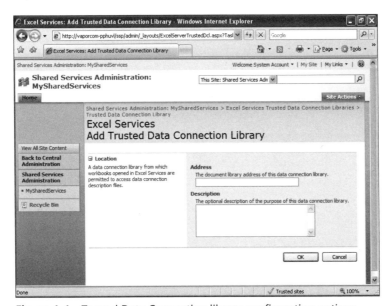

Figure 4-4   Trusted Data Connection library configuration options.

User-Defined Functions in Excel Services

User-defined functions (UDFs) provide a way for users to add custom-built functionality to a workbook. Conceptually, it might help to think of a UDF as an external library that is callable from a cell in a spreadsheet. Excel Services support only managed UDFs, meaning that these libraries must be built using the .NET Framework. UDFs are a powerful way to extend the surface area of the calculation engine.

The main reason for implementing UDFs is that you require functionality that is not provided by Excel. For instance, the ability to import data from a Web service is a good candidate for a UDF implementation. Or consider a requirement to consume data from a legacy business layer.

UDFs can be called from a cell using regular formula syntax such as *=myUDF(A1)*, where *myUDF* is a function defined in an external, managed assembly. The scope of functionality of the UDF is not limited in any way. There is also no limit on the number of UDFs that can be called from an Excel spreadsheet.

For safety and security, Excel Services runs UDFs under a blanket of security so that malicious code cannot compromise the system. We talk more about this security blanket in Chapter 7, "Advanced Concepts with Excel Services." For now, we focus on the basics of developing and deploying a managed UDF.

Creating User-Defined Functions

UDFs are easily created by using the Class Library template in Microsoft Visual Studio. Open Visual Studio, if it is not already opened, and create a project based on a Class Library template named **myUDF**, as shown in the Hello World example of Figure 4-5. Note that you cannot create UDFs that work in Excel Services using Visual Studio 2003.

Notice the reference to *Microsoft.Office.Excel.Server.Udf* in Solution Explorer. The path to the UDF assembly is located at *<Drive>:\Program Files\Common Files\Microsoft Shared\Web Server Extensions\12\ISAPI* for default installations. The referenced assembly is required and was added using the Add Reference dialog box from Visual Studio. The assembly is also found in the global assembly cache (GAC).

> **More Info**   UDFs can have security policy applied to them using Code Access Security (CAS). CAS policy is flexible enough to allow fine-grained control of the UDF assembly, dictating the type of resources and the extent of access that can occur. CAS with UDF is examined in more detail in Chapter 7.

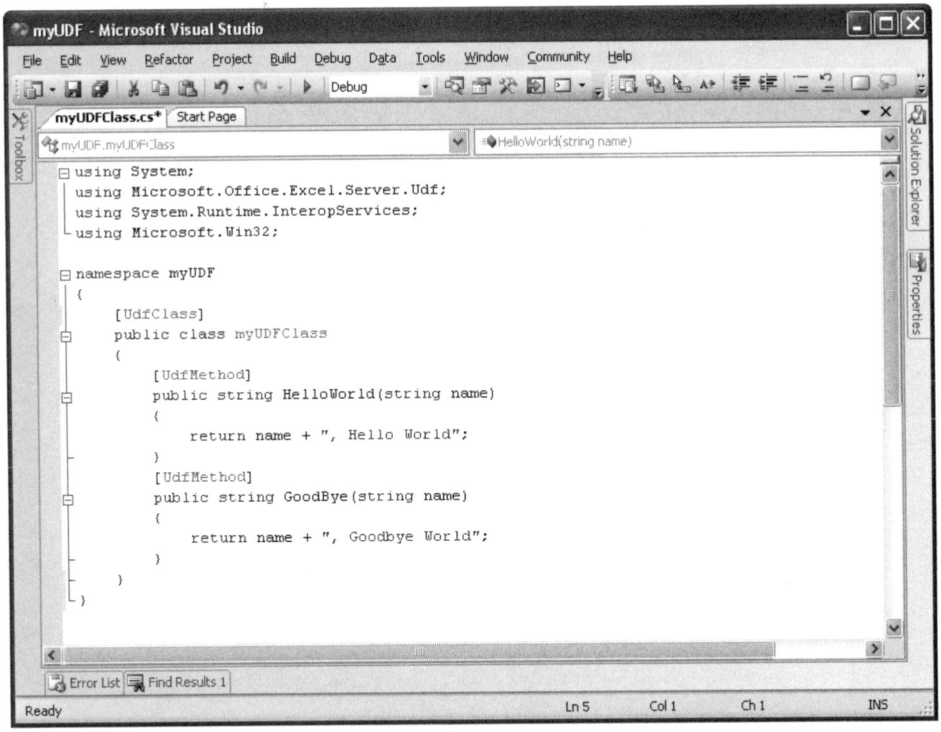

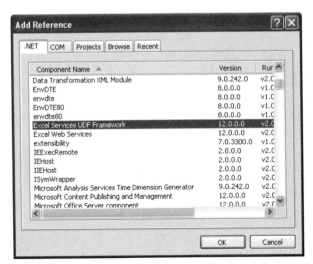

Figure 4-5   Using the Class Library template to create a UDF.

Figure 4-6 Shows the Add Reference dialog box.

Figure 4-6   Add Reference dialog box in Visual Studio .NET.

The code is shown in Listing 4-8.

Listing 4-8   Simple UDF class.

```
C# Snippet
using System;
using System.Collections.Generic;
using System.Text;
using .Office.Excel.Server.Udf;
using System.Runtime.InteropServices;
using .Win32;
namespace myUDF
{
    [UdfClass]
    public class myUDFClass
    {
        [UdfMethod]
        public string HelloWorld(string name)
        {
            return name + ", Hello World";
        }
        [UdfMethod]
        public string GoodBye(string name)
        {
            return name + ", Goodbye World";
        }
    }
}
```

```
Visual Basic Snippet
Imports System
Imports System.Collections.Generic
Imports System.Text
Imports .Office.Excel.Server.Udf
Imports System.Runtime.InteropServices
Imports .Win32

Namespace myUDF
    <UdfClass> _
    Public Class myUDFClass
        <UdfMethod> _
        Public Function HelloWorld(ByVal name As String) As String
            Return name & ", Hello World"
        End Function
        <UdfMethod> _
        Public Function GoodBye(ByVal name As String) As String
            Return name & ", Goodbye World"
        End Function
    End Class
End Namespace
```

The *HelloWorld* method takes a String parameter and appends the text "Hello World" to it. We expect that when we call this function with an argument, the return value in the cell will include "Hello World" appended to the input argument. The example is conceptually simple, but once you learn the basics you will be able to extend it into a real-world library quite easily.

Notice that the class and method are decorated with a special attribute. Only methods that are decorated with this attribute are callable from the spreadsheet. Undecorated methods are hidden. That's it for the code writing part. Let's focus on the deployment steps now.

Deploying User-Defined Functions

After the UDF has been built successfully, it needs to be deployed on a server running SharePoint so that it can be called from a cell in the spreadsheet. The UDF assembly can either be placed in a local folder that SharePoint can access or deployed to the GAC. For GAC deployment, strongly name the assembly using Visual Studio's Signing tab in the project property pages of the project. Alternatively, you can use the .NET Framework's sn.exe utility to sign the assembly. We will focus on simple deployment to a known folder here. The next section will show GAC deployment.

Create a directory called **UDF** in the SharePoint Web site directory to hold the assembly. You should choose the SharePoint directory where your site is located; otherwise, the folder will not be found. "Finding the Web Application Root" on page 33 showed you how to determine the directory path for your Web site. Copy the *myUdf* assembly to the UDF folder that you just created, as shown in Figure 4-7.

Figure 4-7 shows the UDF deployment to the bin folder.

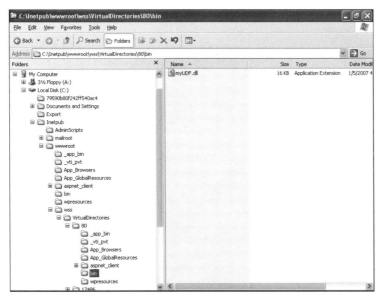

Figure 4-7   Deployment to the bin SharePoint folder.

GAC Deployment for UDFs

If you prefer to deploy your assembly to the GAC, you will gain a slight performance increase because the GAC is at the first point in the probing path of the directory search order when the framework attempts to resolve assembly references. Also, assemblies placed in the GAC are globally available across a farm. To sign the assembly, navigate to the property pages and select the Signing tab, as shown in Figure 4-8. Remember to perform a save. Visual Studio does not save the settings on the Signing tab automatically.

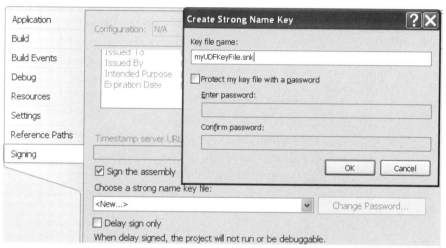

Figure 4-8   Enabling assembly signing in Visual Studio .NET.

Deploy the signed assembly to the GAC by using the Gacutil.exe tool at a Visual Studio command prompt. Confirm that the UDF is in the GAC by navigating to the *myUDF* dynamic-link library (DLL) in the *<Drive>:\<windows>\assembly* folder. (See Figure 4-9.)

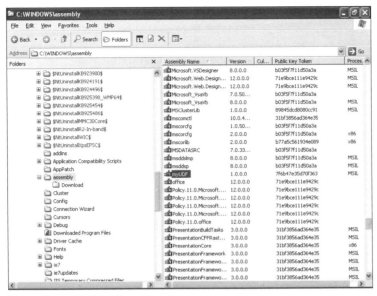

Figure 4-9   GAC UDF confirmation.

Configuring UDFs in SharePoint

To configure a UDF in SharePoint, navigate to the following page: *Central Administration 3.0 > Shared Services Administration: [SharedServices] > Excel Services User-Defined Functions.* Select Add User-Defined Function Assembly to display the next page. (See Figure 4-10.)

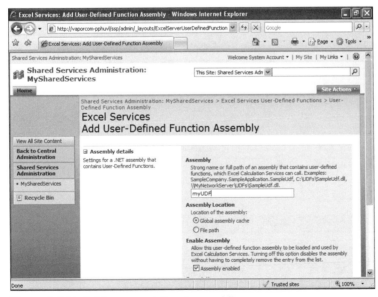

Figure 4-10   Adding user-defined assemblies.

In the Assembly text box, add the path to your assembly and type in an optional description. If you elected to sign the assembly, select the first option, Global Assembly Cache. Otherwise, choose the File Path option. At this point, SharePoint can find your UDF and it is enabled; however, it still cannot be called because calling is disabled by default.

Volatility

UDFs perform volatile calculations by default, meaning that functions are recalculated even if the data has not changed. This results in a significant performance penalty for large spreadsheets. You can force Excel Services to perform nonvolatile calculations as appropriate by using the *UdfMethodAttribute* with the *IsVolatile* property set to a value of true.

Enabling UDFs in SharePoint

UDFs are disabled by default. There is a certain security risk to loading and executing code that is foreign to the SharePoint process. Navigate to *Shared Services Administration: [Shared-Services] > Excel Services Trusted File Locations > Trusted File Location* to perform this step on your own machine, as shown in Figure 4-11.

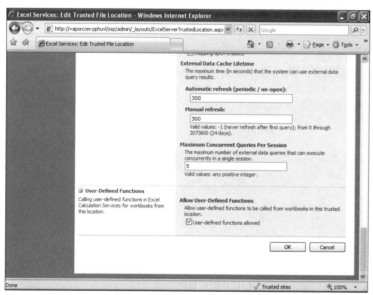

Figure 4-11   Enabling UDF in the CA.

In the Allow User-Defined Functions section, select the User-Defined Functions Allowed check box. Click OK to save your changes. In this step, we have assumed that you already have a trusted location set up on your computer. If the assumption is incorrect, review the material in Chapter 1.

Calling User-Defined Functions from EWS

At this point, the UDF is simply another formula in the cell. There is nothing particularly special about it. You construct the call just like any regular call to the spreadsheet through EWS. The process is identical to reading and writing from a cell and won't be rehashed here. (See Chapter 2 for the details.) Instead, we simply discuss some idiosyncrasies.

Figure 4-12 shows the Excel spreadsheet with the formula. As you can see, Excel does not recognize it, so the #NAME error is shown.

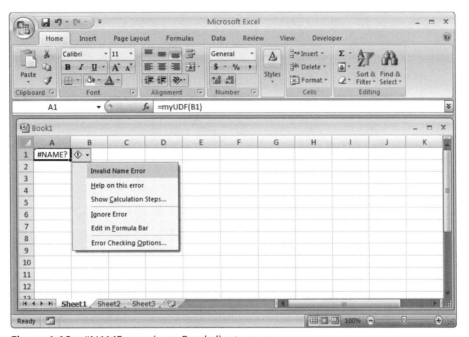

Figure 4-12   #NAME error in an Excel client.

Create a spreadsheet similar to Figure 4-12, and enter the formula **=myUDF(B1)** in cell A1. Notice that you receive a #NAME error. In this current release, Excel cannot dynamically resolve the UDF by default. The call will only be resolved at run time, when the assembly is loaded. This causes some discomfort because it is tedious to determine whether or not your UDF is actually loaded and running without issue. Let us remedy this approach.

Make the following modifications on the code to allow the .NET assembly to be visible to COM Interop. Listing 4-9 shows the code with just the additions.

Listing 4-9 Configuring a UDF for display in Excel 2007.

```csharp
C# Snippet
using System;
using .Office.Excel.Server.Udf;
using System.Runtime.InteropServices;
using .Win32;

namespace myUDF
{
    [UdfClass]
    [Guid(myUDFClass.ClsId)]
    [ProgId(myUDFClass.ProgId)]
    [ClassInterface(ClassInterfaceType.AutoDual)]
    [ComVisible(true)]

    public class myUDFClass
    {
        const string ClsId = "C62931E5-7BCE-41c3-BBFB-015BA0205DB9";
        const string ProgId = "myUDF.myUDFClass";

        [ComRegisterFunction]
        public static void RegistrationMethod(Type type)
        {
            if (typeof(myUDFClass) != type)
            {
                return;
            }

            RegistryKey key = Registry.ClassesRoot.CreateSubKey("CLSID\\{" +
              ClsId + "}\\Programmable");
            key.Close();
        }

        [ComUnregisterFunction]
        public static void UnregistrationMethod(Type type)
        {
            if (typeof(myUDFClass) != type)
            {
                return;
            }
            Registry.ClassesRoot.DeleteSubKey("CLSID\\{" + ClsId +
              "}\\Programmable");
        }

        [UdfMethod]
        public string HelloWorld(string name)
        {
            return name + ", Hello World";
        }
        [UdfMethod]
        public string GoodBye(string name)
        {
            return name + ", Goodbye World";
        }
    }
}
```

Visual Basic Snippet

```vb
Imports System
Imports .Office.Excel.Server.Udf
Imports System.Runtime.InteropServices
Imports .Win32
Namespace myUDF
    <UdfClass, Guid(myUDFClass.ClsId), ProgId(myUDFClass.ProgId),
     ClassInterface(ClassInterfaceType.AutoDual), ComVisible(True)> _
    Public Class myUDFClass
        Private Const ClsId As String = "C62931E5-7BCE-41c3-BBFB-015BA0205DB9"
        Private Const ProgId As String = "myUDF.myUDFClass"

        <ComRegisterFunction> _
        Public Shared Sub RegistrationMethod(ByVal type As Type)
            If Not GetType(myUDFClass) Is type Then
                Return
            End If
            Dim key As RegistryKey = Registry.ClassesRoot.CreateSubKey("CLSID\{" &
                ClsId & "}\Programmable")
            key.Close()
        End Sub

        <ComUnregisterFunction> _
        Public Shared Sub UnregistrationMethod(ByVal type As Type)
            If Not GetType(myUDFClass) Is type Then
                Return
            End If

            Registry.ClassesRoot.DeleteSubKey("CLSID\{" & ClsId & "}\Programmable")
        End Sub

        <UdfMethod> _
        Public Function HelloWorld(ByVal name As String) As String
            Return name & ", Hello World"
        End Function
        <UdfMethod> _
        Public Function GoodBye(ByVal name As String) As String
            Return name & ", Goodbye World"
        End Function
    End Class
End Namespace
```

Let's go through the code. First you need to run the guidgen.exe tool available at a Visual Studio command prompt to provide a GUID for COM Interop. The GUID is assigned to the *clsid* variable. The class is then decorated with attributes that allow for COM Interop. The exact details are not particularly relevant to the discussion. If you care to, you can find more information about each attribute on MSDN. Finally, when your assembly is registered, it will simply add the programmable keyword to the registry key for the component. *Unregister* performs the exact opposite—that is, it removes the term from the keyword.

Build your assembly, and deploy it either to the GAC or to the bin directory in SharePoint as outlined previously. The final step required is to register the .NET assembly so that it is available for COM Interop. From a Visual Studio command prompt, navigate to the myUDF\bin\ debug directory and register the assembly using the regasm.exe utility like so:

```
Regasm /codebase myUDF.dll.
```

You'll get a warning that you can safely ignore followed by a message indicating that type registration succeeded. The assembly is now registered for COM Interop and visible to Excel. You just need to make Excel aware of this add-in. Follow these steps. Open Excel if it is not already opened. Click Excel Options as shown in Figure 4-13.

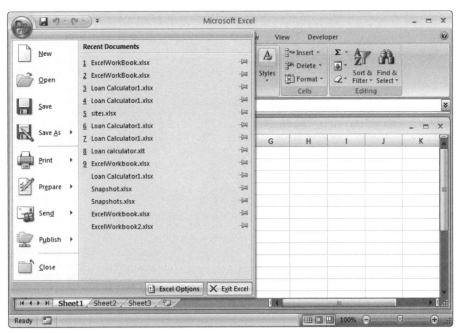

Figure 4-13   Excel save options for UDF.

Click the Add-Ins button in the left window, and click the Go button next to the Excel Add-Ins drop-down control in the right window, as shown in Figure 4-14.

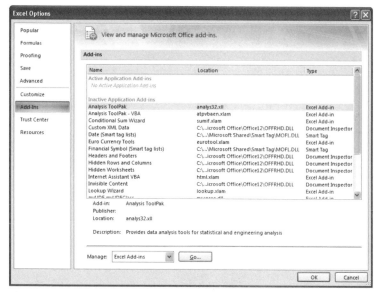

Figure 4-14   Add-Ins dialog box in Excel.

An Add-Ins dialog box appears. Click the Automation button to display the Automation Servers dialog box shown in Figure 4-15.

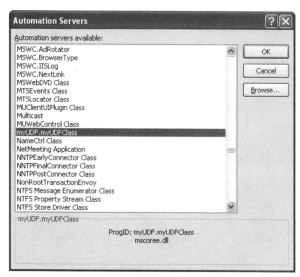

Figure 4-15   Automation Servers dialog box.

In the Automation Servers dialog box, find your custom class, as shown in Figure 4-15. Click OK to dismiss the dialog box.

You will be prompted for *mscoree.dll* because this is a managed library. The reference will be resolved at run time. Click No to continue. Load the Excel workbook. Notice that the #NAME error is gone. Enter your formula, **=myUDF(C1)**, in the cell. It should immediately return the results. You only need to perform these series of steps once. After each build, the update changes will take effect.

> **Caution**   If you make further changes to your custom UDF class library, you need to close Excel 2007 before you can build successfully. Excel 2007 maintains a directory lock on the debug folder, causing your build routine to fail.

In some cases, after performing these steps, you might still receive a #NAME error. To remedy this situation, make sure the selection is not in the cell that contains the formula. Then click the Insert Function button in the spreadsheet address bar. In the Insert Function dialog box, select your assembly and click OK to dismiss the dialog box, as shown in Figure 4-16.

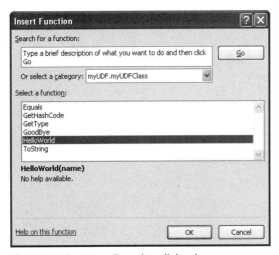

Figure 4-16   Insert Function dialog box.

Excel Services UDFs and Data Types

You need to be aware of certain errors that can occur when variables are passed to or returned from UDFs. Type conversion errors occur when unsupported types are used in UDFs. #NUM errors indicate that the UDF argument cannot be converted because of size constraints. #VALUE errors indicate a type mismatch or an argument type that is not supported.

You should note some key difference between Excel Services and Excel; the primary difference is that the Excel Services object model is a subset of Excel. How does this difference affect UDFs? Recall that Chapter 2 showed that only a few error codes were supported. The data types and type conversion process are also more restrictive. You might even recall that the exception code presented in Chapter 3, "Excel Web Access," returned exceptions as cell enumeration types. These differences mean that you might have to adjust your code to accommodate the restrictive nature of UDFs.

Another interesting feature is that UDFs are loaded in the same application domain as Excel Services, meaning that an errant UDF can cause Excel Services to misbehave. Let's formalize this discussion into a section that details the specifics of type conversion.

Type Restrictions

Following is a list of type restrictions you should be aware of when working with Excel Services:

- Excel Services supports UDFs with one or two dimensions for arguments that are passed of type *Object* array.

- There is no support for types other than *Object*.

- Only contiguous Excel ranges can be passed as arrays.

- UDFs can be passed as single-dimension arrays.

- Single-dimension arrays are converted to two-dimensional arrays.

- UDFs support parameter arrays—for instance, the *params[]* construct.

- UDFs convert return value types to objects of type VARIANT.

- UDFs support numeric data excluding Int64 and UInt64. For all other numerical values, perform a cast to a double type.

Summary

This chapter focused on the holy grail of the Excel Services architecture, the Excel calculation engine. The calculation engine powers Excel Services and exposes myriad functionality to calling applications, including local spreadsheets and remote SOAP clients. The exposure is neatly tucked in under a security umbrella that protects intellectual property, including proprietary formulas and data that might be contained within spreadsheets.

The calculation engine also allows calling code to harvest data based on protected information without exposing the details of the protected information. For instance, an EWS client can use a proprietary formula to perform a calculation request without exposing the intimate details to the client. This flexibility is remarkable.

EWS manages user sessions and is able to flex and scale to impressive numbers across a server farm. However, the calculation engine imposes restrictions on workbooks. These restrictions can cause a certain volatility in data because it is stored in memory. The chapter presented approaches to persisting the data outside of memory. This capability is convenient!

Finally, quite a bit of time and effort was spent working with user-defined functions. UDFs bring extensibility efforts full-circle because they allow calling code to increase the functionality of the spreadsheet. Even with this extensibility, intellectual property that is so important to maintaining a company's competitive advantage is still protected. Chapter 7 will show you how to manage the security aspects of UDFs so that you can actually exercise fine-grained control over the intimate parts of a UDF that is about to execute in SharePoint. This low-risk extensibility is impressive!

The chapters presented so far have laid the groundwork for real-world software. However, the final missing link will be examined next; it provides the ability to extend the SharePoint infrastructure itself so that you can build powerful applications that span the breadth and depth of client requirements in a way that is scalable, flexible, and performant. This is just the beginning!

Chapter 5
Windows SharePoint Services 3.0

As a .NET developer, you are probably intimately connected to software frameworks. You thrive in the depths of these frameworks where others fear to tread. You have learned that intimacy fosters a deep understanding of the foundations of any architecture. And your training and discipline forces you in that direction. Microsoft Windows SharePoint Services (WSS) 3.0 is your ultimate target. And you need to be intimately familiar with it if you intend to bend the infrastructure to suit your needs.

Windows SharePoint Services Overview

Recall that Chapter 1, "An Introduction to Excel Services," introduced WSS (rhymes with "less") as a Microsoft Windows Server 2003 add-on and explained the technology using the grape analogy reproduced here in Figure 5-1 for convenience.

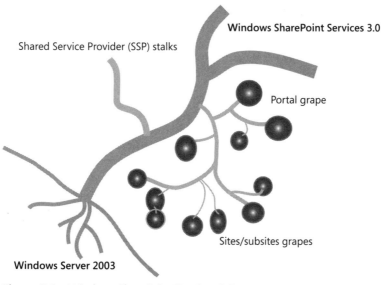

Figure 5-1 Windows SharePoint Services 3.0.

WSS provides a scalable, capable platform that can be extended in any direction to create robust Web-based applications. The new software that you author can integrate with existing applications using a variety of techniques and strategies that are included in Microsoft Office SharePoint Server (MOSS) 2007. These techniques include, but aren't limited to, the following:

- Web Parts that can move data between zones or across pages
- Data caching through intrinsic SharePoint objects
- Services that allow calling code to interact with the SharePoint infrastructure
- Rich feature set that allows authoring and management of documents

The WSS framework addresses two issues. First, it provides a way to manage data contained in SharePoint. *Data management* is an umbrella term that involves storage, enumeration, updating, and deleting SharePoint data structures. One of the prominent data structures is the *List* object. Lists are generic data structures that can hold, display, and operate on data. Most user-interface pieces on a SharePoint page are tied to lists.

Second, WSS provides a way to extend the SharePoint infrastructure. Extensibility allows calling code to hook into the programming platform that drives SharePoint behavior. Without extensibility, there is no elegant way to influence the behavior of the SharePoint infrastructure.

This chapter will provide the final piece of the puzzle that allows you to shape the behavior of SharePoint. Through WSS, you can work your way around Excel Services limitations in an elegant manner that behaves well under load. For instance, although Excel Services allows no way to persist workbooks in session, WSS allows you to work around this limitation.

SharePoint Site Architecture

The key players in the SharePoint site architecture are listed in Table 5-1.

Table 5-1   Object Hierarchy for WSS Site Architecture

Object	Description
SPSite	The object represents a collection of sites on a virtual server, including a top-level site and all its subsites.
SPList	The object represents a list on a SharePoint Web site.
SPWebCollection	The object represents a collection of *SPWeb* objects.
SPWeb	The object represents a SharePoint Web site.
SPListCollection	The object represents a collection of *SPList* objects.
SPField	The object represents a field in a list on a SharePoint Web site.
SPListItem	The object represents an item, or row, in a list.

These objects are relatively easy to use. Most of the functionality that you implement in WSS either starts with these objects or contains heavy doses of them sprinkled throughout production code. To work with any of the types listed in Table 5-1, simply instantiate an object from the type and use the properties associated with the instantiated object. Listing 5-1 provides an example that shows how to change the user name.

Listing 5-1   Changing the user name.

```
C# Snippet
SPWeb Web = SPContext.Current.Web;
SPUser _currentUser = Web.CurrentUser;
//name variable has been declared and passed in to this routine
if (_currentUser.Name.Trim().ToLower() == name.Trim().ToLower())
{
    _currentUser.Name = name;
    _currentUser.Update();

    //display update
    NameField.Text = _currentUser.Name;
}
```

```
Visual Basic Snippet
Dim Web As SPWeb = SPContext.Current.Web
Dim _currentUser As SPUser = Web.CurrentUser
'name variable has been declared and passed in to this routine
If _currentUser.Name.Trim().ToLower() = name.Trim().ToLower() Then
    _currentUser.Name = name
    _currentUser.Update()

    'display update
    NameField.Text = _currentUser.Name
End If
```

From the code, the context object is used to extract an object of type *SPWeb* that represents the current Web site. The context object represents the Http context of an HTTP request in Windows SharePoint Services. It also contains information for the current Web application, site collection, site, list, or list item.

From the *SPWeb* instance, we extract the current user browsing the Web site and store a reference to this user in the *_currentUser* variable. The *if* statement construct is presented for simplicity only. You should prefer the use of the overload of *String.Equals* that takes a *String-Comparison*, and uses a *StringComparison*, which ignores case. Finally, the *name* property is used to change the name variable passed in by the application. Notice that the *Update* method updates the content database with changes made to the properties of the user object. As a general rule, use the *Update* method for changes to the e-mail, name, and notes properties. The *Update* method automatically creates a connection to the content database and updates the property as appropriate. Do not write code to manually perform the database update. We explain the exact reasons for this recommendation in "Content Database Architecture Overview" on page 177.

Another approach to working with new concepts is to start with the result and work backward. For instance, consider the previous example that updates a user name. To update the user name, you need access to some sort of user name object. Prepend the letters **SP** to either

User or *UserName* to locate an associated object. *SPUser* is a match. From this point, you simply need to work backward to obtain an *SPWeb* type that contains information about the user logged in to the Web application.

> **Tip**   To test this code, create an ordinary ASP.NET Web site. Compile, build, and deploy the .aspx and .aspx.cs files to the *C:\Program Files\Common Files\Shared\web server extensions\12\ TEMPLATE\LAYOUTS* directory. Open Central Administration (CA). Copy the link in the current address of the CA page. Choose Add To My Links from the My Links link at the top right corner of the page. Paste the address into the address field, and modify it to point to the _layouts folder—for example: *http://<servername:port>/ssp/admin/default.aspx* changes to *http://<servername:port>/ssp/_layouts/default.aspx*. Fill in the other fields and click Save.
>
> You can test your page easily by selecting the My Links link and choosing the new link that you just added in the menu. All test code that requires a SharePoint context should use this quick test method.

The *SPUser* object can encapsulate different types of data for the user. For instance, the *SPUser* object can provide the following information:

- If returned from either the site collection's *AllUsers* property or *SiteUsers* property of the *SPWeb* class, the *SPUser* object contains all the users of a site or all the users in the site collection, respectively.

- If returned from the *GetAllAuthenticatedUsers* method of the *SPUtility* class, the *SPUser* object contains all the authenticated users of a site.

- If returned from the *GetUniqueUsers* method of the *SPAlertCollection* class, the *SPUser* object contains a list of users for a collection of alerts.

In contrast, the *Users* property of the *SPGroup*, *SPRole*, and *SPWeb* class returns the users in a group, role definition, or site, respectively.

Finally, let's mention that every user has a unique member ID as well as the permissions associated with that membership. These details are encapsulated in the *SPMember* object. You can assign information to or retrieve information from this object as appropriate to your programming needs.

Developing with WSS

We begin a controlled descent into the bowels of the WSS object model, for this is where great applications begin. Our inspection is centered on areas of functionality rather than raw object-definition semantics. The benefit to this approach is that the text can cover the entire suite of available functionality with focused examples that help you to understand how these areas of functionality can be weaved into enterprise applications. We focus on the following key areas:

- Events
- Content migration

- Search

- Logging

- Security

- Administration

When you surface from this deep dive, you will be able to transition an idea from the drawing board to the production server by making effective use of the WSS object model.

Making Use of Events

Most real-world applications have a fair amount of code dedicated to event handling. After all, Windows applications are event driven in nature. The event model in SharePoint allows you to respond to events that fire during the course of code execution. The SharePoint event model is based on the .NET event model and offers the following functionality:

- Rich support for events and delegates

- Schema support for events

- Declarative support for event registration

Before we start writing event code, let's quickly review the event model. Examine Figure 5-2, which shows the object hierarchy for SharePoint events.

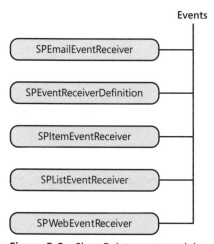

Figure 5-2   SharePoint event model.

There are five top-level types. Each type contains its own subhierarchy, not shown, that exposes deeper nested types. If your intention is to respond to incoming e-mail events, you should make use of the *SPEmailEventReceiver* type. On the other hand, if you are interested in cancelling deletion in the task list, you need to make use of the *SPListEventReceiver* type. This is the general approach for event implementation.

Conceptually, there are a few steps to follow to register interest in a particular event. The steps involve creating the event handler in code by creating an assembly based on a Microsoft Visual Studio Class Library template. Once this is done, you need to register the event and cause the event to fire by triggering some action in a SharePoint Web site. Let's focus on the first part, which is creating event handler. Create a project called *SimpleEventHandler* based on a Visual Studio Class Library template. Listing 5-2 gives you the code.

Listing 5-2   Event coding.

```csharp
C# Snippet
using System;
using Microsoft.SharePoint;

namespace SimpleEventHandler
{
    public class SimpleEventHandler : SPItemEventReceiver
    {
        public override void ItemDeleting(SPItemEventProperties properties)
        {
            properties.Cancel = true;
            properties.ErrorMessage = "Item deletion is not allowed by user: "
                + properties.UserDisplayName;
        }
    }
}
```

```vb
Visual Basic Snippet
Imports System
Imports Microsoft.SharePoint

Namespace SimpleEventHandler
    Public Class SimpleEventHandler
        Inherits SPItemEventReceiver
        Public Overrides Sub ItemDeleting(ByVal properties As SPItemEventProperties)
            properties.Cancel = True
            properties.ErrorMessage = "Item deletion is not allowed by user: " &
                properties.UserDisplayName
        End Sub
    End Class
End Namespace
```

In WSS, .NET types are used to implement event listening behavior. As the code shows, you need to inherit from *SPItemEventReceiver* to set up the necessary plumbing to listen for item-level events.

Important   Item-level events offer the most explicit control. SharePoint defines the following levels of granularity for events: Site level (e.g., SiteDeleted, SiteDeleting), List level (e.g., FieldAdded, FieldAdding), and List Item level (e.g., ItemAdded, ItemAdding).

The code just shown is bare bones and simply shows how to cancel list deletions with a message prompt to the user. Conceptually, you can construct your handler to perform any action. The particular event to override, *ItemDeleting*, performs the custom action.

A word about naming conventions for events in SharePoint is necessary before going further. Naming conventions that use *<event>* with *ing—ItemDeleting*, for instance—are synchronous events that occur before the list item is updated in the content database. This allows you to cancel the event or take any appropriate action. Naming conventions that use *<event>* with *ed—ItemAdded*, for instance—are asynchronous events. In the typical case, you cannot use these types of events to make changes to the item before it is added to the content database because the order of these events is not guaranteed. Synchronous events are new to WSS 3.0.

If you need to, you can access the data associated with the event by extracting data from the object of type *SPItemEventProperties* in the event handler signature. In this particular case, there's no need for data extraction because we intend to only prevent the user from adding items.

The assembly that contains the handler code needs to be deployed in the global assembly cache (GAC). We have already stated several times that GAC deployment is required because it provides governance over executing assemblies. In addition, assemblies that live in the GAC can have security policy applied to them. We talk more about Code Access Security in Chapter 7, "Advanced Concepts with Excel Services." For now, we note that the assembly deployed to the GAC runs with full trust. Sign the code and deploy it to the GAC.

After you have deployed the assembly to the GAC, you have code that is ready to respond to the *ItemDeleting* event when it fires on the Web site. The final step involves actively listening for events. WSS offers two ways to register event handlers. You can think of this step as the rough equivalent of performing an event hookup in .NET like so:

```
Button1.Click += new System.EventHandler(this.button1_Click);
```

You can register the assembly through the object model or by using SharePoint Features. The Features feature in SharePoint is discussed in a lot more detail in Chapter 7.

We proceed with an example based on the object model. Listing 5-3 shows you the client code. It is based on a console application template created in Visual Studio.

Listing 5-3 Client event registration.

```
C# Snippet
private void RegisterForEvent()
{
    string receiverName = "Calendar Event Receiver";
    int sequenceNumber = 1000;
    string assemblyFullName = "SimpleEventHandler,Culture=Neutral, Version=1.0.0.0,
      PublicKeyToken=a0d916ad75d71b3e";
    string assemblyClassName = "SimpleEventHandler.SimpleEventHandler";
    string receiverData = "Some Data";
```

```
        SPSite mySiteCollection = new SPSite("http://<servername:port>");
        SPWeb mySite = mySiteCollection.AllWebs["Title"];
        SPList list = mySite.Lists["Custom List"];

        SPEventReceiverDefinitionCollection eventReceivers = slist.EventReceivers;
        SPEventReceiverDefinition eventReceiver = eventReceivers.Add();
        eventReceiver.Name = receiverName;
        eventReceiver.Type = SPEventReceiverType.ItemDeleting;
        eventReceiver.SequenceNumber = sequenceNumber;
        eventReceiver.Assembly = assemblyFullName;
        eventReceiver.Class = assemblyClassName;
        eventReceiver.Data = receiverData;
        eventReceiver.Update();
}
```

Visual Basic Snippet

```
Private Sub RegisterForEvent()
    Dim receiverName As String = " Event Receiver"
    Dim sequenceNumber As Integer = 1000
    Dim assemblyFullName As String = "SimpleEventHandler,Culture=Neutral,
      Version=1.0.0.0, PublicKeyToken=a0d916ad75d71b3e"
    Dim assemblyClassName As String = "SimpleEventHandler.SimpleEventHandler"
    Dim receiverData As String = "Some Data"

    Dim mySiteCollection As SPSite = New SPSite("http://<servername:port>")
    Dim mySite As SPWeb = mySiteCollection.AllWebs("Title")
    Dim list As SPList = mySite.Lists("Custom List")

    Dim eventReceivers As SPEventReceiverDefinitionCollection = list.EventReceivers
    Dim eventReceiver As SPEventReceiverDefinition = eventReceivers.Add()
    eventReceiver.Name = receiverName
    eventReceiver.Type = SPEventReceiverType.ItemDeleting
    eventReceiver.SequenceNumber = sequenceNumber
    eventReceiver.Assembly = assemblyFullName
    eventReceiver.Class = assemblyClassName
    eventReceiver.Data = receiverData
    eventReceiver.Update()
  End Sub
```

Tip   The code is intentionally verbose so that you have an idea of the extent of functionality available. Production code can use a more streamlined version that involves a single line of code making use of the *list.EventReceivers.Add* method. Notice the *SequenceNumber* property. It is an an integer that represents the relative sequence of the event. Notice also *assembly-FullName*. It takes the fully qualified name of the GAC assembly: Name, Version, Culture, Public Token. You can view the properties of the assembly in Windows Explorer to retrieve these values. *AssemblyClassName* takes a fully qualified class name in the form of *Namespace.Class*. *ReceiverData* contains any type of data that you might want to pass to the event handler. The framework takes care of marshalling the data.

From the site reference, we register interest in a site with the name Title. The code is interested in subscribing to list deletes for a list with the title "Custom Lists." In a moment, we will create the custom list on the site in SharePoint. Notice that the console application in this example is running local to the SharePoint server because we are making use of the object model. If this code were ported to an external server, the code would fail. To hook into the event model from an external server, you need to use the appropriate Web service application programming interface (API). In our case, a Uniform Resource Identifier (URI) pointing to the Web site on MOSS is used to retrieve a site reference.

Finally, we simply need to perform some action that triggers the event we are registered to handle. Open the portal site, and click the Create link on the Site Actions menu. Select Custom Lists from the Custom List menu, and enter a list name and description on the custom list setup page, shown in Figure 5-3.

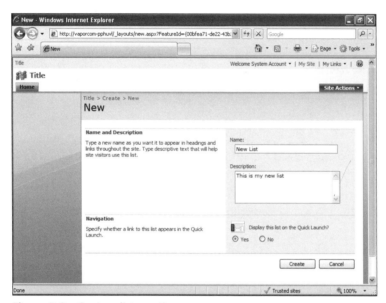

Figure 5-3   Custom list creation.

Click the Create button to add the custom list to the site. Confirm that the Site tab shows the new list as a link on the left menu. To trigger the event, select the Custom List link and add a new item to it. Then try to delete the item. You will receive an error. That's it. Real-world application requirements follow this basic outline, hooking into different events as required.

Guidelines for Programming WSS Events

Eventing code is extremely powerful yet fairly intuitive to program. You should notice the large number of events that are available through the *SPEventReceiverType* enumeration. Although this example applies specifically to lists, you can use a modification of this technique to hook into document libraries and list definitions on any page running on the SharePoint server.

To recap, the following sequence of events allows calling code to hook into the SharePoint event model:

1. Provide an event handler derived from the appropriate event object.

2. Sign the assembly, and deploy it in the GAC.

3. Determine the scope of the event registration.

4. Wire the assembly to a particular event on the SharePoint Web application.

Content Migration Programming

The Content Migration APIs provide a way to migrate content between Windows SharePoint Services Web sites. The migration involves content along with related dependencies. The WSS object model exposes the programmatic equivalent of the functionality available using the stsadm tool. The object model is powerful enough to migrate an entire Web site or a single item in a library and everything in between. (See Figure 5-4.)

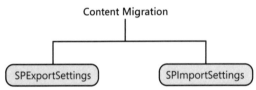

Figure 5-4   Content migration object hierarchy.

The content migration APIs can be used for the following common tasks:

- Content publishing from one server to the next

- Export/import content

Let's examine some code that exports the changes of a portal site to a file on disk using the content migration API. (See Listing 5-4.) The code will give you a feel for the amount of effort required to extend content migration through code.

Listing 5-4   Content migration walk-through.

```
C# Snippet
using System;
using Microsoft.SharePoint;
using Microsoft.SharePoint.Administration;
using Microsoft.SharePoint.Deployment;

namespace Export
{
    class Program
    {
        static void Main(string[] args)
        {
            SPExportSettings exportSettings = new SPExportSettings();
```

```
            exportSettings.SiteUrl = "http://<servername:port>/Title/";
            exportSettings.ExportMethod = SPExportMethodType.ExportChanges;
            exportSettings.ExcludeDependencies = true;
            exportSettings.HaltOnNonfatalError = false;
            exportSettings.BaseFileName = "fileName";
            exportSettings.FileLocation = @"C:\export";

            SPExport export = new SPExport(exportSettings);
            export.Run();
            Console.ReadLine();


        }
    }
}
```

Visual Basic Snippet

```
Imports System
Imports Microsoft.SharePoint
Imports Microsoft.SharePoint.Administration
Imports Microsoft.SharePoint.Deployment

Namespace Export
    Friend Class Program
        Shared Sub Main(ByVal args As String())
            Dim exportSettings As SPExportSettings = New SPExportSettings()
            exportSettings.SiteUrl = "http://<servername:port>/Title/"
            exportSettings.ExportMethod = SPExportMethodType.ExportChanges
            exportSettings.ExcludeDependencies = True
            exportSettings.HaltOnNonfatalError = False
            exportSettings.BaseFileName = "fileName"
            exportSettings.FileLocation = "C:\export"

            Dim export As SPExport = New SPExport(exportSettings)
            export.Run()
            Console.ReadLine()

        End Sub
    End Class
End Namespace
```

Compared with the code we have examined so far, this is very basic. The main method that needs to be called is *run*. The *run* method is part of the *SPExport* object. The *SPExport* object constructor takes an *SPExportSettings* type that contains the particulars of the export task.

The *SPExportMethodType* option indicates the extent of the migration to be performed. For migrations set to *ExportAll*, you should expect a reasonable amount of time to elapse for the migration to complete because the exported file can range in size from a few megabytes (MBs) to several gigabytes (GBs) of data.

As an added benefit, the *SPImport* type, sister to the *SPExport* type, is programmed identical to the approach presented here. An import implementation is left as an exercise to the reader.

> **Tip** For migrations set to *ExportChanges*, only the delta changes are migrated, resulting in a shorter migration time. The migrated file name is set using the *BaseFileName* option. The copied file automatically assumes a .cmp extension. These files contain no human-friendly information.

WSS allows you to take migration to the next level. Instead of simply copying or moving files around to document stores, you can actually check in files to document stores through code. In case you missed this one, let's slow down to examine the impact.

Recall that most files are actually stored in a content database. One of the benefits of that type of storage is that it provides a way to version files. In keeping with the versioning concept, files stored in such repositories typically contain version metadata and check-in/check-out attributes associated with them. The content API allows you to hook into this versioning process.

And this approach is not limited to local direct-link access. Using the WSS 3.0 Software Development Kit (SDK) Help documentation as a guide, you can hook into the appropriate Web service and create the same functionality through a Simple Object Access Protocol (SOAP) client. Examine the code in Listing 5-5, which shows how to check in a file to a document library.

Listing 5-5   Dynamic check-in processing.

```csharp
C# Snippet
private static void ViewFiles()
{
    SPSite site = null;
    SPWeb web = null;

    if (SPContext.Current == null)
    {
        site = new SPSite("http://<servername:port>");
    }
    else
    {
        site = SPContext.Current.Site;
    }

    web = site.AllWebs["Title"];
    SPFolder docLibFolder = web.Folders["Shared Documents"];

    SPFileCollection docLibFiles = docLibFolder.Files;

    for (int i = 0; i < docLibFiles.Count; i++)
    {
        Console.WriteLine("Examining file " + docLibFiles[i].Name + "...");
        if (docLibFiles[i].CheckedOutBy != null &&
          docLibFiles[i].CheckedOutBy.LoginName != "Administrator")
        {
            docLibFiles[i].CheckIn("Force checkin by admin");
            Console.WriteLine("File belonging to " + docLibFiles[i].Name
                + " was checked-in");
```

```
            }
        else
            Console.WriteLine("No action taken");
    }
}
static void Main(string[] args)
{
    ViewFiles();
}
```

Visual Basic Snippet

```
Private Shared Sub ViewFiles()
    Dim site As SPSite = Nothing
    Dim web As SPWeb = Nothing

    If SPContext.Current Is Nothing Then
        site = New SPSite("http://<servername:port>")
    Else
        site = SPContext.Current.Site
    End If

    web = site.AllWebs("Title")
    Dim docLibFolder As SPFolder = web.Folders("Shared Documents")

    Dim docLibFiles As SPFileCollection = docLibFolder.Files

    Dim i As Integer = 0
    Do While i < docLibFiles.Count
        Console.WriteLine("Examining file " & docLibFiles(i).Name & "...")
        If Not docLibFiles(i).CheckedOutBy Is Nothing AndAlso
          docLibFiles(i).CheckedOutBy.LoginName <> "Administrator" Then
            docLibFiles(i).CheckIn("Force checkin by admin")
            Console.WriteLine("File belonging to " & docLibFiles(i).Name
             & " was checked-in")
        Else
            Console.WriteLine("No action taken")
        End If
        i += 1
    Loop
End Sub
Shared Sub Main(ByVal args As String())
    ViewFiles()
End Sub
```

The snippet of code examines the Shared Documents repository for a particular site and checks in all files that were not checked out by the administrator. The code is environment-aware—that is, it determines whether or not there is a valid context and creates one if there isn't. This would be the case for console applications running outside of the SharePoint context. With a valid context, we simply iterate the file list, examining the criteria for a match and taking the appropriate action.

Guidelines for Content Management Programming

Let's make a few notes. Interestingly enough, when you move a file to a repository, a copy of the file is made and moved. The original file remains intact. There are also special cases where files can be versioned in the document repository. If versioning is enabled for the document library that contains the file, calling the *CheckIn* method creates an *SPFileVersion* object.

For added flexibility, you might want to consider accessing the *SPFile* type, not shown here, which allows you to get a byte array of the contents of the file. You should be able to expand this concept to add all sorts of functionality, such as file deletes, uploads, content examination, document migration between repositories, and even creation of new repositories.

You need to be aware of some limitations built into the content migration API. The content migration API is not designed to perform backup and restoration. Configuration and application data cannot be exported or imported. There is also an upper limit on the site object that can be exported. For instance, the *SPWeb* object is the largest object that can be exported. For smaller objects, there are limitations on object types. The following objects cannot be exported or imported: alerts, audit trail, change log history, check-in/check-out state, recycle bin items, recycle bin state, security state, workflow tasks, and workflow state.

It seems a bit odd that the object model allows you to programmatically create and access a document library. After all, security can be compromised by either an ill-conceived application or a well-written application constructed by a nefarious individual. It is worth a closer look. Listing 5-6 contains the code to create the document library.

Listing 5-6   Content library creation.

```
C# Snippet
using System;
using Microsoft.SharePoint;

namespace AddDocLibrary
{
    class Program
    {
        static void Main(string[] args)
        {
            SPSite site = new SPSite("http://<servername:port>");
            SPWeb web = site.AllWebs["Title"];

            string docLibrary= "VaporLibrary";
            web.AllowUnsafeUpdates = true;
            SPListTemplate listTemplate = web.ListTemplates["Document Library"];

            try
            {
                Guid guid = web.Lists.Add(docLibrary, "Document Library",
                    listTemplate);
                Console.WriteLine("Document library " + docLibrary + "<" +
                    guid.ToString() + "> added");
```

```
        }
        catch (SPException ex)
        {
            Console.WriteLine(ex.Message);
        }
        Console.ReadLine();
    }
  }
}
```

Visual Basic Snippet

```
Imports System
Imports Microsoft.SharePoint

Namespace AddDocLibrary
    Friend Class Program
        Shared Sub Main(ByVal args As String())
            Dim site As SPSite = New SPSite("http://<servername:port>")
            Dim web As SPWeb = site.AllWebs("Title")

            Dim docLibrary As String= "VaporLibrary"
            web.AllowUnsafeUpdates = true
            Dim listTemplate As SPListTemplate = web.ListTemplates("Document Library")

            Try
                Dim guid As Guid = web.Lists.Add(docLibrary, "Document Library",
                    listTemplate)
                Console.WriteLine("Document library " & docLibrary & "<" &
                    guid.ToString() & "> added")
            Catch ex As SPException
                Console.WriteLine(ex.Message)
            End Try
            Console.ReadLine()
        End Sub
    End Class
End Namespace
```

There's very little to explain here. By now, you should be familiar with the general approach. A reference to a site is obtained using a URI parameter. We use that reference to add our new document library. These types of objects are built using templates. A GUID is returned if the call was successful. If it fails, we handle the *SPException* exception and print out an appropriate message. The call might fail if, for instance, the document library is not unique.

Finally, notice the *AllowUnsafeUpdates* property. It is not a requirement for code connecting locally through Direct-Linking because that code is implicitly trusted. However, for SOAP clients, the call is required because these calls are untrusted. Although the default for *AllowUnsafeUpdates* is *false*, you should always include it in code to inform others about the context and assumptions being made by the code. Also, future service packs or improvements to the object model may change the default value, resulting in broken code.

Recall that in Chapter 2, "Excel Web Services," we added documents to the trusted location store to load and manipulate workbooks. Following this new strategy presented previously, you can use the object model to create, manipulate, and store documents in trusted stores that were created programmatically. Even more interesting is the fact that you can combine this approach with the security code to govern access to these programmatically created stores. Security is an integral part of the document library process and is handled through the *SPSecurity* object. It is one valuable tool in thwarting the efforts of nefarious thinkers or limiting the adverse effects of ill-conceived software. Use it liberally.

Developing Search Strategies

Search functionality forms a large part of the extensibility package inside MOSS. After all, Web sites based on MOSS can grow very large. You might also recall from Chapter 1 that provisioning the site included running these search services and indexing engines. As it turns out, the functionality inside these services is conveniently exposed through a new *Query* object model. You are at liberty to use either the object model method or the Web service model method to implement search functionality on your site. Figure 5-5 shows the search functionality hierarchy.

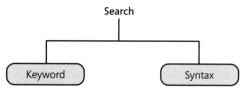

Figure 5-5   Search functionality hierarchy.

In Figure 5-5, observe that search functionality can be provided by using either of two logical approaches. You can choose to search based on a keyword, or you can use syntax. The keyword approach uses an XML format, whereas the syntax approach uses SQL query semantics. Both approaches support data set return values and XML string result types.

We focus on a Web service example implementation that makes use of the keyword approach. The example shows how to search a SharePoint Web site from an ASP.NET Web page. You can safely port this example to a Web Part or Windows application after grasping the basic concepts.

First, we need to create a project based on an ASP.NET Web site template. Name the project **WebSearch**. Add a *GridView* server control, text box, and button to the page. Add a reference to the Web service search service from the *Add Web Reference* property. Select the search Web service for your Web site, and name the reference **WebSearch**. Add the code shown in Listing 5-7 to the button's click event handler.

Listing 5-7   Keyword searching in WSS 3.0.

C# Snippet

```csharp
protected void Search_Click(object sender, EventArgs e)
{
    if(String.IsNullOrEmpty(Search.Text.Trim()))
        return;

    //build specially formatted xml with search parameter
    string qXMLString = "<QueryPacket xmlns='urn:.Search.Query'>" +
      "<Query><SupportedFormats><Format revision='1'>" +
      "urn:.Search.Response.Document:Document</Format>" +
      "</SupportedFormats><Context><QueryText language='en-US' type='STRING'>" +
      SearchResults.Text.Trim() + "</QueryText></Context></Query></QueryPacket>";

    using (<servername>.QueryService queryService = new <servername>.QueryService())
    {
        queryService.Credentials = System.Net.CredentialCache.DefaultCredentials;
        queryService.Timeout = 1500;

        //is the service available?
        if (queryService.Status() == "ONLINE")
        {
            System.Data.DataSet queryResults = queryService.QueryEx(qXMLString);

            //is there data to display
            if (queryResults != null && queryResults.Tables.Count > 0 &&
              queryResults.Tables[0].Rows.Count > 0)
            {
                GridView1.DataSource = queryResults.Tables[0];
                GridView1.DataBind();
            }
        }
    }
}
```

Visual Basic Snippet

```vb
Protected Sub Search_Click(ByVal sender As Object, ByVal e As EventArgs)
    If String.IsNullOrEmpty(Search.Text.Trim()) Then
        Return
    End If

    'build specially formatted xml with search parameter
    Dim qXMLString As String = "<QueryPacket xmlns='urn:.Search.Query'>" &
      "<Query><SupportedFormats><Format revision='1'>" &
      "urn:.Search.Response.Document:Document</Format>" &
      "</SupportedFormats><Context><QueryText language='en-US' type='STRING'>" &
      SearchResults.Text.Trim() & "</QueryText></Context></Query></QueryPacket>"

    Using queryService As <servername>.QueryService = New <servername>.QueryService()
        queryService.Credentials = System.Net.CredentialCache.DefaultCredentials
        queryService.Timeout = 1500

        'is the service available?
        If queryService.Status() = "ONLINE" Then
            Dim queryResults As System.Data.DataSet = queryService.QueryEx(qXMLString)
```

```
            'is there data to display
            If Not queryResults Is Nothing AndAlso queryResults.Tables.Count > 0
              AndAlso queryResults.Tables(0).Rows.Count > 0 Then
                GridView1.DataSource = queryResults.Tables(0)
                GridView1.DataBind()
            End If
        End If
    End Using
End Sub
```

Let's walk through the important parts of the code. Once a reference is added to the Web service (*SPSearch.asmx*), a *using* construct creates a local proxy object. Default credentials are passed in, and a time-out is set appropriately. Next, we explicitly test to see whether the Web service is available before proceeding. That sanity check can quickly eliminate all sorts of connectivity issues. Figure 5-6 shows the search results.

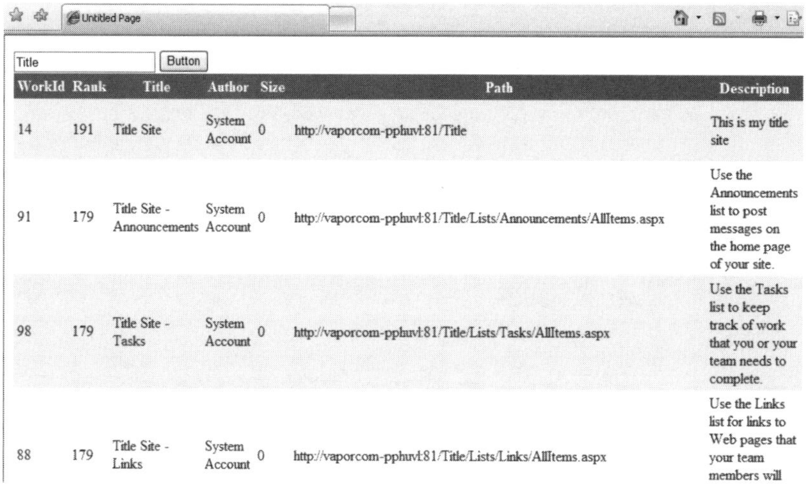

Figure 5-6   Search results data.

If there are results from the XML query, they are bound to the *GridView* server control. The *QueryEx* method returns a data set, so the bind is straightforward. Table 5-2 shows the lean interface of the query Web service.

Table 5-2   Query Web Service Interface Items

Name	Description
Query	Returns a set of results in an XML string for the specified query
QueryEx	Returns a set of results in an ADO.NET *DataSet* object for the specified query
Registration	Returns the name for a specified site
Status	Returns availability of the search service

> **Note**   One interesting part of the Web service is that it follows a schema definition for the query. The complete schema definition is presented here:
>
> ```
> <QueryPacket>
>     <Query>
>         <QueryId />
>         <SupportedFormats>
>             <Format />
>          </SupportedFormats>
>         <Context>
>             <QueryText />
>             <OriginatorContext />
>         </Context>
>         <Range>
>             <StartAt />
>             <Count />
>         </Range>
>         <Properties>
>             <Property />
>         </Properties>
>         <SortByProperties>
>             <SortByProperty />
>         </SortByProperties>
>         <EnableStemming />
>         <TrimDuplicates />
>         <IgnoreAllNoiseQuery />
>         <IncludeRelevantResults />
>     </Query>
> </QueryPacket>
> ```

Based on the schema in this note, you can see why the *qXMLString* variable was constructed the way it was. The code simply uses the appropriate nodes to build a query. The schema syntax is part of Collaborative Application Markup Language (CAML). Although CAML is beyond the scope of this discussion, it is important to understand the basic concepts.

CAML is an XML-based language that is used in Windows SharePoint Services to define sites and lists, including fields, views, or forms. CAML is also used to define tables, as well as the type of data that is contained within a field, and to construct HTML that is displayed in the browser in the Windows SharePoint Services database during site provisioning.

Various programming tasks and activities can be performed by CAML including the following ones:

- Creation of site definitions from existing site definitions
- Customizing the message text for alerts
- Customizing the navigation areas
- Making file additions to site definitions through modules
- Creating list definitions

- Adding a document type and file type icon
- Customizing the toolbar for a list
- Adding a field to a list definition
- Customizing the context menu for list items

Chapter 7 will provide a sample customization using CAML. If you aren't comfortable using this approach, bear in mind that the Web service also supports SQL syntax. You can read more about CAML at this link: *http://caml.inria.fr/*.

Guidelines for Developing Search Strategies

Let's be mindful of a few issues before we move on to the next topic. The search service must be running in order to bind to the Web service. You can minimize discomfort by querying the status as shown in the example. Many services can use the same approach. Exception-handling code is required because a server-side exception is raised if there are no search terms or if the *timeout* property has expired.

An exception is also thrown if you have only provided search stop words—that is, common words that have been eliminated such as "a" and "the." The exception design is a bit draconian in nature because it assumes that an empty result set represents a violated assumption. To prevent your application from crashing due to exceptions, use exception-handling code.

In most cases, the code presented will fail to return any results initially. The reason is that a full crawl of the site must be performed first to construct a searchable index. You can start or configure a full crawl by examining and tweaking the relevant search settings for your Shared Service Provider in the Central Administration Web application.

To recap, a successful search caters to the following sequences:

1. Perform a full site crawl.
2. Choose XML or SQL query syntax.
3. Scope the query to a particular site.
4. Invoke the *Query* or *QueryEx* method.
5. Use exception-handling code.

Logging

Logging is crucial to data management and has become a priority task in many cases, especially after the passage of the Sarbanes-Oxley (SOX) regulations in the U.S. In WSS, logging is handled through the *SPChange* object. Change logs contain information about the type of change that was made to an object or metadata in a Web site, list, site collection, site collection scope, or security policy. Because change log objects can hold sensitive data, the *SPChange* object runs under the SharePoint security context. The implication is that the clients need elevated access rights to successfully retrieve data from the change logs. Figure 5-7 shows the change log object hierarchy.

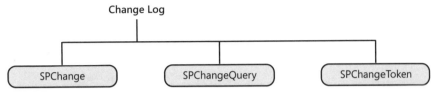

Figure 5-7   Change log object hierarchy.

Figure 5-7 shows that there are three objects in the change log hierarchy. Table 5-3 describes each of these objects.

Table 5-3   Change Object Hierarchy

Object	Description
SPChange	The object represents a change that has been made to objects or metadata within an item, list, Web site, or site collection scope, or a security policy change at the Web application scope that has been recorded in the Windows SharePoint Services change log.
SPChangeQuery	The object defines a query that will be passed as a parameter through a *GetChanges* method of the *SPList*, *SPWeb*, *SPSite*, or *SPContentDatabase* class.
SPChangeToken	The object represents the unique sequential location of a change within the change log.

Consider the example shown in Listing 5-8, which uses the *GetChanges* method to display information about items that have been added to lists within the Web site, including the names of the lists and when the additions were made.

Listing 5-8   Custom list iteration with the *GetChanges* method in WSS 3.0.

```
C# Snippet
SPSite siteCollection = new SPSite("http://<servername:port>");
SPWeb site = siteCollection.AllWebs["Title"];
SPListCollection lists = site.Lists;
SPTimeZone timeZone = site.RegionalSettings.TimeZone;

SPChangeQuery query = new SPChangeQuery(false,false);
query.Item = true;
query.Add = true;

SPChangeCollection changes = site.GetChanges(query);

foreach (SPChange change in changes)
{
    SPChangeItem changeItem = (SPChangeItem)change;
    Console.WriteLine(lists[changeItem.ListId]);
}
```

```
Visual Basic Snippet
Dim siteCollection As SPSite = New SPSite("http://<servername:port>")
Dim site As SPWeb = siteCollection.AllWebs("Title")
Dim lists As SPListCollection = site.Lists
Dim timeZone As SPTimeZone = site.RegionalSettings.TimeZone

Dim query As SPChangeQuery = New SPChangeQuery(False,False)
query.Item = True
query.Add = True

Dim changes As SPChangeCollection = site.GetChanges(query)

For Each change As SPChange In changes
    Dim changeItem As SPChangeItem = CType(change, SPChangeItem)
    Console.Writeline(lists(changeItem.ListId))
Next change
```

The important parts of the code deal with the *SPListsCollection* object. It is populated using a site reference. From this, a time zone object reference is extracted and stored in an object of type *SPTimeZone*. You should use the *TimeZone* property of the *SPRegionalSettings* class to return the time zone used in a specific site. For nonspecific sites, use the *TimeZone* property of either the *SPRegionalSettings* or *SPGlobalAdmin* class to return the collection of time zones used in the site or in the deployment of Windows SharePoint Services. Finally, the code sets up a loop to iterate through the change logs.

Guidelines for Developing with Change Logs

As usual, we need to be mindful of quite a few things. Change logs can be used only to return changes that occurred in items, files, folders, metadata, and security objects. Change logs do not record changes for configuration files, global administrative settings, binaries, Web Parts, Web sites, and databases. Finally, the type of change in a change log can be obtained through the *SPChangeType* enumeration. The scope of the change is restricted to lists, sites, site collections, and content databases.

You need to pay special attention to the *SPTimeZone* object discussed previously. The attention is required not because of a faulty implementation as such, but rather, because time zones are complicated beasts. Throw Daylight Saving Time into the mix, and you could have issues with time management on your hands that you are suddenly not prepared to handle. Let's consider an example before an explanation. Examine the code in Listing 5-9.

Listing 5-9   Time zone usage scenario.

```
C# Snippet
[WebMethod]
public string GetTime()
{
    SPSite siteCollection = SPControl.GetContextSite(Context);
    SPWeb site = siteCollection.AllWebs["site"];
    SPRegionalSettings regSettings = site.RegionalSettings;
```

```
        SPTimeZone timeZone = regSettings.TimeZone;

        return timeZone.LocalTimeToUTC(DateTime.Now).ToString();
}
```

Visual Basic Snippet
```
<WebMethod> _
Public Function GetTime() As String
    Dim siteCollection As SPSite = SPControl.GetContextSite(Context)
    Dim site As SPWeb = siteCollection.AllWebs("site")
    Dim regSettings As SPRegionalSettings = site.RegionalSettings
    Dim timeZone As SPTimeZone = regSettings.TimeZone

    Return timeZone.LocalTimeToUTC(DateTime.Now).ToString()
End Function
```

The code in Listing 5-9 requires a reference to *System.Web.Services* to compile. The reference exposes the *WebMethod* attribute, which allows the method to be called via a Web service. As you can see, the code queries the local time on the server and returns it as a string. This string, containing the current time in UTC format, is serialized and returned to the client as an XML stream. It is important to understand that the code in Listing 5-9 might display incorrect time values in some clients, depending on where these clients are located around the world.

The reason is that the time zone object allows local time to be converted to UTC time. Although time conversion to UTC format is a recommended best practice, it fails to produce the correct results here because of the .NET XML serializer. The XML serializer used to serialize the date/time value always assumes that *DateTime* values being serialized represent local machine time. During the serialization process, the .NET serializer applies the machine local time-zone offset as the offset portion of the encoded XML time. For SOAP clients that deserialize the returned value to a client machine, the original offset is subtracted from the value being parsed. Then the current machine's time-zone offset is added to the deserialized value.

Because we have converted the value to UTC format before serialization, the XML string being deserialized is off by the number of hours equal to the time-zone offset of the server where the code runs. To repair the code, simply return the local time and not the local time in UTC format.

Incorporating Security

We have mentioned that SharePoint runs applications under an umbrella of security. The concept is not new and refers to security-in-depth strategies, where one or more levels of security are interwoven to form a blanket of protection that is used to cover a software system. SharePoint uses this same concept to provide greater security for a Web site. Review the security object hierarchy presented in Figure 5-8.

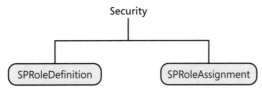

Figure 5-8   SharePoint security object hierarchy.

At its core, security is encapsulated in two top-level objects. The *SPRoleDefinition* object defines a single role definition, including a name, a description, management properties, and a set of rights. The *SPRoleAssignment* object defines the role assignments for a user or group on the current object. These two objects can be combined to support authentication and authorization for resources by clients. Examine Table 5-4.

Table 5-4   *SPRoleAssignment* Definitions

Element	Description
User authentication	The process used to validate the user account that is attempting to gain access to a Web site or network resource. Security is managed using Windows NT users and security groups.
SharePoint administrators group	A Windows user group authorized to perform administrative tasks for Windows SharePoint Services.
Site groups	A means of controlling the rights assigned to particular users or groups in a Web site based on Windows SharePoint Services. SharePoint contains a predefined list of site groups for each Web site (Administrators, Web Designers, and so on).
Administrative port security	A way to control access to the administrative port for Windows SharePoint Services.
SQL Server computer connection	SharePoint relies on Microsoft SQL Server security to protect data. Either Integrated Windows authentication or SQL Server authentication can be used to connect securely.
Firewall protection	A firewall helps protect your data from exposure to external access. Windows SharePoint Services can work inside or through your organization's firewall.

Table 5-4 shows a further level of security built in to SharePoint Web sites. Access to resources can be governed through a set of groups. These groups have permissions applied to them as a whole. End users and clients are assigned to these groups as appropriate. Resource requests that target SQL Server are protected separately through SQL Server security. At the hardware level and software level, firewalls help to protect data by gating access to internal networks. When viewed as a unit, these various layers weave together a security blanket that reduces the surface area of a potential attack.

> **Warning**   You cannot use distribution lists to control access to content in Windows SharePoint Services because distribution lists are not used for authentication in Windows.
>
> Also, the SharePoint Administrators group does not have access to the Internet Information Services (IIS) metabase, so they cannot perform the following actions for Windows SharePoint Services:
>
> ❑   Extend virtual servers.
>
> ❑   Manage paths.
>
> ❑   Change the SharePoint Administrators group.
>
> ❑   Change the configuration database settings.
>
> ❑   Use the *stsadm.exe* command-line tool.
>
> By using the HTML Administration pages or the object model for Windows SharePoint Services, members of the SharePoint Administrators group can perform any other administrative action, including creating a top-level Web site, changing settings for a virtual server, reading documents or list items, changing survey settings, deleting a site, or performing any action on a site that the site administrator can perform.

Table 5-4 also displays user authentication as one of the levels of security in depth. WSS supports Windows, Forms, and Delegated authentication schemes. You should be intimately familiar with these concepts because they are based heavily on the same model used by the .NET Framework. SharePoint incorporates this security even at the object-model level. Let's have a look at some code to demonstrate security. The example shown in Listing 5-10 uses a new feature known as *elevation of security*.

Listing 5-10   Dynamic security elevation.

```
C# Snippet
using System;
using System.Web;
using Microsoft.SharePoint;
using Microsoft.SharePoint.WebControls;

public partial class _Default : System.Web.UI.Page
{
    private static void GetGroups()
    {
        SPWeb site = SPControl.GetContextSite(HttpContext.Current).RootWeb;
        SPGroupCollection groups = site.SiteGroups;
        SPUser user = site.Users["Administrator"];
        SPMember member = site.Users["Administrator"];
        groups.Add("Group Name", member, user, "Group Description");
    }
    protected void Page_Load(object sender, EventArgs e)
    {
        try
        {
            GetGroups();
        }
```

```
        catch (SPException)
        {
            SPSecurity.RunWithElevatedPrivileges(GetGroups);
        }
    }
}
```

Visual Basic Snippet

```
Imports System
Imports System.Web
Imports Microsoft.SharePoint
Imports Microsoft.SharePoint.WebControls

Public Partial Class _Default
    Inherits System.Web.UI.Page
    Private Shared Sub GetGroups()
        Dim site As SPWeb = SPControl.GetContextSite(HttpContext.Current).RootWeb
        Dim groups As SPGroupCollection = site.SiteGroups
        Dim user As SPUser = site.Users("Administrator")
        Dim member As SPMember = site.Users("Administrator")
        groups.Add("Group Name", member, user, "Group Description")
    End Sub
    Protected Sub Page_Load(ByVal sender As Object, ByVal e As EventArgs)
        Try
            GetGroups()
        Catch e1 As SPException
            SPSecurity.RunWithElevatedPrivileges(AddressOf GetGroups)
        End Try
    End Sub
End Class
```

To run this code, you need to place this code in the _layout folder, as described in the "SharePoint Site Architecture" section, so that you can gain access to a valid context object. If you are a security-conscious individual and you spend time thinking about this code, the very thought of what is programmatically possible is enough to keep you up all night. In case you missed it, the code tries to delete a list item, and if this fails with a security exception, the code promptly overrides the security safeguard by adorning the context of the security account to enforce a list delete.

> **Important** Do not use the *Dispose* or *Close* method of the *SPSite* class to close the object returned through the *GetContextSite* method. This is because the *SPSite* object may contain a reference to a shared resource that calling code is not aware of. Instead, let Windows SharePoint Services or your portal application manage the object.

If you are wondering why the object model would expose that type of functionality, think for a bit about the principle of *least privilege*. A fundamental rule of security is to provide the least amount of privilege possible to the running application. In this case, you can have the application run under an account with deprived privileges and simply use this call to perform a particular task requiring more privilege. The benefit here is that only the single task is affected with increased privilege, not the entire application. The advantage of this approach over impersonation is that the password management burden is avoided and the attack surface is restricted.

On the other hand, if calling code has unauthorized access to administrative credentials, the system has already been compromised. Nothing more can be done at this point except to tally the damages caused by carelessness on somebody's part. Credentials help to keep the bad guys out—they were not meant to protect against carelessness.

One of the more important additions is the ability to perform role-based item-level security. For instance, consider a request to create an item in a list based on a user permission set. The code, which is shown in Listing 5-11, requires minimal effort but is well rewarded.

Listing 5-11   Role-based item-level security.

```csharp
C# Snippet
SPSite Site = new SPSite("http://<servername:port>/Title/");
SPWeb Web = Site.OpenWeb();
SPRoleDefinition RoleDefinition =
  Web.RoleDefinitions.GetByType(SPRoleType.Administrator);

//Get SPListItem
SPList List = Web.Lists["Calendar"]; //e.g., "Announcements"

SPListItem ListItem;

if (List.ItemCount > 0)
{
ListItem = List.Items["My Test Item"];
    //Create new Role Assignment
    SPRoleAssignment RoleAssignment = new SPRoleAssignment(@"<servername>\
      Administrator", string.Empty, "Admin", "Add some notes here");

    RoleAssignment.RoleDefinitionBindings.Add(RoleDefinition);
    if (!ListItem.HasUniqueRoleAssignments)
    {
        ListItem.BreakRoleInheritance(true);
    }
    //Add Role Assignment
    ListItem.RoleAssignments.Add(RoleAssignment);
    ListItem.Update();
}
```

```vbnet
Visual Basic Snippet
Dim Site As SPSite = New SPSite("http://<servername:port>/Title/")
Dim Web As SPWeb = Site.OpenWeb()

Dim RoleDefinition As SPRoleDefinition = Web.RoleDefinitions.
  GetByType(SPRoleType.Administrator)
'Get SPListItem
Dim List As SPList = Web.Lists("Calendar") 'e.g., "Announcements"
Dim ListItem As SPListItem

If List.ItemCount > 0 Then
    ListItem = List.Items("My Test Item")
```

```
Dim RoleAssignment As SPRoleAssignment = New SPRoleAssignment("<servername>\
    Administrator",
  String.Empty, "Admin", "Add some notes here")
RoleAssignment.RoleDefinitionBindings.Add(RoleDefinition)
If (Not ListItem.HasUniqueRoleAssignments) Then
    ListItem.BreakRoleInheritance(True)
End If
ListItem.RoleAssignments.Add(RoleAssignment)
ListItem.Update()
End If
```

The code creates a role definition object based on an existing account. The role definition is the list of rights or permissions levels associated with the role. The existing account derives its value from the *SPRoleType.Administrator* value. You might have noticed the *if* block in the code with a test for *HasUniqueRoleAssignments*. If the role has already been assigned, an exception is thrown. To avoid this potentially troubling situation, we need to break the role inheritance. Once this is done, we can simply assign the role to the list and update the list item. This approach provides an easy way to create list items and to provide security for the list based on an existing account.

Guidelines for Developing with Security

Let's make a few notes before moving on. The Web service API, specifically the *Permissions* Web service, cannot be used to set item-level permissions. It can be used only to set permissions on sites or lists. There is no way to validate the user account being passed in. If the account does not exist, an exception of type *SPException* is thrown when you attempt to assign the role to the list.

The *SPRoleDefinition* type supports inheritance from its parent. Only direct inheritance is supported. For instance, an object can inherit permissions only from its parent, not from any other object. The role inheritance mechanism forces subclasses to necessarily inherit role definitions if permissions inheritance is available. Put another way, it is not possible to inherit permissions without inheriting role definitions. Unique role definitions also cannot be created without creating unique permissions.

Extensible Administration Object Model

For quite a while now, we have been harping on the fact that MOSS is extensible programmatically. And the code presented so far in this chapter should lead you to believe that even more is possible. We have explored various parts of the object model and the Web service API. However, many administrative tasks have yet to be covered from a programmatic perspective. SharePoint invests heavily in administration. The investment is apparent in features such as the Extensible Administration Store, Extensible Administration Site, and Extensible Administration Command Line. Let's have a look at some key players. Figure 5-9 shows the extensible administration object model hierarchy.

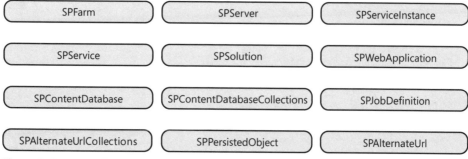

Figure 5-9   Extensible administration object model hierarchy.

The objects in Figure 5-9 provide the functionality for implementing administrative function-ality. By combining this functionality with the Web service API, you can extend administration outside of the SharePoint domain. Listing 5-12 provides an example.

Listing 5-12   Extending administration through code.

```csharp
C# Snippet
private static void EnumerateSolutions(string target)
{
    if(!String.IsNullOrEmpty(target))
    {
        target = target.Trim();
        SPWebService cs = SPWebService.ContentService;
        SPFarm mySPFarm = null;

        if (cs != null)
        {
            mySPFarm = cs.Farm;
        }

        foreach (SPSolution spSol in mySPFarm.Solutions)
        {
            if (spSol.Name.Trim().ToLower() == target.ToLower())
            {
                Console.WriteLine("Solution " + target + " found");
                if (!spSol.Deployed)
                {
                    try
                    {
                        spSol.Retract(DateTime.Now);
                    }
                    catch (Microsoft.SharePoint.SPException ex)
                    {
                        spSol.Delete();
                    }
                    Console.WriteLine(spSol.Name + " has been uninstalled");
                }
            }
        }
        Console.ReadLine();
    }
}
```

Visual Basic Snippet

```vb
Private Shared Sub EnumerateSolutions(ByVal target As String)
    If (Not String.IsNullOrEmpty(target)) Then
        target = target.Trim()
        Dim cs As SPWebService = SPWebService.ContentService
        Dim mySPFarm As SPFarm = Nothing

        If Not cs Is Nothing Then
            mySPFarm = cs.Farm
        End If
        For Each spSol As SPSolution In mySPFarm.Solutions
            If spSol.Name.Trim().ToLower() = target.ToLower() Then
                Console.WriteLine("Solution " & target & " found")
                If (Not spSol.Deployed) Then
                    Try
                        spSol.Retract(DateTime.Now)
                    Catch ex As Microsoft.SharePoint.SPException
                        spSol.Delete()
                    End Try
                    Console.WriteLine(spSol.Name & " has been uninstalled")
                End If
            End If
        Next spSol
        Console.ReadLine()
    End If
End Sub
```

Note the use of the *SPWebService* object in the code snippet. It is a container for *SPWebApplication* projects. *SPWebApplication* objects represent an IIS load-balanced Web application installed on a farm. What this all means in a nutshell is that you have programmatic access to objects running on the SharePoint Web site.

This snippet of code is as powerful and elegant as it is simple. The idea is to find a particular solution that exists in a farm and retract it. The retraction could fail if resources in the solution are scoped to a Web application. To override this bothersome condition, the code simply catches the error and forces a delete of the solution.

> **Tip**   Permutations of this approach can be used to schedule jobs and to manage the retraction and deployment of solutions on a farm. You can think of its functionality as the loose equivalent of the stsadm functionality that controls solution management. Recall that we modified batch files in Chapter 1 to control solution deployment.

It's easy to take this concept of programmatic administration further to probe the internals of a Web site. For instance, consider the piece of code shown in Listing 5-13, which enumerates a Web application extracting site, a Web service, and content database information.

Listing 5-13   Web site enumeration code.

C# Snippet

```csharp
private static void WebSiteEnumeration()
{
    SPWebApplicationCollection mySPWebAppCollection =
      SPWebService.ContentService.WebApplications;
    if (mySPWebAppCollection != null)
    {
        foreach (SPWebApplication mySPWebApp in mySPWebAppCollection)
        {
            Console.WriteLine("WebApplication:\t" + mySPWebApp.Name);
            Console.WriteLine("\tFarm:" + mySPWebApp.Farm.Name);
            Console.WriteLine(" PublicFolderRootUrl:\t" +
              mySPWebApp.PublicFolderRootUrl);
            Console.WriteLine("\tApplication Pool: " +
              mySPWebApp.ApplicationPool.Name);
            Console.WriteLine("\tApplication Pool Status: " +
              mySPWebApp.ApplicationPool.Status);
            Console.WriteLine("Probing Content Database attached to Web Application");
            SPContentDatabaseCollection mySPContentDBCollection =
              mySPWebApp.ContentDatabases;

            foreach (SPContentDatabase mySPContentDB in mySPContentDBCollection)
            {
                Console.WriteLine(" Database Name: " + mySPContentDB.Name);
                Console.WriteLine(" Database Server: " + mySPContentDB.Server);
                Console.WriteLine(" DSN: " + mySPContentDB.DatabaseConnectionString);
            }

            Console.WriteLine("Enumerating Webservices attached to Web Application");
            SPWebService service = mySPWebApp.WebService;
            Console.WriteLine("\tName: " + service.DisplayName);
            Console.WriteLine("\tDatabase Username: " +
              service.DefaultDatabaseUsername);
            Console.WriteLine("\tStatus: " + service.Status);

            Console.WriteLine("Extracting Webservice details");
            foreach (SPSite s in mySPWebApp.Sites)
            {
                Console.WriteLine(" Root Web: " + s.RootWeb.Title);
                Console.WriteLine(" Url: " + s.Url);
                Console.WriteLine(" ServerRelativeUrl: " + s.ServerRelativeUrl);
                Console.WriteLine(" Port: " + s.Port);
                Console.WriteLine(" Portal Name: " + s.PortalName);
                Console.WriteLine(" Portal Url: " + s.PortalUrl);
            }
        }
    }
}
```

Visual Basic Snippet

```vb
Private Shared Sub WebSiteEnumeration()
    Dim mySPWebAppCollection As SPWebApplicationCollection =
      SPWebService.ContentService.WebApplications
    If Not mySPWebAppCollection Is Nothing Then
        For Each mySPWebApp As SPWebApplication In mySPWebAppCollection
            Console.WriteLine("WebApplication:" & Constants.vbTab + mySPWebApp.Name)
            Console.WriteLine(Constants.vbTab & "Farm:" & mySPWebApp.Farm.Name)
            Console.WriteLine(" PublicFolderRootUrl:" & Constants.vbTab +
              mySPWebApp.PublicFolderRootUrl)
            Console.WriteLine(Constants.vbTab & "Sites: " & mySPWebApp.Sites.Count)
            Console.WriteLine(Constants.vbTab & "Application Pool: " &
              mySPWebApp.ApplicationPool.Name)
            Console.WriteLine(Constants.vbTab & "Application Pool Status: " &
              mySPWebApp.ApplicationPool.Status)
            Console.WriteLine("Probing Content Database attached to Web Application")
            Dim mySPContentDBCollection As SPContentDatabaseCollection =
              mySPWebApp.ContentDatabases

            For Each mySPContentDB As SPContentDatabase In mySPContentDBCollection
                Console.WriteLine(" Database Name: " & mySPContentDB.Name)
                Console.WriteLine(" Database Server: " & mySPContentDB.Server)
                Console.WriteLine(" DSN: " & mySPContentDB.DatabaseConnectionString)
            Next mySPContentDB

            Console.WriteLine("Enumerating Webservices attached to Web Application")
            Dim service As SPWebService = mySPWebApp.WebService
            Console.WriteLine(Constants.vbTab & "Name: " & service.DisplayName)
            Console.WriteLine(Constants.vbTab & "Database Username: " &
              service.DefaultDatabaseUsername)
            Console.WriteLine(Constants.vbTab & "Status: " & service.Status)

            Console.WriteLine("Extracting Webservice details")
            For Each s As SPSite In mySPWebApp.Sites
                Console.WriteLine(" Root Web: " & s.RootWeb.Title)
                Console.WriteLine(" Url: " & s.Url)
                Console.WriteLine(" ServerRelativeUrl: " & s.ServerRelativeUrl)
                Console.WriteLine(" Port: " & s.Port)
                Console.WriteLine(" Portal Name: " & s.PortalName)
                Console.WriteLine(" Portal Url: " & s.PortalUrl)
            Next s
        Next mySPWebApp
    End If
End Sub
```

The code is not that interesting considering the enormous power behind this approach. With an *SPWebApplication* object, we simply iterate the hierarchical structure. However, what is more interesting is the intuitive approach to getting this type of functionality working. The concept of programmatic administration is quite simple to understand. You need to figure out which object you are interested in and then find this object in the object model. The naming convention follows the logical behavior of the object. For instance, access to your site is through the *Site* object, access to the Web is through *SPWeb*, and access to a service is through *SPService*. Then use a reference to that object to probe its internals as the previous body of code shows. Combine that with a healthy dose of Visual Studio .NET IntelliSense and you should be able to craft robust, working code.

Content Database Architecture Overview

Let's wrap up by discussing the content database architecture. There is exactly one content database per SharePoint Web application installed by default. You might recall from Chapter 1 that portions of the setup and installation screen referred to this database. The role of the content database is to store site content for customized pages, including site documents or files in document libraries, list data, and Web Part properties, as well as user names and rights.

In addition, Windows SharePoint Services 3.0 stores all end user data in the content database. The approach provides the following advantages:

- Storage of list data, documents, and metadata in normalized tables
- Transactional updates of documents and document metadata
- Consistent backups of documents and document metadata
- A programmable storage layer
- Deadlock detection and resolution

Access to the content database is provided through the object model *SPContentDatabase* object. Access to the content database comes with the strongest of warnings. You should not read, write, update, or delete data from the content database directly. Instead, you should use the object model or Web service API.

There are several valid reasons why you should heed this warning. The content database has been optimized for performance. Custom code that writes to and reads from the database can interfere with this tuning. In addition, updating the database in a scalable way implies the use of locking constructs from calling code that can interfere with the deadlock detection mechanism. The latter is particularly difficult to isolate when sites begin to scale upwards to include several thousand Web sites. If you don't care to heed these warnings, you should note that Microsoft Product Support will not assist in troubleshooting issues related to SharePoint if you have developed ways to interact with the content database outside of the object model or Web service API.

In addition, changes made to the database contents might be overwritten when updates or service packs for Windows SharePoint Services are installed, causing your application to break. For these reasons, changes made to the database schema or database structures are not supported.

Not all content is stored in the content database. Configuration information that applies across all servers in a deployment of Windows SharePoint Services is stored in the configuration database. The configuration database is set up at installation time by the installation wizard.

When a user addresses a particular virtual directory in SharePoint, what happens next depends entirely on the state of the page. If the page has not been customized by the user in any way, a cached version of the page is used to service the request. The cache is first populated on process startup of IIS. Caching allows these types of uncustomized pages to be reused across an entire site, improving scalability and performance. The content database does not play a role in uncustomized pages.

If the user has added customizations to the page, the customizations are stored in the content database attached to the site. Client requests that address this particular virtual directory cause the SharePoint run time to retrieve the contents for the page from the content database and hand off the request to the ASP.NET run time. The ASP.NET run time invokes the safe-mode parser to parse the contents of the page.

The safe-mode parser does not dynamically compile the page. Instead, it parses the contents of the page in an attempt to determine which controls to render to the user interface. The safe-mode parser uses the Safe Control List that is cached in memory to determine which controls present in the form can be created. Recall that the Safe Control List is found in the *web.config* file on disk and populated with a list of controls that are safe to be run. As an optimization technique, the safemode parser disables any server-side execution of code.

Because of the extra parsing involved and content database retrieval, you should expect customized pages to lag a click or two behind uncustomized pages. However, this lag is not usually noticeable. In fact, page performance is more closely related to the functionality being implemented in the page. Legacy literature refers to customized pages as *unghosted pages* and uncustomized pages as *ghosted pages*. These references are deprecated and should not be used to describe .aspx pages anymore.

Summary

The WSS 3.0 API is as wide as your favorite ocean and equally as deep. In this chapter, you learned about the Windows SharePoint Services infrastructure and how to program to this sophisticated model. Much of the code was built on snippets that outlined approaches that can be used in enterprise software to build powerful extensible applications.

Along the way, we learned quite a bit about the SharePoint site architecture. The model was divided into areas, and some code was provided to help you align theory with practice. We also spent some time discussing the inner plumbing of the SharePoint architecture. You'll need to be familiar with that architecture if you intend to push the envelope. Now that you have the theory, the remaining chapters will show you how to integrate this functionality with .NET applications.

Chapter 6
Advanced Web Parts Programming

Web Parts are much like building blocks. Each is an independent, atomic unit that can be plugged into a page to extend the functionality of the page. A network of Web Parts on a page provides functional depth without sacrificing page size. This chapter explores the types of functionality that can be built into a Web Part and the types of customizations that are possible.

Advanced Web Part Development

If you have made it this far, you should be able to comfortably create, deploy, and debug Web Parts. These activities form the foundation of programming in Microsoft Office SharePoint Server 2007. However, as we will soon see, there is a lot more that can be accomplished. For instance, you might want to exchange data between Web Parts, subscribe to events on other Web Parts, or embed different types of controls in Web Parts to overcome certain application limitations.

One such limitation is the restriction of the Microsoft Office System spreadsheet to accept end user input directly in spreadsheet cells. Consider Figure 6-1, which shows a published spreadsheet.

As you can see, user input is accepted in the controls located on the far right. The spreadsheet cells are rendered in read-only mode. Although Excel Services is a giant leap forward, limitations such as these are more than a passing inconvenience.

In Chapter 1, "An Introduction to Excel Services," I pointed out that this design decision presents some discomfort to the knowledge worker. It is a design that is not especially intuitive. Further, some form of training is required. Old habits need to be broken, and new habits need to be formed—the net effect being a throttling of productivity. This scenario is symptomatic of any software that imposes drastic changes on the end user, and Excel Services is no different in that regard.

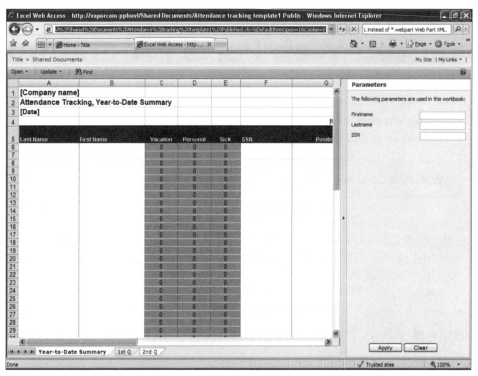

Figure 6-1   Published spreadsheet in Office Professional Plus version.

Let us begin a quest to see if we can ease these restrictions. Bearing in mind that the interactive restrictions are internally built, we need to think creatively to provide a feasible solution for knowledge workers who might find this new design a bitter pill to swallow.

Programmatic Manipulation of Spreadsheets

First, we need to learn how to load a spreadsheet programmatically. The idea is that if we understand the process, it might provide some clues about easing the limitations of interactivity. Consider the code in Listing 6-1.

Listing 6-1   Programmatic loading of spreadsheets.

```
C# Snippet
using System;
using System.Drawing;
using System.Windows.Forms;
using Microsoft.SharePoint;
using Microsoft.SharePoint.WebPartPages;

namespace WindowsExcel
{
    public partial class Form1 : Form
    {
        string siteurl = "http://<site>";
```

```
string bookuri = "http:// <servername:port>/shared
documents/Attendance tracking template1.xlsx";

SPSite site;
SPWeb myWeb;
SPLimitedWebPartManager sharedWebParts;
private void AddEWAButton_Click(object sender, EventArgs e)
{
    site = new SPSite(siteurl);

    if (site != null)
    {
        myWeb = site.OpenWeb();

        //Get the collection of shared Web Parts
        sharedWebParts = myWeb.GetLimitedWebPartManager("Default.aspx",
          System.Web.UI.WebControls.WebParts.PersonalizationScope.Shared);
        SPLimitedWebPartCollection collection = sharedWebParts.WebParts;

        bool found = false;
        foreach(System.Web.UI.WebControls.WebParts.WebPart wp in collection)
        {
            if(wp != null && wp.DisplayTitle.ToLower().Trim() == "ExcelPart")
            {
                found = true;
                break;
            }
        }

        if (!found)
        {
            //Add an Excel Web Access Web Part in a shared view
            Microsoft.Office.Excel.WebUI.ExcelWebRenderer ewaWebPart = new
              Microsoft.Office.Excel.WebUI.ExcelWebRenderer();
            ewaWebPart.ZoneID = "Left";
            ewaWebPart.WorkbookUri = bookuri;
            ewaWebPart.Title = "ExcelPart";

            sharedWebParts.AddWebPart(ewaWebPart, ewaWebPart.ZoneID, 1);

            MessageBox.Show("Added Web Part. Please refresh page.");
        }
    }
}
```

Visual Basic Snippet

```
Imports System
Imports System.Drawing
Imports System.Windows.Forms
Imports Microsoft.SharePoint
Imports Microsoft.SharePoint.WebPartPages

Namespace WindowsExcel
```

```vb
Public Partial Class Form1
    Inherits Form
    Private siteurl As String = "http://<site>"
    Private bookuri As String = "http://<servername:port>/shared documents/
        Attendance tracking template1.xlsx"
    Private site As SPSite
    Private myWeb As SPWeb
    Private sharedWebParts As SPLimitedWebPartManager
    Private Sub AddEWAButton_Click(ByVal sender As Object, ByVal e As EventArgs)
        site = New SPSite(siteurl)

        If Not site Is Nothing Then
            myWeb = site.OpenWeb()
            'Get the collection of shared Web Parts
            sharedWebParts = myWeb.GetLimitedWebPartManager("Default.aspx",
                System.Web.UI.WebControls.WebParts.PersonalizationScope.Shared)
            Dim collection As SPLimitedWebPartCollection = sharedWebParts.WebParts

            Dim found As Boolean = False
            For Each wp As System.Web.UI.WebControls.WebParts.WebPart In
                collection
                    If Not wp Is Nothing AndAlso wp.DisplayTitle.ToLower().Trim() =
                        "ExcelPart" Then
                            found = True
                            Exit For
                    End If
            Next wp

            If (Not found) Then
                'Add an Excel Web Access Web Part in a shared view
                Dim ewaWebPart As Microsoft.Office.Excel.WebUI.ExcelWebRenderer =
                    New Microsoft.Office.Excel.WebUI.ExcelWebRenderer()
                ewaWebPart.ZoneID = "Left"
                ewaWebPart.WorkbookUri = bookuri
                ewaWebPart.Title = "ExcelPart"

                sharedWebParts.AddWebPart(ewaWebPart, ewaWebPart.ZoneID, 1)

                MessageBox.Show("Added Web Part. Please refresh page.")
            End If
        End If
    End Sub
End Class
End Namespace
```

Warning   To compile this code, you need to add a reference to the *Microsoft.Office.Excel. WebUI.dll* assembly. This assembly is installed in the global assembly cache (GAC) when Microsoft Office SharePoint Server (MOSS) 2007 is installed. Extract the assembly into a local folder using the walk-through outlined in the MSDN article at this link: *http://msdn2.microsoft.com/en-us/library/aa549922.aspx*.

The code in Listing 6-1 shows how to add a Web Part to a site. The Web Part contains an Excel spreadsheet similar to the one shown in Figure 6-1. The code is based on a Microsoft Windows Application template project, and essentially it uses the Windows SharePoint Server (WSS) 3.0 object model to load a custom Web Part onto the home page.

Notice that the code performs a sanity check by iterating the Web Part collections on the page. If that Web Part does not exist, an Excel Web Access (EWA) Web Part is created dynamically and added to the page. There are certainly more elegant ways to determine whether or not a Web Part exists; however, this approach suffices nicely because it demonstrates how to iterate a Web Part collection. The URL passed to the Excel Web Access object points to an Excel spreadsheet residing in a trusted location.

Notice, too, that the code inside the body of the loop holds a reference to each Web Part in the collection during the iteration process. That reference allows you, as a developer, to perform any type of operation on the Web Part, such as minimizing or opening the Web Part.

> **Tip**   In case you haven't noticed by now, each click on the Web page forces your Web Part initialization code to be executed again. This condition is certainly not ideal, especially if your initialization routines are expensive. You can remedy that by simply caching the data in the control or using a flag variable to indicate whether or not a refresh is required.

The user will see the changes the next time the page is reloaded. It would be nice to force the page to refresh from the Windows client application. However, this is simply not technically possible. The executing application is not part of SharePoint and contains no knowledge of the user session required to force a refresh.

In case you missed the magic, the ability to programmatically manipulate a Web Part on a SharePoint page is significant. Consider the case where the application performs certain types of personalization. One example might be that the application remembers the selected value in a custom control. Or consider the case where the common Web Parts used by a knowledge worker are automatically loaded when the user logs in. These personalization tidbits can set an application apart from the usual run-of-the-mill applications out there. Using the code presented here, your application can be extended to do beautiful things, things that require minimal effort while providing maximum usability from an end user perspective.

However, let's not get distracted. Getting back on track, I'll note here a significant limitation with the ExcelWebRenderer Web Part. It exposes no access to the spreadsheet. For instance, it does not allow calling code to manipulate spreadsheet cells. It simply displays a spreadsheet where the cells of the spreadsheet operate in read-only mode. The EWA toolbar allows the user to perform a limited range of functionality, such as sorting and formatting.

Programming the *xlViewer* Object

The last example showed how to load a spreadsheet that did not immediately allow cell input. Maybe we can find a way to do this by examining how Excel publishes a spreadsheet. We already know that a published spreadsheet offers interactivity only through the toolbar and the tool pane. However, understanding the process might yield some clues. It's worth a try. Let's publish a spreadsheet and shake it vigorously to see what falls off:

1. Open a spreadsheet in Microsoft Excel.

2. On the Publish menu, select Excel Services as shown in Figure 6-2.

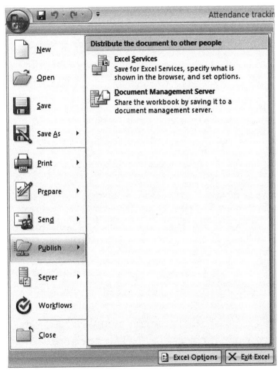

Figure 6-2   Excel Services Publish menu in Office Professional Plus version.

3. In the Save As dialog box, click the Excel Services Options button as shown in Figure 6-3.

Figure 6-3   Excel Services Options button in Office Professional Plus version.

4. Select the cells that require end user input, as shown in Figure 6-4, by using the Parameters and Show tabs at the top of the dialog box.

5. Click OK.

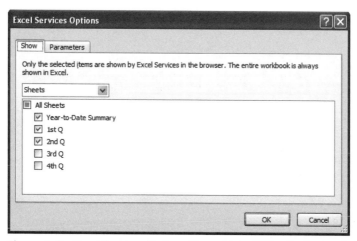

Figure 6-4   Excel Services Options Show tab in Office Professional Plus version.

If you examine the Web Part in Figure 6-5, you will notice the spreadsheet is being rendered with the help of an *xlViewer* object. Consider the URL address bar for Figure 6-1, which is copied here for convenience:

```
http://<sitename:port>/_layouts/xlviewer.aspx?<path to spreadsheet>
```

Note   If you're running on the same machine you publish to, you'll get an error saying, "Unable to display the workbook in the browser." Excel Services cannot open workbooks saved on the local machine.

It seems that the *xlViewer* object accepts a URI that points to a spreadsheet. This is certainly interesting because it provides an internal way to load spreadsheets. Maybe we can access some method or property that allows us to work around the interactivity limitation.

The path on disk given by *<Drive>:\Program Files\Common Files\Microsoft Shared\Web Server Extensions\12\TEMPLATE\LAYOUTS* points to the *xlViewer.aspx* file for default installs. The associated *.cs* file is located in the content database as usual because the page is uncustomized. Recall that we talked briefly about the underpinnings of uncustomized pages in Chapter 5, "Windows SharePoint Services 3.0."

If you care to examine the *.aspx* file, it simply invokes the Excel Web Access Web Part to load the spreadsheet. It should be possible to customize the *xlViewer* object to control the loading process, and perhaps even remove the read-only mode protection. Figure 6-5 shows the Excel Viewer object.

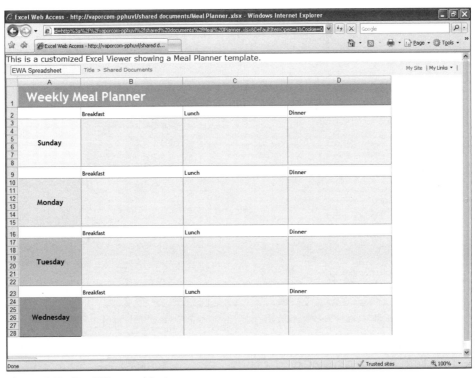

Figure 6-5   Excel Viewer object.

The *.aspx* code modification is shown in Listing 6-2. Only the relevant parts are shown. Feel free to examine the complete *.aspx* file on your machine.

Listing 6-2   ASPX *xlViewer* modification.

C# Snippet

```
<%-- Copyright (c) Microsoft Corporation. All rights reserved. --%>
<%@ Register Tagprefix="SharePoint" Namespace="Microsoft.SharePoint.WebControls"
Assembly="Microsoft.SharePoint, Version=12.0.0.0,
Culture=neutral, PublicKeyToken=71e9bce111e9429c" %>
…
<%@ Page language="C#" Codebehind="XlViewer.aspx.cs" AutoEventWireup="true"
Inherits="Microsoft.Office.Excel.WebUI.XlViewer,Microsoft.Office.Excel.WebUI,
Version=12.0.0.0,Culture=neutral,PublicKeyToken=71e9bce111e9429c" %>
<html id="m_htmlTag" runat="server">
<head>
    <meta name="WebPartPageExpansion" content="full" />
    …
    <link type="text/xml" rel="alternate" href="_vti_bin/spdisco.aspx" />
    <script runat="server">

    </script>
</head>
<body style="overflow:auto;">
    <form runat="server">
        <SharePoint:FormDigest runat="server"/>
        <table cellpadding="0" cellspacing="0" width="100%" height="100%" border="0">
        <tr>
        <td>
            <!-- begin global breadcrumb -->
    …
            <td nowrap="nowrap">
                <asp:TextBox id="myTextBox" runat="server"></asp:TextBox>
            </td>
    …
        </tr>
        </table>
        </form>
</body>
</html>
```

Visual Basic Snippet

```
<%-- Copyright (c) Microsoft Corporation. All rights reserved. --%>
<%@ Register Tagprefix="SharePoint" Namespace="Microsoft.SharePoint.WebControls"
Assembly="Microsoft.SharePoint, Version=12.0.0.0,
Culture=neutral, PublicKeyToken=71e9bce111e9429c" %>
…
<%@ Page language="VB" Codebehind="XlViewer.aspx.vb" AutoEventWireup="true"
Inherits="Microsoft.Office.Excel.WebUI.XlViewer,Microsoft.Office.Excel.WebUI,
Version=12.0.0.0,Culture=neutral,PublicKeyToken=71e9bce111e9429c" %>
<html id="m_htmlTag" runat="server">
<head>
    <meta name="WebPartPageExpansion" content="full" />
    …
    <link type="text/xml" rel="alternate" href="_vti_bin/spdisco.aspx" />
```

```
    <script runat="server">

    </script>
</head>
<body style="overflow:auto;">
    <form runat="server">
        <SharePoint:FormDigest runat="server"/>
        <table cellpadding="0" cellspacing="0" width="100%" height="100%" border="0">
        <tr>
        <td>
            <!-- begin global breadcrumb -->
 …
            <td nowrap="nowrap">
                <asp:TextBox id="myTextBox" runat="server"></asp:TextBox>
            </td>
 …
        </tr>
    </table>
    </form>
</body>
</html>
```

The *.aspx* contents show that we have adjusted the *AutoEventWireup* property to a value of *true*. This allows us to hook into the page-level events so that we can have our custom code called in response to page events.

Listing 6-3 shows the code-beside file modification for the *xlViewer* object.

Listing 6-3 CS *xlViewer* modification.

```
C# Snippet
private void Page_Load(object sender, System.EventArgs e)
{
    m_excelWebRenderer.AllowInExcelOperations = true;
    m_excelWebRenderer.AllowEdit = true;
    m_excelWebRenderer.AllowParameterModification = true;
    m_excelWebRenderer.ToolTip = "Customized Excel Viewer";
    m_title.InnerText = "a title";
    m_excelWebRenderer.Description = "this is my description";
    m_excelWebRenderer.ToolbarStyle = ToolbarVisibilityStyle.None;
    m_excelWebRenderer.RowsToDisplay = 28;
    m_excelWebRenderer.ColumnsToDisplay = 4;
    m_excelWebRenderer.ToolbarStyle =  ToolbarVisibilityStyle.None;
    m_excelWebRenderer.AllowMinimize = false;

    Response.Write("This is a customized Excel Viewer showing a Meal Planner
        template.");

    myTextBox.BackColor = System.Drawing.Color.Yellow;
    myTextBox.Text = "EWA Spreadsheet";
    myTextBox.BorderStyle = BorderStyle.Groove;
    myTextBox.ReadOnly = true;
}
```

```vb
Visual Basic Snippet
Private Sub Page_Load(ByVal sender As Object, ByVal e As System.EventArgs)
    m_excelWebRenderer.AllowInExcelOperations = True
    m_excelWebRenderer.AllowEdit = True
    m_excelWebRenderer.AllowParameterModification = True
    m_excelWebRenderer.ToolTip = "Customized Excel Viewer"
    m_title.InnerText = "a title"
    m_excelWebRenderer.Description = "this is my description"
    m_excelWebRenderer.ToolbarStyle = ToolbarVisibilityStyle.None
    m_excelWebRenderer.RowsToDisplay = 28
    m_excelWebRenderer.ColumnsToDisplay = 4
    m_excelWebRenderer.ToolbarStyle = ToolbarVisibilityStyle.None
    m_excelWebRenderer.AllowMinimize = False

    Response.Write("This is a customized Excel Viewer showing a Meal Planner
      template.")

    myTextBox.BackColor = System.Drawing.Color.Yellow
    myTextBox.Text = "EWA Spreadsheet"
    myTextBox.BorderStyle = BorderStyle.Groove
    myTextBox.ReadOnly = True
End Sub
```

For the page load event, we add a *page_load* handler that allows us to customize the Excel Viewer object. We insert the handler inside the *.aspx* page because SharePoint is hard-wired to source the code-beside file from the content database. Though you certainly can modify the content database, Chapter 5 specifically recommends against doing so.

The *m_excelWebRenderer* object declared in the body of the *.aspx* page represents the Excel viewer control that will contain the Excel spreadsheet. The code provided to customize the *m_excelWebRenderer* object is bare-bones but it does provide a good idea for the range of functionality that you can implement. Remember, this is no different than a regular *.aspx* page so you should treat it no differently.

If you care to scan the properties of the *xlViewer* object using IntelliSense, you'd realize that it offers no way to lift the read-only restrictions of the spreadsheet. This is a dead end! It seems, for now at least, that these interactivity doors are firmly locked. It also seems that this restriction applies to all versions of the Office system.

You shouldn't be disappointed because it wasn't all a fruitless run; we learned of the location where *.aspx* files live. And we learned that we can customize these pages to suit our needs by hooking into the page events and adding server script code. You'll use this technique to customize any one of the several dozen *.aspx* files that can be found in this location. Chapter 7, "Advanced Concepts with Excel Services," will build upon this concept by showing you how to add your own custom pages to SharePoint.

Object Embedding in Web Parts

Continuing the discussion around interactivity, the option to publish to Excel Services shown earlier in Figure 6-2 allows end users to publish a spreadsheet with interactivity so that team members can work with the spreadsheet, entering data and performing calculations as needed. If the version on the client desktop is not the Enterprise edition or the Professional Plus version, the end user will see a read-only version of the spreadsheet.

In addition, the end user will not see a parameter list in the published spreadsheet. Although the Enterprise edition is available for purchase or for download from MSDN, it is available only for specific volume-licensed MSDN subscribers.

Why should you care about this? It is very likely that you or your company might purchase MOSS 2007 without purchasing the 2007 Microsoft Office system. Although these earlier versions of Office allow you to save and load the document from the trusted location, the ability to publish spreadsheets is not available.

> **Important**   Client computers that access MOSS applications do not require any specific version of Office to be installed to use many of the Windows SharePoint Services 3.0 features. However, the 2007 Microsoft Office system provides tighter integration with SharePoint. Outlook 2007 in particular allows you to synchronize most of the content from a Windows SharePoint Services site to an offline folder. There is even tight integration with Real Simple Syndication (RSS). You also do not have to deploy Microsoft Exchange Server to take advantage of many of the Windows SharePoint Services e-mail integration features. A Simple Mail Transfer Protocol (SMTP) server will suffice. Other features, such as the option to automatically synchronize public folder contents to a Windows SharePoint Services document library, do require Exchange Server.

In case you missed the earlier discussion, let's restate the obvious. Published spreadsheets that are interactive tend to foster better collaboration while providing the knowledge worker with the ability to perform extensive data analysis on demand. In actual fact, if you are a knowledge worker with Office 2003 and access to the MOSS 2007 platform, you haven't gained much from a collaboration perspective. To publish spreadsheets, you either need to upgrade or adjust your programming strategies.

So far, our strategies to work around the limited interactivity have come up empty handed. But there is still hope. We still have a juicy carrot that we can dangle on a stick to entice Mr. Interactivity out from hiding.

We have found out, albeit the hard way, that the Office system is locked down with respect to interactivity and that interactivity is hard-wired to the Office version. We have seen this type of interactivity restriction before in the Office Web Components architecture. It is more subtle here. The *xlViewer* tool also exposes no hooks to allow interactivity, but it triggers a light bulb that provides the break we need. Maybe we need to look outside of the 2007 Office system, perhaps at a third-party component or an older Office technology that isn't so locked down.

One suitable candidate is the Office Web Components spreadsheet. It is capable of running in a browser, is not tied to a specific Office version, and also allows the end user to interact with the spreadsheet. For those of us who find ourselves with MOSS 2007 and a lesser version of Office, this type of approach holds a lot of promise because it means that we can take advantage of the MOSS platform while providing our clients the interactivity they are accustomed to. It also allows us to save the cost of updating our Office system. This is especially important for budget-conscious shops. Take a look at Listing 6-4.

Listing 6-4   Embedding objects in a Web Part.

```csharp
C# Snippet
using System;
using System.Runtime.InteropServices;
using System.Web.UI;
using System.Web.UI.WebControls.WebParts;
using System.Xml.Serialization;
using Microsoft.SharePoint;

namespace SpreadsheetControl
{
    [Guid("b6103eab-1d21-4dbf-bb28-5d917d8e96b5")]
    public class ExcelWeb_Part : System.Web.UI.WebControls.WebParts.WebPart
    {
        System.Text.StringBuilder scripter = new System.Text.StringBuilder();
        string spreadsheet = "<object classid=
          'clsid:0002E559-0000-0000-C000-000000000046' id='sp' ></object>";

        protected override void Render(HtmlTextWriter writer)
        {
            writer.Write(spreadsheet);
            writer.Write(LoadData("Programming Microsoft® Office
            Excel 2007 Services "));

            writer.Write(System.Environment.NewLine + "<script language='vbscript'>" +
               System.Environment.NewLine + "call loadData()" +
               System.Environment.NewLine + "</script>");
        }
        public string LoadData(string payload)
        {
            System.Text.StringBuilder script = new System.Text.StringBuilder();

            script.Append(System.Environment.NewLine).Append("<script
              type='text/vbscript' language='vbscript'>Sub loadData()");
            script.Append(System.Environment.NewLine).Append("  Dim chConstants");
            script.Append(System.Environment.NewLine).Append("  Dim Spreadsheet1");
            script.Append(System.Environment.NewLine).Append("  set Spreadsheet1 =
              document.all(\"sp\").object");
            script.Append(System.Environment.NewLine).Append(" Spreadsheet1.
              ActiveSheet.Cells(1, 1).Value = \"ISBN: 0-7356-2407-0\"");
            script.Append(System.Environment.NewLine).Append(" Spreadsheet1.
              ActiveSheet.Cells(2, 1).Value = \"").Append(payload).Append("\"");
            script.Append(System.Environment.NewLine).Append("End Sub");
            script.Append(System.Environment.NewLine).Append(System.Environment.
              NewLine).Append(System.Environment.NewLine).Append("</script>");
```

```
                return script.ToString();
            }
        }
}
```

Visual Basic Snippet

```vb
Imports System
Imports System.Runtime.InteropServices
Imports System.Web.UI
Imports System.Web.UI.WebControls.WebParts
Imports System.Xml.Serialization
Imports Microsoft.SharePoint

Namespace SpreadsheetControl
    <Guid("b6103eab-1d21-4dbf-bb28-5d917d8e96b5")> _
    Public Class ExcelWeb_Part
        Inherits System.Web.UI.WebControls.WebParts.WebPart
        Private scripter As System.Text.StringBuilder =
          New System.Text.StringBuilder()
        Private spreadsheet As String = "<object classid=
          'clsid:0002E559-0000-0000-C000-000000000046' id='sp' ></object>"
        Protected Overrides Sub Render(ByVal writer As HtmlTextWriter)
            writer.Write(spreadsheet)
            writer.Write(LoadData("Programming Microsoft® Office Excel 2007
              Services "))

            writer.Write(System.Environment.NewLine & "<script language='vbscript'>"
              & System.Environment.NewLine & "call loadData()"
              & System.Environment.NewLine & "</script>")
        End Sub
        Public Function LoadData(ByVal payload As String) As String
            Dim script As System.Text.StringBuilder = New System.Text.StringBuilder()

            script.Append(System.Environment.NewLine).Append("<script type='text/
              vbscript' language='vbscript'>Sub loadData()")
            script.Append(System.Environment.NewLine).Append("  Dim chConstants")
            script.Append(System.Environment.NewLine).Append("  Dim Spreadsheet1")
            script.Append(System.Environment.NewLine).Append("  set Spreadsheet1 =
              document.all(""sp"").object")
            script.Append(System.Environment.NewLine).Append(" Spreadsheet1.
              ActiveSheet.Cells(1, 1).Value = ""ISBN: 0-7356-2407-0""")
            script.Append(System.Environment.NewLine).Append(" Spreadsheet1.
              ActiveSheet.Cells(2, 1).Value = """).Append(payload).Append("""")
            script.Append(System.Environment.NewLine).Append("End Sub")
            script.Append(System.Environment.NewLine).Append(System.Environment.
              NewLine).Append(System.Environment.NewLine).Append("</script>")

            Return script.ToString()
        End Function
    End Class
End Namespace
```

Figure 6-6 shows a legacy spreadsheet embedded inside a Web Part hosted on SharePoint.

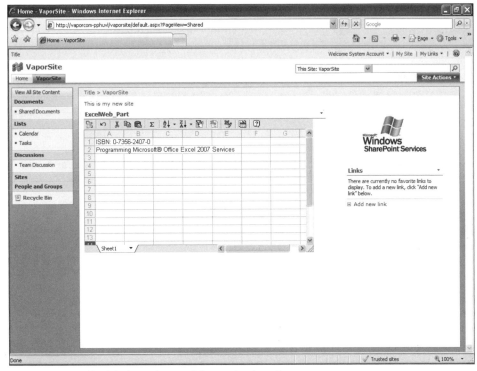

Figure 6-6   Embedded Excel spreadsheet, classic style.

The driving logic behind the page is that it writes an ActiveX COM object out to the response stream for the Web Part. Once this stream reaches the client, the browser takes care of deserializing the stream into the appropriate object and hosting an instance of it on the Web page. For this to work, the client needs to have the Office Web Component (OWC) COM object registered on the local machine. With the object rendered in the browser, the rest of the script code is concerned with loading data into the control.

Important   To run this example, you need to install the Office Web Components from the Microsoft SQL Server installation application located in the tools folder. Or you can download the free package from the Microsoft Office Web site. You should be aware that there are certain licensing restrictions regarding the use of OWC spreadsheets that present an interactive surface.

As a convenience to the user, you can even offer this extended spreadsheet functionality as a "Classic Spreadsheet" option that complements the new Ribbon spreadsheet with the 2007 Office system, similar to the way Microsoft offers Microsoft Windows classic themes with its current operating system. That type of flexibility works well with end users who have grown accustomed to, and achieved a high level of productivity with, existing technology.

While we are on the subject of hosting unmanaged controls in a browser, you shouldn't frown upon the idea of targeting ActiveX COM components with managed code. First, you don't have much of a choice. Managed versions of controls such as Windows Media Player or Flash are not yet available. Second, the .NET platform is not ubiquitous, meaning that it is not yet deployed to all versions of Windows operating systems. Third, .NET managed code was built to interoperate with COM components. Fourth—and this is perhaps the most important—the future is definitely a managed world, but the present and the past are built on COM.

Programming Real-Time Web Part Components

Frankly, while this isn't exactly what we had hoped for in terms of cracking the interactivity nut, this type of functionality is interesting enough to warrant a more thorough look. You can extend the depth and breadth of hosted objects through moderate tweaks to the code presented previously. The driving logic remains the same. Consider the code shown in Listing 6-5.

Listing 6-5   Embedding objects in a Web Part.

```
C# Snippet
namespace LiveChart
{
    [Guid("56c19d9c-0323-4d69-b99a-eb8926aa505e")]
    public class LiveChart : System.Web.UI.WebControls.WebParts.WebPart
    {
        System.Text.StringBuilder scripter = new System.Text.StringBuilder();
        string spreadsheet = "<object classid= 'clsid:0002E559-0000-0000-C000-
          000000000046' id='sp' ></object>";
        string chart = "<object classid= 'clsid:0002E55D-0000-0000-C000-000000000046'
          id='cs' ></object>";

        protected override void Render(HtmlTextWriter writer)
        {
            //embed a chart and a spreadsheet control
            writer.Write(spreadsheet);
            writer.Write(chart);
            writer.Write(LoadData());

            writer.Write(System.Environment.NewLine + "<script language='vbscript'>"
                + System.Environment.NewLine + "call loadData()"
                + System.Environment.NewLine + "</script>");
        }
```

```csharp
public string LoadData()
{
    System.Text.StringBuilder script = new System.Text.StringBuilder();

    script.Append(System.Environment.NewLine + "<script type='text/vbscript'
      language='vbscript'>Sub loadData()");
    script.Append(System.Environment.NewLine + "Dim chConstants");
    script.Append(System.Environment.NewLine + "Dim Spreadsheet1");
    script.Append(System.Environment.NewLine
      + "set Spreadsheet1 = document.all(\"sp\").object");
    script.Append(System.Environment.NewLine
      + "Spreadsheet1.ActiveSheet.Cells(2, 1).Value = \"Mexico\"");
    script.Append(System.Environment.NewLine
      + "Spreadsheet1.ActiveSheet.Cells(3, 1).Value = \"Canada\"");
    script.Append(System.Environment.NewLine
      + "Spreadsheet1.ActiveSheet.Cells(4, 1).Value = \"America\"");
    script.Append(System.Environment.NewLine
      + "Spreadsheet1.ActiveSheet.Cells(1, 2).Value = \"Domestic\"");
    script.Append(System.Environment.NewLine
      + "Spreadsheet1.ActiveSheet.Cells(2, 2).Value = 0.02");
    script.Append(System.Environment.NewLine
      + "Spreadsheet1.ActiveSheet.Cells(3, 2).Value = 0.05");
    script.Append(System.Environment.NewLine
      + "Spreadsheet1.ActiveSheet.Cells(4, 2).Value = 0.10");
    script.Append(System.Environment.NewLine
      + "Spreadsheet1.ActiveSheet.Cells(1, 3).Value = \"Long-Distance\"");
    script.Append(System.Environment.NewLine
      + "Spreadsheet1.ActiveSheet.Cells(2, 3).Value = 0.09");
    script.Append(System.Environment.NewLine
      + "Spreadsheet1.ActiveSheet.Cells(3, 3).Value = 0.82");
    script.Append(System.Environment.NewLine
      + "Spreadsheet1.ActiveSheet.Cells(4, 3).Value = 0.28");
    script.Append(System.Environment.NewLine
      + "Spreadsheet1.ActiveSheet.Cells(1, 4).Value = \"International\"");
    script.Append(System.Environment.NewLine
      + "Spreadsheet1.ActiveSheet.Cells(2, 4).Value = 0.42");
    script.Append(System.Environment.NewLine
      + "Spreadsheet1.ActiveSheet.Cells(3, 4).Value = 0.12");
    script.Append(System.Environment.NewLine
      + "Spreadsheet1.ActiveSheet.Cells(4, 4).Value = 0.55");
    script.Append(System.Environment.NewLine + "Dim ChartSpace1");
    script.Append(System.Environment.NewLine
      + "set ChartSpace1 = document.all(\"cs\").object");
    script.Append(System.Environment.NewLine + "ChartSpace1.Charts.Add");
    script.Append(System.Environment.NewLine
      + "Set chConstants = ChartSpace1.Constants");
    script.Append(System.Environment.NewLine
      + "ChartSpace1.DataSource = Spreadsheet1");
```

```
                script.Append(System.Environment.NewLine
                    + "Set oSeries1 = ChartSpace1.Charts(0).SeriesCollection.Add");
                script.Append(System.Environment.NewLine
                    + "oSeries1.Type = chConstants.chChartTypeLine3D");
                script.Append(System.Environment.NewLine
                    + "ChartSpace1.Charts(0).SeriesCollection.Add");
                script.Append(System.Environment.NewLine
                    + "ChartSpace1.Charts(0).SeriesCollection.Add");
                script.Append(System.Environment.NewLine
                    + "ChartSpace1.Charts(0).SeriesCollection(0).SetData
                    chConstants.chDimSeriesNames, chConstants.chDataBound, \"B1\"");
                script.Append(System.Environment.NewLine
                    + "ChartSpace1.Charts(0).SeriesCollection(0).SetData
                    chConstants.chDimCategories, chConstants.chDataBound, \"A2:A5\"");
                script.Append(System.Environment.NewLine
                    + "ChartSpace1.Charts(0).SeriesCollection(0).SetData
                    chConstants.chDimValues, chConstants.chDataBound, \"B2:B5\"");
                script.Append(System.Environment.NewLine
                    + "ChartSpace1.Charts(0).SeriesCollection(1).SetData
                    chConstants.chDimSeriesNames, chConstants.chDataBound, \"C1\"");
                script.Append(System.Environment.NewLine
                    + "ChartSpace1.Charts(0).SeriesCollection(1).SetData
                    chConstants.chDimCategories, chConstants.chDataBound, \"A2:A5\"");
                script.Append(System.Environment.NewLine
                    + "ChartSpace1.Charts(0).SeriesCollection(1).SetData
                    chConstants.chDimValues, chConstants.chDataBound, \"C2:C5\"");
                script.Append(System.Environment.NewLine
                    + "ChartSpace1.Charts(0).SeriesCollection(2).SetData
                    chConstants.chDimSeriesNames, chConstants.chDataBound, \"D1\"");
                script.Append(System.Environment.NewLine
                    + "ChartSpace1.Charts(0).SeriesCollection(2).SetData
                    chConstants.chDimCategories, chConstants.chDataBound, \"A2:A5\"");
                script.Append(System.Environment.NewLine
                    + "ChartSpace1.Charts(0).SeriesCollection(2).SetData
                    chConstants.chDimValues, chConstants.chDataBound, \"D2:D5\"");
                script.Append(System.Environment.NewLine
                    + "ChartSpace1.Charts(0).HasLegend = True");
                script.Append(System.Environment.NewLine + "ChartSpace1.Charts(0)
                    .Axes(chConstants.chAxisPositionLeft).NumberFormat = \"0%\"");
                script.Append(System.Environment.NewLine + "ChartSpace1.Charts(0)
                    .Axes(chConstants.chAxisPositionLeft).MajorUnit = 0.2");
                script.Append(System.Environment.NewLine + "End Sub");
                script.Append(System.Environment.NewLine + System.Environment.NewLine
                    + System.Environment.NewLine + "</script>");

                return script.ToString();
            }
        }
    }
```

Visual Basic Snippet

```
Namespace LiveChart
    <Guid("56c19d9c-0323-4d69-b99a-eb8926aa505e")> _
    Public Class LiveChart
        Inherits System.Web.UI.WebControls.WebParts.WebPart
```

```vb
Private scripter As System.Text.StringBuilder
  = New System.Text.StringBuilder()
Private spreadsheet As String = "<object classid=
  'clsid:0002E559-0000-0000-C000-000000000046' id='sp' ></object>"
Private chart As String = "<object classid=
  'clsid:0002E55D-0000-0000-C000-000000000046' id='cs' ></object>"

Protected Overrides Sub Render(ByVal writer As HtmlTextWriter)
    'embed a chart and a spreadsheet control
    writer.Write(spreadsheet)
    writer.Write(chart)
    writer.Write(LoadData())

    writer.Write(System.Environment.NewLine & "<script language='vbscript'>"
      & System.Environment.NewLine & "call loadData()"
      & System.Environment.NewLine & "</script>")
End Sub

Public Function LoadData() As String
    Dim script As System.Text.StringBuilder = New System.Text.StringBuilder()
    script.Append(System.Environment.NewLine & "<script type='text/vbscript'
      language='vbscript'>Sub loadData()")
    script.Append(System.Environment.NewLine & "Dim chConstants")
    script.Append(System.Environment.NewLine & "Dim Spreadsheet1")
    script.Append(System.Environment.NewLine &
      "set Spreadsheet1 = document.all(""sp"").object")
    script.Append(System.Environment.NewLine
      & "Spreadsheet1.ActiveSheet.Cells(2, 1).Value = ""Mexico""")
    script.Append(System.Environment.NewLine
      & "Spreadsheet1.ActiveSheet.Cells(3, 1).Value = ""Canada""")
    script.Append(System.Environment.NewLine
      & "Spreadsheet1.ActiveSheet.Cells(4, 1).Value = ""America""")
    script.Append(System.Environment.NewLine
      & "Spreadsheet1.ActiveSheet.Cells(1, 2).Value = ""Domestic""")
    script.Append(System.Environment.NewLine
      & "Spreadsheet1.ActiveSheet.Cells(2, 2).Value = 0.02")
    script.Append(System.Environment.NewLine
      & "Spreadsheet1.ActiveSheet.Cells(3, 2).Value = 0.05")
    script.Append(System.Environment.NewLine
      & "Spreadsheet1.ActiveSheet.Cells(4, 2).Value = 0.10")
    script.Append(System.Environment.NewLine
      & "Spreadsheet1.ActiveSheet.Cells(1, 3).Value = ""Long-Distance""")
    script.Append(System.Environment.NewLine
      & "Spreadsheet1.ActiveSheet.Cells(2, 3).Value = 0.09")
    script.Append(System.Environment.NewLine
      & "Spreadsheet1.ActiveSheet.Cells(3, 3).Value = 0.82")
    script.Append(System.Environment.NewLine
      & "Spreadsheet1.ActiveSheet.Cells(4, 3).Value = 0.28")
    script.Append(System.Environment.NewLine
      & "Spreadsheet1.ActiveSheet.Cells(1, 4).Value = ""International""")
    script.Append(System.Environment.NewLine
      & "Spreadsheet1.ActiveSheet.Cells(2, 4).Value= 0.42")
    script.Append(System.Environment.NewLine
      & "Spreadsheet1.ActiveSheet.Cells(3, 4).Value = 0.12")
```

```
script.Append(System.Environment.NewLine
  & "Spreadsheet1.ActiveSheet.Cells(4, 4).Value = 0.55")
script.Append(System.Environment.NewLine & "Dim ChartSpace1")
script.Append(System.Environment.NewLine
  & "set ChartSpace1 = document.all(""cs"").object")
script.Append(System.Environment.NewLine & "ChartSpace1.Charts.Add")
script.Append(System.Environment.NewLine
  & "Set chConstants = ChartSpace1.Constants")
script.Append(System.Environment.NewLine
  & "ChartSpace1.DataSource = Spreadsheet1")
script.Append(System.Environment.NewLine
  & "Set oSeries1 = ChartSpace1.Charts(0).SeriesCollection.Add")
script.Append(System.Environment.NewLine
  & "oSeries1.Type = chConstants.chChartTypeLine3D")
script.Append(System.Environment.NewLine
  & "ChartSpace1.Charts(0).SeriesCollection.Add")
script.Append(System.Environment.NewLine
  & "ChartSpace1.Charts(0).SeriesCollection.Add")
script.Append(System.Environment.NewLine
  & "ChartSpace1.Charts(0).SeriesCollection(0).SetData
  chConstants.chDimSeriesNames, chConstants.chDataBound, ""B1""")
script.Append(System.Environment.NewLine
  & "ChartSpace1.Charts(0).SeriesCollection(0).SetData
  chConstants.chDimCategories, chConstants.chDataBound, ""A2:A5""")
script.Append(System.Environment.NewLine
  & "ChartSpace1.Charts(0).SeriesCollection(0).SetData
  chConstants.chDimValues, chConstants.chDataBound, ""B2:B5""")
script.Append(System.Environment.NewLine
  & "ChartSpace1.Charts(0).SeriesCollection(1).SetData
  chConstants.chDimSeriesNames, chConstants.chDataBound, ""C1""")
script.Append(System.Environment.NewLine
  & "ChartSpace1.Charts(0).SeriesCollection(1).SetData
  chConstants.chDimCategories, chConstants.chDataBound, ""A2:A5""")
script.Append(System.Environment.NewLine
  & "ChartSpace1.Charts(0).SeriesCollection(1).SetData
  chConstants.chDimValues, chConstants.chDataBound, ""C2:C5""")
script.Append(System.Environment.NewLine
  & "ChartSpace1.Charts(0).SeriesCollection(2).SetData
  chConstants.chDimSeriesNames, chConstants.chDataBound, ""D1""")
script.Append(System.Environment.NewLine
  & "ChartSpace1.Charts(0).SeriesCollection(2).SetData
  chConstants.chDimCategories, chConstants.chDataBound, ""A2:A5""")
script.Append(System.Environment.NewLine
  & "ChartSpace1.Charts(0).SeriesCollection(2).SetData
  chConstants.chDimValues, chConstants.chDataBound, ""D2:D5""")
script.Append(System.Environment.NewLine
  & "ChartSpace1.Charts(0).HasLegend = True")
script.Append(System.Environment.NewLine & "ChartSpace1.Charts(0).
  Axes(chConstants.chAxisPositionLeft).NumberFormat = ""0%""")
script.Append(System.Environment.NewLine
  & "ChartSpace1.Charts(0).Axes(chConstants.chAxisPositionLeft)
  .MajorUnit = 0.2")
script.Append(System.Environment.NewLine & "End Sub")
script.Append(System.Environment.NewLine & System.Environment.NewLine
  & System.Environment.NewLine & "</script>")
```

```
            Return script.ToString()
        End Function
    End Class
End Namespace
```

The code structure is framed on the previous example with the exception that the *LoadData* method call no longer contains an input parameter. We have also added a chart object in the *Render* method. Its *clsid* is declared in the same manner as the spreadsheet. The *LoadData* method is extended to build an X/Y axis, more accurately described as a category/value axis. The rest of the code is concerned with filling the cells with data and formatting it appropriately.

Pay special attention to this line:

```
script.Append(System.Environment.NewLine & "ChartSpace1.DataSource = Spreadsheet1")
```

This is where the magic happens. This line of code causes the chart to source its data from the cells in the spreadsheet. As the data in the cells change, the chart updates in real time. Picture this type of functionality in a financial application where a Web service feeds the spreadsheet with stock values and symbols. The instant the spreadsheet cell changes, the bound chart reflects these changes, transforming the data into impact in real time.

In addition, you can simply allow the end user to change the type of chart being rendered to show a pie, linear, 2D/3D, combination, or multiseries chart. (See Figure 6-7.) The possibilities are endless. The development effort for the features mentioned will cost, at most, a couple of lines of code each, but the payoff is that it gives a competitive advantage to your product offering by differentiating it from your competitor's paltry, static analysis tool suite.

As far as code complexity is concerned, the code is trivial to understand. A chart rendered to the client is based on an ActiveX COM object. This object must create a *Chartspace* container to hold the chart. Data to be rendered in the chart control is loaded into category and value axes, and some customizations are performed. Finally, the contents are rendered to the client. All charting components follow the same basic approach, which is why this example is a valuable tool in understanding how charts are rendered in Web Parts. SharePoint does not ship with a native Chart Web Part.

However, you shouldn't get carried away. The data in the spreadsheet, the gloss of an Excel chart, and the lure of real-time data aren't really what is important. The important point is that ActiveX objects can be hosted in Web Parts. That's not available in any of the stock Office Web Parts, at least not with that degree of sophistication and appeal.

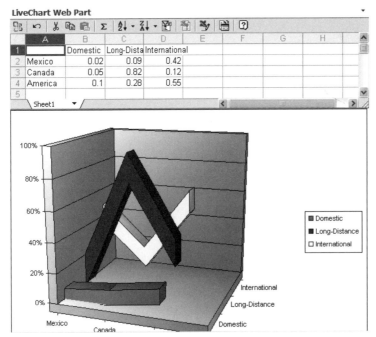

Figure 6-7   Interactive spreadsheet and chart.

Guidelines for Developing with ActiveX Controls

There are some lessons that you need to learn if you intend to step up to this level of programming:

- The value assigned to the spreadsheet cells should not contain single quotes if you choose to use VBScript because these demarcate comments in the VBScript language. You should use escaped quotes as the code shows.

- Function calls need to use the *call method* notation. If you don't need the *'call'* statement, you can invoke the function by using the function name *loadData*.

- Pay special attention to the way in which ActiveX objects are called—for instance:

```
Set Spreadsheet1 = document.all(\"mytest_sp\").object.
```

Another bombshell of sorts is that intrinsic 2007 Office system objects are unavailable to calling code. And this is a bitter disappointment! Yet it is the reason why we focused time and energy on embedding objects into Web Parts. The 2007 Office system contains impressive components to include charts, spreadsheets, and Pivot tables. However, there is currently no way to hook into these native objects with managed code. Naysayers often advise against using ActiveX components. However, enterprise-level alternatives are not in abundance.

While you can certainly draw charts manually in code, realistically speaking, it is an unwise decision to require developers to resort to Graphical Device Interface (GDI)-level constructs to render charts for enterprise-level applications. These developers are not in the business of constructing charts. Neither MOSS 2007 nor WSS 3.0 answers these questions with any sort of authority. For instance, you cannot embed a 2007 Office system chart into a Web Part. The choices at present are third-party components or legacy ActiveX objects. Do the best you can based on the tools you have before you. Hopefully, that type of functionality will be supported in future versions.

> **Caution**   The MOSS architecture explicitly prevents the Excel object from being embedded inside a Web Part. What this means exactly will be fully explained in a while, but it is significant enough to the discussion that I mention it here. As a workaround, the *xlViewer* object allows clients with the ability to load spreadsheets in Web Parts without breaking the tenets of the MOSS architecture.

Automating ActiveX Objects in Web Parts

As I mentioned previously, any ActiveX object can be displayed using the techniques described here. Consider the code in Listing 6-6.

Listing 6-6   Embedding ActiveX controls in Web Parts.

```
C# Snippet
private void DisplayWindowsMediaPlayer(HtmlTextWriter writer)
{
    string windowsMedia = "<object classid=
      'clsid:22d6f312-b0f6-11d0-94ab-0080c74c7e95' id='wm' >" +
      "<PARAM NAME='animationatStart' VALUE='true'>" +
      "<PARAM NAME='autoStart' VALUE='true'>" +
      "<PARAM NAME='shO.W.Controls' VALUE='true'>" + "<PARAM NAME='fileName'
      VALUE='http://wm.microsoft.com/ms/evnet/LanguageFutures_s_ch9.wmv'></object>";

    writer.Write(windowsMedia);
}
Visual Basic Snippet
Private Sub DisplayWindowsMediaPlayer(ByVal writer As HtmlTextWriter)

    Dim windowsMedia As String = "<object classid=
      'clsid:22d6f312-b0f6-11d0-94ab-0080c74c7e95' id='wm' >" &
      "<PARAM NAME='animationatStart' VALUE='true'>" &
      "<PARAM NAME='autoStart' VALUE='true'>" &
      "<PARAM NAME='shO.W.Controls' VALUE='true'>" &
      "<PARAM NAME='fileName' VALUE='http://wm.microsoft.com/ms/evnet/
      LanguageFutures_s_ch9.wmv'></object>"
    writer.Write(windowsMedia)
End Sub
```

Figure 6-8 shows Windows Media Player operating in a Web Part hosted on SharePoint.

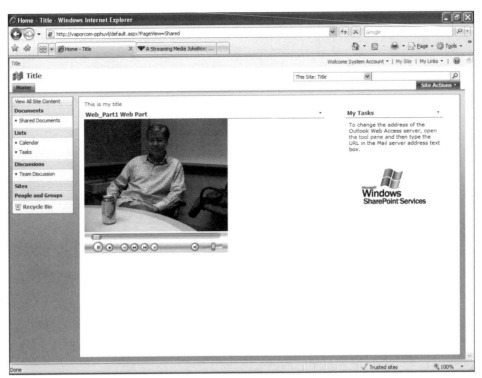

Figure 6-8   Windows Media Player in a Web Part.

The code reuses the same principles discussed earlier, except that the class ID is changed to target the Windows Media Player on the desktop. If this ActiveX object is installed on the end user's desktop, Windows Media Player is launched and immediately starts playing a media file sourced from the Microsoft Channel9 Web site (*http://channel9.msdn.com/*).

Automating Managed User Controls in Web Parts

ActiveX controls like the ones shown so far come in handy when Web applications need to interact with the desktop. For instance, multimedia content can be wired to Web Parts to provide an immersive experience—just think Flash plug-ins. However, you should note that ActiveX controls are not without issues, some of which were mentioned in Chapter 1.

One of the main issues with ActiveX controls is that policy cannot be applied to the executing code. Managed user controls, the .NET equivalent of ActiveX controls, overcomes this obstacle by allowing Code Access Security (CAS) policy to govern the execution of code. In stark contrast, an ActiveX control is either allowed to execute, in which case it has full access to the machine resources, or it is not allowed to execute at all. There is no middle ground.

This chapter neatly side-steps the CAS policy issue for good reason. A theoretical probe of the implications of CAS is best left for Chapter 7. For now, we can suppress security policy and simply demonstrate how to build embedded managed user controls that might be deployed in a SharePoint environment.

Here is a high-level overview of the steps involved in running managed Web controls from Web Parts based on SharePoint. First, we need to create a user control that loads inside a Web Part. Then we deploy this Web Part to SharePoint. The user control contains a link to an embedded Windows object so that it can be loaded when SharePoint loads the Web Part. Finally, we create the embedded object and deploy these various assemblies to the SharePoint Web application. Don't worry; the coding effort is significantly less than that required by ActiveX controls.

A fair amount of procedure and indirection is involved, but it is based on steps you have already performed leading up to this chapter. The final experience rides the bleeding edge of Web development and is well worth the entrance fee, as these types of applications rival Windows-based applications running on the desktop. You will soon see why. A word of caution is in order. You need to be grounded in the foundations of Web Part programming before proceeding beyond this point.

Creating the Web Part Loader   Create a Web Part application called **ManagedPart**. The entire code follows in Listing 6-7.

Listing 6-7   Web Part user control project.

```
C# Snippet
namespace ManagedPart
{
    [Guid("3b9477c7-7763-4d05-ace7-cd6d981270c9")]
    public class ManagedPart : System.Web.UI.WebControls.WebParts.WebPart
    {
        protected override void Render(HtmlTextWriter writer)
        {
            writer.Write("<object id='myControl1' name='myControl1'
                classid='/Controls/MyCustomWinControl.dll#MyCustomWinControl.
                UserControl1'></object>");
        }
    }
}
```

```
Visual Basic Snippet
Namespace ManagedPart
    <Guid("3b9477c7-7763-4d05-ace7-cd6d981270c9")> _
    Public Class ManagedPart
        Inherits System.Web.UI.WebControls.WebParts.WebPart
        Protected Overrides Sub Render(ByVal writer As HtmlTextWriter)
            writer.Write("<object id='myControl1' name='myControl1'
            classid='/Controls/MyCustomWinControl.dll
            #MyCustomWinControl.UserControl1'></object>")
        End Sub
    End Class
End Namespace
```

Interestingly, there is only a single, salty line of code. You will notice that this code is similar to the ActiveX control code. This is more than a passing similarity because, from the point of view of the Web browser, it is an ActiveX object. In fact, when the control finally loads, the code flavor tricks the browser into believing this is an ActiveX object.

Before moving on, note that the code to load a *System.Web.UI.UserControl*, reproduced here for convenience, won't work in this situation:

```
(UserControl)Page.LoadControl(@"/<folder>/<usercontrol.ascx>")
```

The safe-mode parser will promptly throw an exception when it encounters this type of control. The workaround is to avoid the safe-mode parser by using a piggyback approach of writing the object into the response stream.

The Windows control, not yet created by us, must be delivered by Internet Information Services (IIS) to the Web Part. This step requires the creation of a virtual directory. We won't need to explicitly create this step because the Web Part runs on SharePoint. However, the code does load a control from the controls folder (see the file path in Listing 6-7), which is a physical directory on disk. This physical directory needs to map to a virtual directory. The virtual directory must contain the appropriate permissions that allow IIS to retrieve and deliver the .NET assembly to the client download cache.

Creating the Virtual Directory   As mentioned previously, the Windows user control needs to be delivered via IIS to the Web Part so that when the Web Part is added to the page, the appropriate assembly can be downloaded to the client's machine. The delivery mechanism relies on a virtual folder. The virtual folder path points to a folder that contains the Web control assembly. You need to configure IIS appropriately. The control is delivered by IIS using the path *http://<servername:port/site/controls/webpartassembly.dll*.

Create a folder, **controls**, in the Web application for your site. This physical folder can be located anywhere on disk, but it is usually a good idea to create the folder in the application directory. The folder will map to a virtual folder given by the object path in the single line of code presented earlier. You need to make sure the controls virtual folder has Execute Permissions set to Scripts Only in IIS and not Scripts And Executables; otherwise, the control will not be loaded. Figure 6-9 shows the required permission settings. The setting instructs IIS to simply deliver the assembly to the client. IIS should not attempt to execute the code in the assembly.

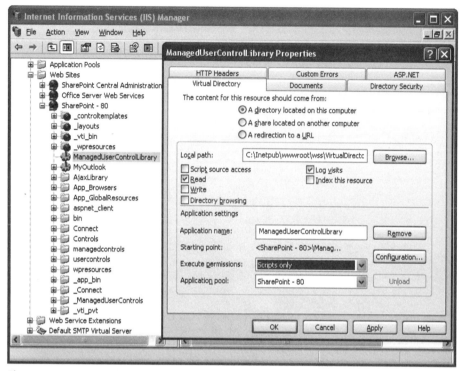

Figure 6-9   IIS virtual directory permissions configuration.

Creating the Managed User Control Application   The managed user control is built to interact with the resources running on the client machine. It makes no sense to go through this rigmarole if you do not intend to access desktop resources. Nonclient resources can be accessed in the regular way with less effort—that is, by building a regular ASP.NET application or Web Part control.

The application being developed here requires *System.Forms.Windows* controls. You can't use Web server controls here because Web server controls cannot access desktop resources. The idea here is to trick the controls into thinking that they are running on the desktop when, in truth, they are running embedded in the Web browser. The controls are none the wiser, so they continue to perform Windows-type functionality such as directory browsing, file manipulation, registry manipulation, and the myriad activities that Windows controls can perform, except that this will all occur inside a Web browser. If we succeed, the end effect is that the Web browser is elevated in status to a Windows application.

As a disclaimer, it is quite possible that we might be unsuccessful in our attempts because that type of functionality was surely absent from the SharePoint design philosophy. But we suspect it can work because managed user controls can be hosted in Internet Explorer in ASP.NET. It is certainly worth a shot, or two. The return on this investment is just too good to pass up. Enough of the theory, let's get on with the practical application of it.

Create a Windows application based on a Windows User Control template. For now, we simply add a Windows button control and an *OpenFileDialog* control. Add some code to the click event so that the *FileDialog* control is displayed. Handle the OK event in the *FileDialog* control, and add some code to open the selected file. We will keep it simple for now. Later, once you have the basics, we will build some amazing software. Listing 6-8 shows the complete code.

Listing 6-8   Web Part user control project.

```
C# Snippet
private void button1_Click(object sender, EventArgs e)
{
    openFileDialog1.ShowDialog();
}

private void openFileDialog1_FileOk(object sender, CancelEventArgs e)
{
    System.Diagnostics.Process.Start(openFileDialog1.FileName);
}
```
```
Visual Basic Snippet
Private Sub button1_Click(ByVal sender As Object, ByVal e As EventArgs)
    openFileDialog1.ShowDialog()
End Sub
Private Sub openFileDialog1_FileOk(ByVal sender As Object, ByVal e As CancelEventArgs)
    System.Diagnostics.Process.Start(openFileDialog1.FileName)
End Sub
```

This is the advanced chapter of the book, so I'll spare you the tedium of a code explanation. Suffice it to say that any type of code functionality can be implemented here. There are no bounds. For all intents and purposes, the common language runtime (CLR) considers this a Windows application. Ignorance is bliss—the CLR should not be made any wiser to the fact that we intend to run this application embedded in a Web Form on the SharePoint platform. It might get confused and start asking silly questions, or worse, it might throw foolish exceptions.

Exercise the application. The ActiveX Control Test Container (tstcon32.exe) will be invoked to host your newly created control. If you pretend that the ActiveX Control Test Container is actually a SharePoint page, you will have a good idea of what is at stake here. Click the button to make sure the code is executing as intended. Figure 6-10 shows the Windows application in the ActiveX Control Test Container.

We are halfway there. If you recall, the Windows control will actually be embedded inside a Web Part. The code will be allowed to execute once the Web Part is added to a page.

If this all seems a bit confusing to you, let's spend a moment talking about what is happening here. You must understand the difference between a managed user control application and an ordinary ASP.NET application. ASP.NET application code typically executes on the server and pushes formatted output to the client browser. Web Parts behave no differently.

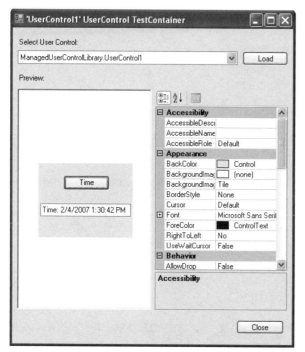

Figure 6-10 Windows control in the ActiveX Control Test Container.

In contrast, managed user controls run embedded in a browser—that is, they execute in the process space of the client machine, not on the server. The term *embedded* is adequate because it exactly captures the technical aspects of the process. An object is now living in the browser! This is far different from lifeless HTML or tired JavaScript that sits much like a prisoner in the Web page. The user control actually has a pulse and can react to stimuli such as mouse clicks and event notification.

Unfortunately, a single control cannot be in two places at once. These managed user controls have no way of interacting with the server even if they appear to use a code-beside model. It is this gem that interests us; the ability to access client resources while running in a Web browser. It is this gem that we are trying to exploit for our selfish benefit of creating killer applications.

If you cared to run the code, you would most likely see a button in a Web Part. If you click the button, the CLR promptly throws a security exception. From a theoretical perspective, IIS is responsible for delivering the managed assembly to the client. For Internet Explorer, managed assemblies are downloaded to a special cache in the *<Drive>:\Windows\Assembly\download* folder. This is the equivalent of the GAC for Web applications. As soon as the assembly tries to execute, CAS policy steps in to govern the process. Because we haven't configured CAS policy for the assembly, the assembly isn't even loaded. Contrast that to the ActiveX approach and you can see why .NET is infinitely superior from a security perspective.

It's nice to think that we could trick the run time into executing code for us. That isn't possible, though, because the CLR executes code based on the evidence that the assembly presents to the run time. There is no way for the assembly on disk to spoof the identity of another assembly. When the assembly is questioned by the run time, it must inform the run time that it is a file being sourced from the intranet zone.

The CLR consults CAS policy on the local machine to determine whether or not there are any special provisions for files being downloaded from the intranet. There are no defined permissions, so the CLR permits the control to run with default permissions for an assembly downloaded from the intranet—meaning that the control might render correctly but any other action that requires elevated permissions isn't allowed. You might see a button on screen, but clicking the button will result in a security exception.

Note that I am side-stepping the various CAS policy issues that come into play. I'll tackle them head-on in Chapter 7 by explicitly walking through the permissions configuration changes with a full explanation. For now, let's simply turn CAS policy off on the local machine so that we can test our application. To do so, open a Microsoft Visual Studio command prompt and enter **caspol -s off**, as shown in Figure 6-11.

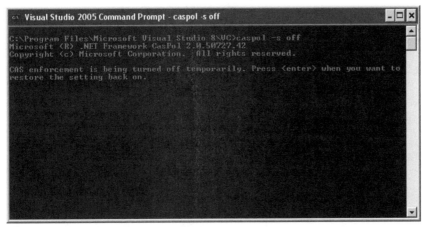

Figure 6-11   CAS policy override.

Notice how the command prompt remains open in Figure 6-11. This behavior is noticeably different from previous versions of the framework where the command prompt could be closed, resulting in CAS policy being turned off on the local machine. For .NET 2.0, if the command window is closed or the process is stopped, CAS policy is immediately re-enabled.

In case you are wondering, the ability to turn CAS policy off is not necessarily a security risk. If you can turn the policy off on your machine, you obviously have the authority to do much more. And you do so at your own risk. However, a number of Windows applications that rely on .NET will cease to function correctly, so you should make a mental note to turn CAS policy on when you are through with the exercise. For instance, Visual Studio will not load any projects, and the SharePoint configuration database will begin to throw access exceptions when it is accessed. In any case, enterprise policy for corporations usually avoids granting administrative privilege to users. Without administrative privilege, end users cannot tamper with CAS policy.

> **Tip**   From time to time when developing managed *UserControls*, it is necessary to clear the download cache just described to prevent issues resulting from caching. For instance, changes to the appearance of a control might cause the run time to use the cached assembly. This can lead to situations where the design-time change is not reflected in the Web page. Purging the download cache fixes this problem. The download cache can be cleared from the command prompt by typing "<*Drive*>:\Program Files\Microsoft Visual Studio .NET [version]\SDK\[version]\Bin\gacutil.exe" /cdl or by clearing the assembly folder in Windows Explorer.

Running the Managed User Control Application   As far as plumbing goes, that is it. You simply need to copy the relevant files to the virtual folder that you created on MOSS. For clarity, this is the MyCustomWinControl.dll that needs to be placed in the Web application bin folder and the usercontrol1.cs file that needs to be placed in the controls folder. You do not need any other files. You can run the application by navigating to your SharePoint site and adding the ManagedPart Web Part control to the page.

The control will appear in the browser window embedded in the Web Part. (See Figure 6-12.) Clicking the Browse button should display a client *FileDialog* control that you can use to select a file on your machine. Clicking OK causes the application associated with that file extension to be invoked on the client machine. If you are still getting security exceptions at this point, clear the download cache, restart IIS, and refresh the page.

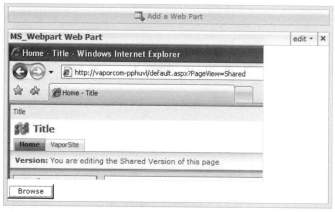

Figure 6-12   Managed user control showing image of a Web application embedded in a Web Form.

Guidelines for Developing Managed User Controls

Several things here are worth mentioning. First, because the managed user control is executing on the client, not on the server, the .NET Framework is required on the client. If you attempt to execute this Web Part on a machine that does not contain the .NET Framework, the application will fail.

Second, client code that requires elevated security privileges must contain configured CAS policy to allow the code to execute successfully. Without the necessary policy, the code is crippled. The default CAS policy provides bare-minimum privileges that are insufficient to run this type of application successfully.

Registry Access Using Managed User Controls in a Web Page

Let's crank up the complexity a notch or two; it might help to convince you that there is power in this technique. One really impressive application that can be created in this way allows a Web page to access the Windows registry on the client machine. For all Windows applications, the registry is hallowed ground. In fact, tampering with the registry can cause your computer to fail to start. Would an example of a SharePoint Web application manipulating the Windows registry on the client machine be enough to convince you?

Figure 6-13 shows just such an application in all its glory.

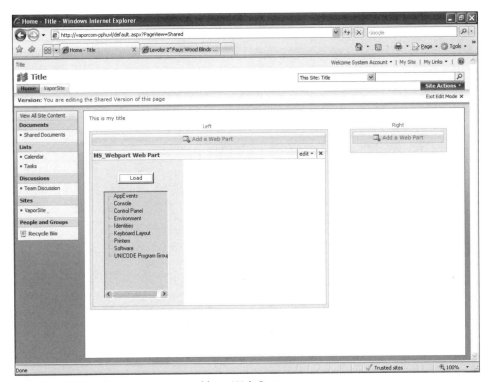

Figure 6-13   Registry output created by a Web Part.

This is certainly not a mocked-up image. In fact, the approach described previously that opens a *FileDialog* control on the client can be reused here. We simply changed part of the code to allow the control to probe the registry. The code is shown in Listing 6-9.

Listing 6-9   Automating registry entries from a Web Part.

C# Snippet
```csharp
private void GetSubKeys(RegistryKey SubKey, TreeView keysStructure)
{
    foreach (string sub in SubKey.GetSubKeyNames())
    {
        keysStructure.Nodes.Add(sub);
    }
}

public void PopulateRegistryKeys(string key, TreeView yourKeys)
{
    RegistryKey OurKey = Registry.Users;
    OurKey = OurKey.OpenSubKey(key, true);
    GetSubKeys(OurKey, yourKeys);
}
private void button1_Click(object sender, EventArgs e)
{
    PopulateRegistryKeys(".DEFAULT", keysStructure);
}
```
Visual Basic Snippet
```vb
Private Sub GetSubKeys(ByVal SubKey As RegistryKey,
ByVal keysStructure As TreeView)
    For Each [sub] As String In SubKey.GetSubKeyNames()
        keysStructure.Nodes.Add([sub])
    Next [sub]
End Sub

Public Sub PopulateRegistryKeys(ByVal key As String, ByVal yourKeys As TreeView)
    Dim OurKey As RegistryKey = Registry.Users
    OurKey = OurKey.OpenSubKey(key, True)
    GetSubKeys(OurKey, yourKeys)
End Sub
Private Sub button1_Click(ByVal sender As Object, ByVal e As EventArgs)
    PopulateRegistryKeys(".DEFAULT", keysStructure)
End Sub
```

Instead of the *FileDialog* control, we substitute a Windows *TreeView* control named **keys-Structure**. When the button in the Web Part is clicked, we iterate the registry, building a view of the registry hives as we go along. We will keep it simple and restrict our code to top-level hives—that is, we won't recurse the depth of the registry. Also, we will be sure to not perform any deletes or additions, but you should know that it is technically quite possible.

The *PopulateRegistryKeys* method accepts a parameter that indicates where to start the registry probe. The *TreeView* control is also passed into the method as a parameter so that it can be populated with the results of the probe. Because objects are passed by value by default but the value parameter is actually a pointer, we expect the changes made in the routine to remain when the method exits scope.

As is the case with most registry-access applications, the code first needs to open the appropriate subkeys and iterate its contents. Let's contrast this with the ActiveX approach. For the ActiveX control, if it is allowed to execute, it can delete every key in the registry because it has free reign on the system. The end user provided the free reign by accepting the ActiveX prompt. Not so for a managed user control. The managed user control runs in a fortified sandbox. It must perform exactly what it is cleared to perform and absolutely nothing more. For instance, CAS policy can even indicate which keys in the registry the application can access. Chapter 7 will prepare you for the beast that is CAS. For now, because CAS policy is turned off, the behavior mirrors that of an ActiveX control.

Creating a New Breed of Web Part Software   Aside from the dazzle of having a Windows control embedded in a Web Form, why would you want to run a Web Part that can interact with the desktop? It's easier to simply have the user open a file in Notepad, as opposed to writing a Web Part application that performs the same function. Although this line of reasoning certainly has merit in a narrow context, it does not account for applications that require client object automation or manipulation of data outside of the SharePoint process. Applications with this type of scope frequently run in the enterprise context.

Or consider the case where a company spends millions of dollars shipping updated CD installation software to its client base. These millions of dollars, significant for large companies, can be reduced to zero by using this approach while maintaining the equivalent functionality of the desktop application.

Further, there is a larger issue at stake here. In the real world, if you ask search engines such as Google and MSN Search about the data that they pursue, they will tell you that data is elusive. During the "chase," it is common for data to scale the Internet fence, land on the desktop, and take cover in a folder. Search engines today have no choice but to call off the search at the Internet boundary. They can pick up the search on the desktop only as another application, such as Google Desktop. This is both inconvenient and suboptimal because it requires at least a separate installation program, such as Google Desktop, and an extra step by the end user.

Search applications built today lack the heavy-duty equipment needed to perform such functionality efficiently, making it somewhat of a challenge for Web-based applications to find elusive data that isn't necessarily confined to the Web. The time is ripe to begin building applications that follow the form and function of the data that it pursues. This is the crux of the matter. Without this, search engines will always hold the short end of the stick. Search engines will always return suboptimal results because they cannot possibly retrieve all the data.

To frame this discussion in the real world, consider a file that starts off in a SharePoint context on an intranet and is downloaded to the user desktop, modified, and saved in a folder. That file has essentially jumped across the intranet chasm, far from the custom search Web Part built to provide search functionality. A custom-built Web Part searching for this file is necessarily limited to the SharePoint intranet domain—it does not even entertain the possibility that the file could have been saved to a local folder. But the file hiding in the folder is also a valid search result and should be part of the search results returned to the end user. You see, there is an inherent limitation in design that applies boundaries to the application. This limitation curses the application with inherent inferiority.

But it doesn't have to be so. That type of limitation can be repaired by applications built on managed user controls. These applications allow Web Parts to be empowered to scale the Internet fence so that it becomes entirely possible for a Web Part control that is built to search for a file to perform the search operation both in the SharePoint context as well as outside of the context, such as on the desktop or anywhere that data could have jumped to.

And what is more, this is easily accomplished. You can simply present a managed user control that hooks into the Windows search and indexing engine. At the same time, the code-beside file can spawn a thread that hooks into the WSS search infrastructure via one of the many Web Services targeting the intranet portal. Or, with the help of the Business Data Catalog, your Web Part can hook into SharePoint functionality that indexes databases from custom applications, Customer Resource Management CRM, and Enterprise Resource Planning (ERP) data sources in an effort to provide optimal search results. And this is the true worth of these types of applications. Read more about Microsoft Dynamics CRM at this link: *http://www.microsoft.com/dynamics/crm/default.mspx.*

Managed user Web Part controls are infinitely more powerful. I have presented only one example based on search. There are many, many more permutations. However, I won't present advanced concepts such as events that occur with these managed user controls in this chapter because there are implications that apply to CAS policy. I'll tackle these and other issues in Chapter 7.

Exploring Web Part Fundamentals

Let's take a break from this torrid pace to unwind for a bit. SharePoint ships with an extensive list of Web Parts out of the box. You program these various Web Parts using the same techniques discussed in this book. Admittedly, it is a bit intimidating to entertain the extensive list of available Web Parts. However, SharePoint allows you to perform filters and groupings on the list of Web Parts to process the information. You should first perform this type of activity if you are considering building, extending, or purchasing a Web Part. If it is already being offered by SharePoint, you have paid for it, so you can just use it. Otherwise, if the stock implementation does not fit your purpose, consider extending it.

Follow these steps to organize the Web Part list offering. Navigate to Shared Services Administration > Web Part Gallery from the Central Administration Web application. Click the Modify This View option as shown in Figure 6-14.

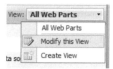

Figure 6-14 Modify This View option.

Clicking the Modify This View option that is shown in Figure 6-14 brings you to the page shown in Figure 6-15. In the View Name text box, create a view by typing **Web Parts By Group Type**. This will serve as the caption for our special group. We also provision a special page that will display our new group by typing **GroupingType** in the Web Address text box. Our view consists simply of the first four options selected below these text boxes. For now, we will accept the Positions From Left options in the right-hand column for each item. (See Figure 6-15.)

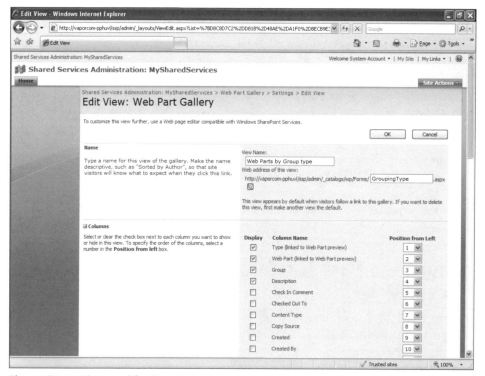

Figure 6-15 View modification options.

In the Sort section of the page, shown in Figure 6-16, we apply the actual filter that creates the view. We sort by a Web Part group. This is a simple view, so we accept the Filter section default values. However, you should note that the expressions can grow in complexity to include group by, totals, styles, folders, and item limit expressions.

Click OK to execute the view. Figure 6-17 shows the results of the applied view.

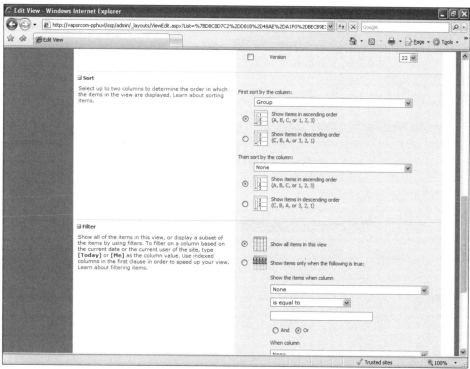

Figure 6-16   Additional view modification options.

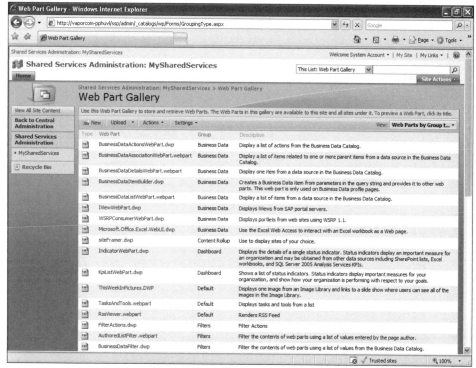

Figure 6-17   Applied view for a Web Part Gallery.

With this new view, you can easily see that the default offering is eight Web Parts for the Business Data Catalog and so on. Because we have chosen the Description field, we can immediately see what each Web Part brings to the table. Perform that type of analysis first before you blindly start building or purchasing Web Parts.

Configuring Web Parts Permissions

For each Web Part available to you, it is possible to customize a set of permissions to restrict access to these Web Parts. You can perform the permissions configuration from the Web Part Gallery. Navigate to the Web Part Gallery. Select Manage Permissions. Figure 6-18 shows the Permissions: Customizations page. Choose the appropriate settings to govern access to the Web Part control.

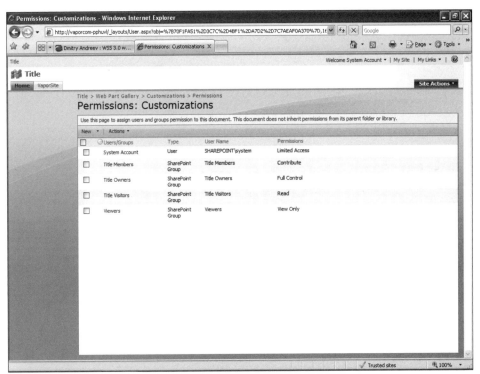

Figure 6-18   Applying permissions to Web Parts.

If you select an item, say System Account, shown in Figure 6-18, and click the Site Actions tab, you will be able to configure permissions for that particular account as shown in Figure 6-19.

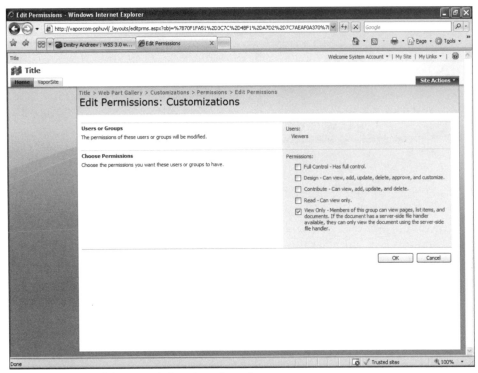

Figure 6-19   Applying permissions based on views.

The configuration process is really straightforward.

Exporting and Importing Web Parts

Let's suppose that, being the guru that you are, you can now build any Web Part. However, there is the pretty sexy ASP.NET Web Part that you desperately want to take advantage of which is already built and deployed. As it turns out, because ASP.NET Web Parts and SharePoint Web Parts have a common lineage, you can swap, reuse, or perform export/import operations on them.

Exporting Web Parts

By default and as a security measure, Web Part exports are disabled. To enable export functionality, you need to make a configuration file change to the *web.config* file:

```
<webParts enableExport="true"></webParts>
```

You also need to make a code change in the Web Part, as shown in Listing 6-10.

Listing 6-10   Programmatically preparing a Web Part for export.

```
C# Snippet
protected void Page_Load(object sender, EventArgs e)
{
    this.ExportMode = WebPartExportMode.All;
}
Visual Basic Snippet
Protected Sub Page_Load(ByVal sender As Object, ByVal e As EventArgs)
    Me.ExportMode = WebPartExportMode.All
End Sub
```

The *WebPartExportMode* is an enumeration. To enable exporting all properties for the control, set the *ExportMode* value of the *WebPartExportMode* enumeration to a value of All. To exercise more control over the export, set the property value to *NonSensitiveData*. The *NonSensitive-Data* exports only attributes that are not decorated with the *PersonalizableAttribute* attribute. To protect sensitive data in a Web Part, apply the *PersonalizableAttribute* attribute. A sample implementation is best left as an exercise to the reader.

Figure 6-20 shows the *.dwp* file representing an exported Web Part.

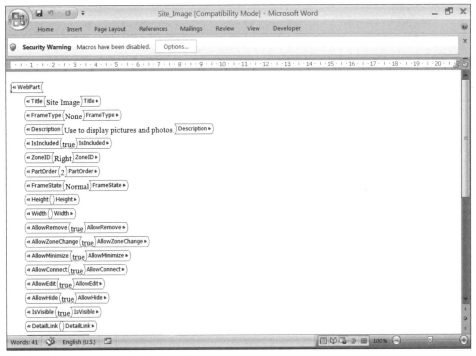

Figure 6-20   Contents of the *.dwp* file.

As you can see, the Web Part assembly is not exported. The file merely contains references and internal plumbing that allow the run time to find and load your assembly. From an intellectual property perspective, the run time takes adequate steps to protect your intellectual investment.

Importing Web Parts

As you might have already guessed, exported Web Parts can be imported into a site or subsite. This process does not involve code. Here are the steps:

1. Click Site Actions on the portal site.

2. Click Site Settings.

3. Under the Galleries column, click Web Part and then Manage Web Part Gallery in the Site Collection Galleries section.

4. On the Web Part Gallery page, click Upload Web Part. Figure 6-21 shows the upload option in the Web Part Gallery.

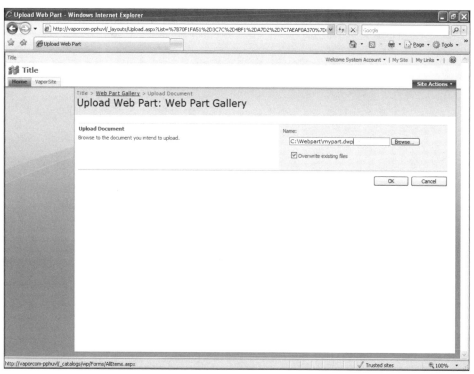

Figure 6-21   Web Part upload option.

5. Click Browse, and select the modified Web Part you want to import.

6. On the Web Part Gallery page, choose the most appropriate options. Figure 6-22 shows the Web Part Gallery and associated options.

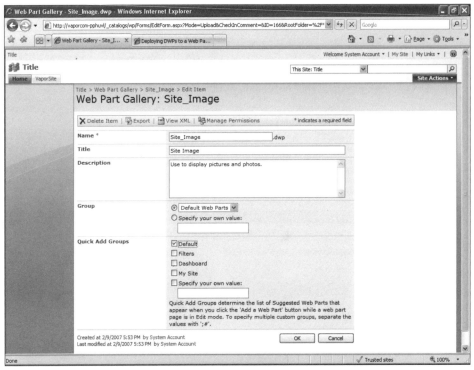

Figure 6-22   Web Part Gallery options.

7. Click OK. The action closes the dialog box and returns you to the design view.

Troubleshooting Import/Export Issues

As is the typical case, simple exercises like those can, and do, go wrong. Let's discuss some approaches that might help resolve these bumps in the SharePoint road. If an import fails, the chief culprit might be the fact that the assembly is not installed on the server. Without an installed assembly, the Web Part will not be loaded. You shouldn't confuse a *.dwp* file for an assembly, as explained earlier.

Another issue is that you might not have the correct permissions to perform the export or import operations. SharePoint runs every line of code under an umbrella of security. The implication here is that not all functionality is permitted for the account on whose behalf the code is executing. In the case of inadequate privileges, consult your SharePoint administrator.

Web Parts that run on SharePoint must be declared as safe controls. If this isn't the case, the Web Part will fail to load. Safe controls were discussed in Chapter 3, "Excel Web Access." Web Parts that are imported must have a *.dwp* extension; otherwise, the load will fail. Finally, if you encounter errors during an import, verify that the XML Web Part file is well-formed.

As a side note, Web Part classes that inherit from *Microsoft.SharePoint.WebPartPages.WebPart* have the Export item automatically inserted into Web Part menus as shown in Figure 6-23. All other Web Part classes that derive from other base classes—for instance, *System.Web.UI.Web-Controls.WebParts*—do not expose this menu item by default.

Figure 6-23   Web Part Export menu item.

About Web Part File Types

You might have noticed that there are two types of Web Part files. Let's focus on some minor details about these file types. The discussion is aimed at providing a clear picture of how these different file types fit into the Web Part architecture.

The .*dwp* File Type   As you know, a Web Part is a .NET assembly. The Web Part uses a Web Part description file (.*dwp*) that can be stored independent of the assembly. The .*dwp* file contains XML metadata that describes an instance of the Web Part. The actual assembly or DLL file must be installed and registered on each computer running Windows SharePoint Services that uses the Web Part. You can read more about .*dwp* files at this link: *http://msdn2.microsoft.com/en-us/office/aa209897(office.11).aspx*.

The previous sections have shown you how to import or export a Web Part. The export function implicitly creates a file with a .dwp extension. To re-iterate, the assembly or Intellectual Property that implements the business logic, is not part of the .*dwp*. You are free to edit the file in any text editor to change the descriptions or properties of the Web Part. It's only a description of the functionality contained in the assembly. These changes typically show up in the Web Part Gallery after the Web Part has been imported. Figure 6-24 shows a download dialog box for a *.dwp* file representing a Web Part.

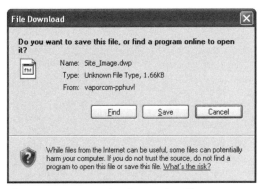

Figure 6-24   Downloading a *.dwp* file.

The .*webpart* File Type   Every Web Part should have a *.webpart* file. A *.webpart* file is an XML file that describes the Web Part. The *.webpart* file also allows the Web Part to appear in the Web Part Gallery. Figure 6-25 shows the contents of a *.webpart* file.

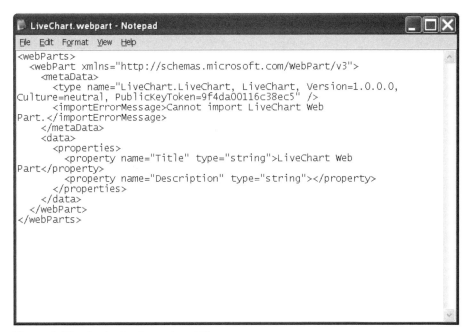

Figure 6-25   Contents of a *.webpart* file.

Because this is an XML file, it is human-readable and does not really merit an explanation.

Although you can create a .*webpart* file by modifying the contents of an existing file, you should exercise care in the process. In fact, it is recommended that you let the run time create the .*webpart* file for you. This occurs automatically when you build and deploy a Web Part to SharePoint.

In any case, to manually create a .*webpart* file, first build and deploy a Web Part. After the Web Part is deployed, navigate to http://<*sitename:port*>myserver/_layouts/newdwp.aspx, where <*sitename:port*> is the name of the server on which your SharePoint site is deployed. Select the check box next to the Web Part that you have just deployed. Click Populate Gallery. This will create a .*webpart* file for the Web Part. Figure 6-26 shows the page for populating the gallery.

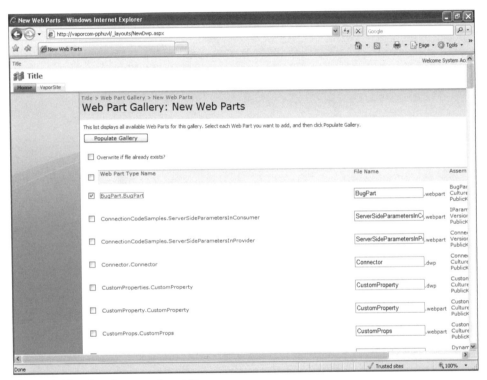

Figure 6-26   Creating a .*webpart* file.

Web Part Customization

For the most part, the examples presented so far have allowed you to build sophisticated functionality into your application. The art of embedding objects into Web Parts adds polish to otherwise dull Web pages, with the added benefit that the platform used to build these hosted objects can vary widely. For instance, a hosted object can be built using Java, Visual Basic, C++, or Flash. However, there is still room for improving the user experience. We have yet to really allow the knowledge worker to drive the aesthetics of the Web Part.

One good way to put the knowledge worker in the driver's seat is through customizations. Customizations can be performed through the Web Part tool pane. You should recall from

Chapter 3 that the Tool Pane dialog box contains a property sheet that might be used to adjust certain default properties on the Web Part.

Customizing the Look and Feel of Web Parts

Let's build a rudimentary image viewer for the knowledge worker. This application is conceptually simple. It allows the user to load images into a Web Part by providing an *openFileDialog* control that can be used to find and select image files on the client disk or network share. The idea is not to replace the standard image viewer Web Part, but to show how you can outsource the responsibility of imaging to a managed user control. Once the basic framework is up and running, we address the look and feel through code.

For simplicity, we reuse the existing managed user control from the past example in this chapter. There is no need to change the project code; we will simply replace some controls. Instead of the *TreeView* control in the previous example, we add a *pictureBox* control. We keep the *openFileDialog* control because it will be used to browse the client file system. We modify the code to reflect the change and deploy the control to the controls directory for our Web site. The modified code is shown in Listing 6-11.

Listing 6-11   Managed user control image viewer.

```
C# Snippet
private void button1_Click(object sender, EventArgs e)
{
    openFileDialog1.CheckFileExists = true;
    openFileDialog1.CheckPathExists = true;
    openFileDialog1.Title = "Load your image.";
    openFileDialog1.ShowDialog();
}

private void openFileDialog1_FileOk(object sender, CancelEventArgs e)
{
    if (openFileDialog1.FileName.Length > 0)
    {
        pictureBox1.Load(openFileDialog1.FileName);
    }
}
```

```
Visual Basic Snippet
Private Sub button1_Click(ByVal sender As Object, ByVal e As EventArgs)
    openFileDialog1.CheckFileExists = True
    openFileDialog1.CheckPathExists = True
    openFileDialog1.Title = "Load your image."
    openFileDialog1.ShowDialog()
End Sub

Private Sub openFileDialog1_FileOk(ByVal sender As Object, _
  ByVal e As CancelEventArgs)
    If openFileDialog1.FileName.Length > 0 Then
        pictureBox1.Load(openFileDialog1.FileName)
    End If
End Sub
```

The code isn't rocket science. In fact, it is intellectually cheap and requires very little effort. When the Browse button is clicked, a file dialog box allows the user to choose an image on disk. The user is able to browse for a particular file or type in the name of a file. The file dialog box automatically checks to see whether the file exists on disk controlled by the *CheckFile-Exists* and *CheckPathExists* properties.

In the case of erroneous input, the end user is gently prompted for a valid path or file. This is handled automatically; we don't need to write any code. Although we could have set appropriate file filters, we skip this step and focus on the task at hand. However, you should bear in mind that this type of functionality is available to the *openFileDialog* control.

With the example up and running, let's have a look at the customizations that we can apply to this Web Part. It is possible to customize the Edit menu assigned to the Web Part. The Edit menu consists of a collection of verbs such as Close, Export, and Modify Shared Web Part, and it usually appears in the upper right-hand corner of a Web Part. The code listed next demonstrates how to add your own verb to the collection. Listing 6-12 shows the code.

Listing 6-12   Verb customization.

```csharp
C# Snippet
public MS_Webpart()
{
    this.AllowEdit = false;
    this.AllowMinimize = false;
    this.AllowZoneChange = false;
    this.ChromeType = PartChromeType.TitleAndBorder;
    this.BackColor = Color.Beige;
    this.BorderStyle = System.Web.UI.WebControls.BorderStyle.Double;
}
public override WebPartVerbCollection Verbs
{
    get
    {
        WebPartVerb CustomizedVerb = new WebPartVerb("AddBorder",
          new WebPartEventHandler(AddBorder));
        CustomizedVerb.Text = "Add Border";

        //Add the verb into the collection
        WebPartVerb[] newVerbs = new WebPartVerb[] { CustomizedVerb };

        //Add the collection of verbs to the Web Part collection
          WebPartVerbCollection verbs =
        new WebPartVerbCollection(base.Verbs, newVerbs);

        return verbs;
    }
}
```

```csharp
protected void AddBorder(object sender, WebPartEventArgs args)
{
    this.Title = "Modified Image. ";
    this.BorderStyle = System.Web.UI.WebControls.BorderStyle.Ridge;
    this.BorderColor = Color.Black;
}
```

Visual Basic Snippet

```vb
Public Sub New()
    Me.AllowEdit = False
    Me.AllowMinimize = False
    Me.AllowZoneChange = False
    Me.ChromeType = PartChromeType.TitleAndBorder
    Me.BackColor = Color.Beige
    Me.BorderStyle = System.Web.UI.WebControls.BorderStyle.Double
End Sub
Public Overrides ReadOnly Property Verbs() As WebPartVerbCollection
    Get
        Dim CustomizedVerb As WebPartVerb = New WebPartVerb("AddBorder",
            New WebPartEventHandler(AddressOf AddBorder))

        CustomizedVerb.Text = "Add Border"

        'Add the verb into the collection
        Dim newVerbs As WebPartVerb() = New WebPartVerb() { CustomizedVerb }

        'Add the collection of verbs to the Web Part collection
        Dim verbs_Renamed As WebPartVerbCollection =
          New WebPartVerbCollection(MyBase.Verbs, newVerbs)

        Return newverbs
    End Get
End Property

Protected Sub AddBorder(ByVal sender As Object,
ByVal args As WebPartEventArgs)
    Me.Title = "Modified Image. "
    Me.BorderStyle = System.Web.UI.WebControls.BorderStyle.Ridge
    Me.BorderColor = Color.Black
End Sub
```

As you can see, the code is pretty basic. The code in the class constructor applies certain types of functionality to the Web Part at load time. In our case, the code chooses a few random properties from a very large range of properties so that you get a good feel for what is possible. As an example, one of the properties, *AllowMinimize*, is set to false, with the effect that the Web Part cannot be minimized by the user.

Notice how we override the *Verbs* method. This allows us to inject our customized verb into the collection of verbs. As we perform the surgical injection, we also provide a delegate that ties the action associated with the event to a handler that is able to execute customized code.

Do not underestimate the power of the association of *action* plus *event*. It allows us to build applications that cater to a wide variety of functionality. For instance, you might have noticed that the *WebPartVerb* constructor has an overload that allows the action to be connected to client-side events as opposed to server-side events. The implication here is that script can be attached to the verb so that it executes on the client. Think of this in the context of a dialog prompt to the end user for list deletes, for instance. An example is trivial and best left as an exercise to the reader.

To paint this approach in broader strokes, you can hook into the Web Part behavior by simply overriding interesting methods. The hook allows you to impose your own customizations on the Web Part at run time. You simply need to identify the functionality that you are after—customizing Web Part verbs, for instance—find the associated method (*Verbs*), and override it. Figure 6-27 shows the verb customization code in action.

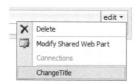

Figure 6-27   Verb customization.

A word of caution is in order. Think deeply about the functionality you add here. For instance, you can simply prevent the Close option in a Web Part by setting the *close* property to false. However, that leaves the end user with no way to remove the Web Part from the page. Such functionality, or lack of it, really detracts from the otherwise pleasant SharePoint experience because it takes away the control that the end user enjoys. A frustrated user can quickly grow to develop ill will toward a Web Part. The result is a bitter user whose productivity suffers.

Creating Custom Properties   Much of the power of Web Parts is derived from the control they provide the end user. And so far, this has been our theme. The chief instrument of this control is the property items that display in the Web Part Tool Pane dialog box. You can view the Tool Pane dialog box by clicking on the Modify Shared Web Part property on the Edit menu of a Web Part.

Each Web Part has a default set of properties that are categorized neatly into sections with titles such as Appearance, Layout, and Advanced. It's possible to both add properties to these categories and to build your own categories that contain custom properties. I'll present both approaches.

The next few sections break up a single example into functional parts. You put these different parts together to understand the complete customization picture. The example shown in Listing 6-13 is based on a Web Part template project being developed for a car dealership. We pretend that our Web Part allows clients to pick a vehicle and customize its appearance. If they like the final product, they can order the vehicle online.

Listing 6-13 Custom properties.

```csharp
C# Snippet
public class CustomPropertyWebPart : Microsoft.SharePoint.WebPartPages.WebPart
{
    public enum suvTypes
    {
        Lexus = 0,
        Toyota= 1,
        Kia  = 2,
        Hyundai=3
    };

    protected suvTypes _myEnum;
    string _stringDescription;
    int intInStock;
    const bool _constBoolOnSale = false;
    bool _boolOnSale;

    private System.Drawing.KnownColor _exteriorColors =
      System.Drawing.KnownColor.Red;

    [Category("Custom Section")]
    [WebPartStorage(Storage.Personal)]
    [FriendlyNameAttribute("Vehicle Description")]
    [Description("Enter a description.")]
    [Browsable(true)]
    new public string Description
    {
        get
        {
            return _stringDescription;
        }
        set
        {
            _stringDescription = value;
        }
    }

    [Category("Custom Section")]
    [WebPartStorage(Storage.Personal)]
    [FriendlyNameAttribute("On Sale")]
    [Description("Select sale availability.")]
    [Browsable(true)]
    public bool OnSale
    {
        get
        {
            return _boolOnSale;
        }
        set
        {
            _boolOnSale = value;
        }
    }
    [Category("Custom Section")]
    [WebPartStorage(Storage.Personal)]
```

```
[FriendlyNameAttribute("In Stock")]
[Description("Enter number.")]
[Browsable(true)]
public int InStock
{
    get
    {
        return intInStock;
    }
    set
    {
        throw new WebPartPageUserException("Please enter an integer.");
    }
}


[Category("Custom Section")]
[DefaultValue(WebLibrary2.CustomPropertyWebPart.suvTypes.Toyota)]
[WebPartStorage(Storage.Personal)]
[FriendlyName("SUV Type")]
[Description("Select an SUV make.")]
[Browsable(true)]
public suvTypes SUVType
{
    get
    {
        return _myEnum;
    }
    set
    {
        _myEnum = value;
    }
}


[Category("Extra")]
[WebPartStorage(Storage.Personal)]
[FriendlyNameAttribute("Exterior Color")]
[Description("Select a color from the dropdown list.")]
[Browsable(true)]
public System.Drawing.KnownColor MyColor
{
    get
    {
        return _exteriorColors;
    }
    set
    {
        _exteriorColors = value;
    }
}

public bool ShouldSerializeMyColor()
{
    return true;
}
}
```

Visual Basic Snippet

```vb
Public Class CustomPropertyWebPart
    Inherits Microsoft.SharePoint.WebPartPages.WebPart
        Public Enum suvTypes
            Lexus = 0
            Toyota= 1
            Kia = 2
            Hyundai=3
        End Enum

        Protected _myEnum As suvTypes
        Private _stringDescription As String
        Private intInStock As Integer
        Private Const _constBoolOnSale As Boolean = False
        Private _boolOnSale As Boolean

        Private _exteriorColors As System.Drawing.KnownColor =
          System.Drawing.KnownColor.Red

        <Category("Custom Section"), WebPartStorage(Storage.Personal),
          FriendlyNameAttribute("Vehicle Description"),
          Description("Enter a description."), Browsable(True)>
        Shadows Public Property Description() As String
            Get
                Return _stringDescription
            End Get
            Set
                _stringDescription = Value
            End Set
        End Property
        <Category("Custom Section"), WebPartStorage(Storage.Personal),
          FriendlyNameAttribute("On Sale"), Description("Select sale availability."),
          Browsable(True)>
        Public Property OnSale() As Boolean
            Get
                Return _boolOnSale
            End Get
            Set
                _boolOnSale = Value
            End Set
        End Property


        <Category("Custom Section"), WebPartStorage(Storage.Personal),
          FriendlyNameAttribute("In Stock"), Description("Enter number."),
          Browsable(True)>
        Public Property InStock() As Integer
            Get
                Return intInStock
            End Get
            Set
            Throw New WebPartPageUserException("Please enter an integer.")
            End Set
        End Property
```

```
        <Category("Custom Section"), DefaultValue(WebLibrary2.CustomPropertyWebPart.
          suvTypes.Toyota), WebPartStorage(Storage.Personal), FriendlyName("SUV
          Type"), Description("Select an SUV make."), Browsable(True)>
        Public Property SUVType() As suvTypes
            Get
                Return _myEnum
            End Get
            Set
                _myEnum = Value
            End Set
        End Property
        <Category("Extra"), WebPartStorage(Storage.Personal),
          FriendlyNameAttribute("Exterior Color"), Description("Select a color from
          the dropdown list."), Browsable(True)>
        Public Property MyColor() As System.Drawing.KnownColor
            Get
                Return _exteriorColors
            End Get
            Set
                _exteriorColors = Value
            End Set
        End Property

        Public Function ShouldSerializeMyColor() As Boolean
            Return True
        End Function
    End Class
```

From the top of the source code listing, the code shows that a regular .NET property is constructed in the usual way. However, these properties are decorated with special attributes that transform the properties into property sheet items in the tool pane. The attributes themselves are easy to understand, so we simply list the choices with a short explanation in Table 6-1.

Table 6-1   Tool Pane Attributes

Attribute	Function
Browsable	Determines whether or not the property is displayed
Category	Determines the section where the custom property will appear on the property sheet
Description	Sets the ToolTip text for the property
DefaultValue	Sets the default value for the custom property
FriendlyNameAttribute	Sets the title for the custom property
ReadOnly	Determines the read-only state of the custom property
WebPartStorage	Determines the storage mode of the property
HtmlDesignerAttribute	Allows the custom property to customize the input from the property

> **Important** In Listing 6-13, notice that the *Description* property uses the *new* keyword. This is because our description clashes with the *WebPart.Description* property. By using the *new* keyword, we indicate to the compiler that this is by choice.

Let's spend some time focusing on the code. The *suvType* enumeration holds values for sport utility vehicles (SUVs) that are available. The run time automatically converts the enumeration into a drop-down control, as shown in Figure 6-28.

Figure 6-28   New custom properties in the Tool Pane property sheet.

Notice the *InStock* property has both *get* and *set* accessors. The *get* accessor is valid; the *set* accessor is not. Any value that is assigned to this property promptly throws an exception. The point of the code is to show that an exception of type *WebPartPageUserException* is intercepted by SharePoint and displayed neatly in the tool pane as shown in Figure 6-29. You do not have to write any custom code to help with the error message display.

After the error message is displayed, the exception is considered handled and does not proceed further up the chain. The exception to the rule occurs when the property triggers an exception but the Tool Pane dialog box is not visible or is unavailable to handle the exception. In this particular case, the exception is considered unhandled and the entire page fails.

Figure 6-29   New custom property error message.

Focus on the *MyColor* property. This property returns an intrinsic type defined in the *System.Drawing* namespace. The run time is aware that this type is known to the system, so it intercepts these values, determines that the type is an enumeration, and renders the values in a drop-down control.

Notice the *ShouldSerializeMyColor* method. The method forms part of the *ShouldSerializeXXX* family of methods. In this particular case, this method is provided to help with the serialization of the property. If you define an attribute of type *[DefaultValue]* as shown in the code, it automatically overrides the *ShouldSerializeXXX* property.

Notice the *InStock* property. One of the attributes, *[HtmlDesigner("sales.aspx")]*, adds an ellipsis button next to the property as shown in Figure 6-30.

Figure 6-30   HtmlDesigner button in the Tool Pane property sheet.

When you click inside the *InStock* text box control, the ellipses button appears. When the ellipsis button is clicked, the sales.aspx page is invoked and displays on screen as a popup.

The page can perform any function, but it typically accepts or displays values related to the property. In our case, the sales.aspx page can actually retrieve the number of SUVs that are on sale. It's up to you how you pass the values back to the calling page. One approach might be to add a reference to the *ToolPart* class and SharePoint services assembly. Then build a simple

Web page called sales.aspx. Your sales.aspx page will contain some UI widgets and a Submit button. The code for the Submit button could look like the code in Listing 6-14.

Listing 6-14 Custom ToolPart page.

```
C# Snippet
protected void Button1_Click(object sender, EventArgs e)
{
    WebLibrary2.CustomPropertyWebPart w1 = new WebLibrary2.CustomPropertyWebPart();
    w1.Description = TextBox1.Text;

    Response.Write("<script>window.close()</script>");
}
```
```
Visual Basic Snippet
Protected Sub Button1_Click(ByVal sender As Object, ByVal e As EventArgs)
    Dim w1 As  = New WebLibrary2.CustomPropertyWebPart()
    w1.Description = TextBox1.Text

    Response.Write("<script>window.close()</script>")
End Sub
```

The code is self-explanatory. You should note also that the *HtmlDesigner* attribute accepts named parameters in one of the overloaded methods so that you can exercise more control over the designing process, such as sizing the popup. You can read more on the *HtmlDesigner-Attribute* class at *http://msdn2.microsoft.com/en-us/library/microsoft.sharepoint.web-partpages.htmldesignerattribute.aspx.*

Table 6-2 is a property map table that the run time uses to determine how to render each property in the property sheet of the tool pane. The determination is made automatically based on the property return type. You do not have to write any code.

Table 6-2 Property Map Table

Type	Control
Enumeration	Displays as a drop-down control
Boolean	Displays as a check box control
String, Integer, DateTime	Display as a text box control

These are the only supported types that can display in a property sheet. Other property types are ignored.

Creating Custom Tool Parts   Figure 6-31 shows the Tool Pane dialog box with a custom section that contains a text box. When the Apply button is clicked, the text in the text box is sent to the Web Part control. The text box control changes its background to indicate that an update occurred.

Figure 6-31   New custom properties in the Tool Pane property sheet.

Let's review the code presented in Listing 6-14 that shows how to build such functionality. First, we need to create a class that inherits from the SharePoint *ToolParts* class. This new class will manage the process of updating the Tool Pane dialog box. However, you should note that this new class is not the Web Part control. It simply complements the Web Part control by allowing the Web Part to provide tool pane functionality.

Create a Web Part template, and add a new class named *CustomToolParts*. The code is shown in Listing 6-15.

Listing 6-15   Custom properties using classes.

```
C# Snippet
class CustomToolPart : Microsoft.SharePoint.WebPartPages.ToolPart
 {
     // declaring a sample variable
     private string customControl;
     private bool _updateUI;

     // an event handler for the Init event
     private void ToolPart1_Init(object sender, System.EventArgs e )
     {
         customControl = "customUniqueID";
     }
```

```csharp
    public CustomToolPart()
    {
        // Set default properties
        this.Title="Custom Property";

        this.Init += new EventHandler(ToolPart1_Init);
    }
    public override void ApplyChanges()
    {
        MyCustProperty wp = (MyCustProperty)this.ParentToolPane.SelectedWebPart;

        // Send the custom text to the Web Part.
        wp.AString = Page.Request.Form[customControl];
    }
    public override void SyncChanges()
    {
        _updateUI = true;
    }
    public override void CancelChanges()
    {
        _updateUI = false;
    }

    protected override void RenderToolPart(System.Web.UI.HtmlTextWriter output)
    {
        // Establish a reference to the Web Part.
        CustomProperties.MyCustProperty wp =
          (CustomProperties.MyCustProperty)this.ParentToolPane.SelectedWebPart;
        output.Write("Enter data: ");
        output.Write("<input name= '" + customControl );
        if (_updateUI)
            output.Write("' type='text' style='background-color: yellow' value='" +
                SPEncode.HtmlEncode(wp.AString) + "'> <br>");
        else
            output.Write("' type='text' style='background-color: white' value='" +
                SPEncode.HtmlEncode(wp.AString) + "'> <br>");
    }
}
```

Visual Basic Snippet

```vb
Friend Class CustomToolPart
Inherits Microsoft.SharePoint.WebPartPages.ToolPart
    ' declaring a sample variable
    Private customControl As String
    Private _updateUI As Boolean

    ' an event handler for the Init event
    Private Sub ToolPart1_Init(ByVal sender As Object, ByVal e As System.EventArgs)
        customControl = "customUniqueID"
    End Sub
    Public Sub New()
        ' Set default properties
        Me.Title="Custom Property"
        AddHandler Init, AddressOf ToolPart1_Init
    End Sub
```

```
Public Overrides Sub ApplyChanges()
    Dim wp As MyCustProperty =
      CType(Me.ParentToolPane.SelectedWebPart, MyCustProperty)

    ' Send the custom text to the Web Part.
    wp.AString = Page.Request.Form(customControl)
End Sub
Public Overrides Sub SyncChanges()
    _updateUI = True
End Sub
Public Overrides Sub CancelChanges()
    _updateUI = False
End Sub

Protected Overrides Sub RenderToolPart(ByVal output As
  System.Web.UI.HtmlTextWriter)
    ' Establish a reference to the Web Part.
    Dim wp As CustomProperties.MyCustProperty =
      CType(Me.ParentToolPane.SelectedWebPart, CustomProperties.MyCustProperty)
    output.Write("Enter data: ")
    output.Write("<input name= '" & customControl)
    If _updateUI Then
        output.Write("' type='text' style='background-color: yellow' value='"
          & SPEncode.HtmlEncode(wp.AString) & "'> <br>")
    Else
        output.Write("' type='text' style='background-color: white' value='"
          & SPEncode.HtmlEncode(wp.AString) & "'> <br>")
    End If
End Sub
End Class
```

We begin with the *Class* constructor. The code in the constructor sets the title that appears in the Tool Pane dialog box and wires up an Initialization event. The event handler simply names the control with a unique string. We use this unique name to render the correct control later in the event chain when we write the controls to the output stream.

If you care to examine the code, you will see that there are three methods begging for a bit of attention, so let's satisfy those needs. The *ApplyChanges* method is invoked by the tool pane to apply property changes to the selected Web Part. If the *ApplyChanges* method succeeds, the *SyncChanges* method is called by the tool pane to refresh the specified property values in the tool part user interface. Otherwise, the *SyncChanges* method is not called. *CancelChanges* performs the obvious.

Based on this sequence of events, we have set up our code to simply mark a flag that indicates whether the changes succeeded. The flag is marked as true only in the *ApplyChanges* event because, as noted earlier, it is called on success. When the *RenderToolPart* method is called, the code examines this flag variable and paints the background of the text box appropriately.

For the *ApplyChanges* event, we rely on the run time to provide the selected Web Part to us. Casting appropriately, we set the properties on the Web Part. After this sequence of events has fired successfully, the Web Part is updated and the tool pane reflects the updated changes.

You might have noticed that the custom section we provided is somewhat of an ugly duckling. It does not resemble its prettier siblings because we chose to do our own thing with the custom *ToolPart* class. If you want to provide custom tool pane functionality that blends in with the stock offering, you need to follow this next approach.

Consider the code in Listing 6-16.

Listing 6-16   *GetToolParts* code structure.

```csharp
C# Snippet
public override ToolPart[] GetToolParts()
{
    ToolPart[] toolparts = new ToolPart[3];

    //this object represents the tool parts for custom properties
    CustomPropertyToolPart custom = new CustomPropertyToolPart();
    custom.Expand(1);
    custom.Expand(0);

    //allow the custom tool part to be visible
    toolparts[0] = custom;

    //this object represents the tool part for custom properties
    //Appearance, Layout, Advanced
    WebPartToolPart wp = new WebPartToolPart();
    //expand appearance
    wp.Expand(WebPartToolPart.Categories.Appearance);
    toolparts[1] = wp;
    toolparts[1].BackColor = Color.White;

    //disable the expanded appearance section
    toolparts[1].Enabled = false;

    WebLibrary2.CustomToolPart ctp = new WebLibrary2.CustomToolPart();
    ctp.BackColor = Color.White;
    ctp.ForeColor = Color.Gray;
    ctp.ScrollBars = System.Web.UI.WebControls.ScrollBars.Both;
    ctp.AllowMinimize = false;
    ctp.ChromeType = PartChromeType.BorderOnly;

    //display the tool part
    toolparts[2] = ctp;
    return toolparts;
}
```

Visual Basic Snippet

```vb
Public Overrides Function GetToolParts() As ToolPart()
    Dim toolparts As ToolPart() = New ToolPart(2){}

    'this object represents the tool parts for custom properties
    Dim custom As CustomPropertyToolPart = New CustomPropertyToolPart()
    custom.Expand(1)
    custom.Expand(0)

    'allow the custom tool part to be visible
    toolparts(0) = custom

    'this object represents the tool part for custom properties
    'Appearance, Layout, Advanced
    Dim wp As WebPartToolPart = New WebPartToolPart()
    'expand appearance
    wp.Expand(WebPartToolPart.Categories.Appearance)
    toolparts(1) = wp
    toolparts(1).BackColor = Color.White

    'disable the expanded appearance section
    toolparts(1).Enabled = False

    Dim ctp As WebLibrary2.CustomToolPart = New WebLibrary2.CustomToolPart()
    ctp.BackColor = Color.White
    ctp.ForeColor = Color.Gray
    ctp.ScrollBars = System.Web.UI.WebControls.ScrollBars.Both
    ctp.AllowMinimize = False
    ctp.ChromeType = PartChromeType.BorderOnly

    'display the tool part
    toolparts(2) = ctp

    Return toolparts
End Function
```

This snippet of code shows a method that returns the custom *ToolParts* for a Web Part by overriding the *GetToolParts* method of the *WebPart* base class. If a Web Part implementing one or more custom properties does not override the *GetToolParts* method, an instance of the *WebPartToolPart* class and an instance of the *CustomPropertyToolPart* class is returned.

The *WebPartToolPart* determines which tool parts are displayed in the tool pane and also the order that these objects appear in the tool pane user interface. By default, the *WebPartToolPart* class automatically displays the Web Part's standard properties. These properties are derived from the properties of the *WebPart* base class.

The *CustomPropertyToolPart* represents the default *ToolPart* that is displayed in the property sheet for a Web Part that implements one or more custom properties. The *CustomPropertyTool-Part* class automatically displays the Web Part's custom properties. An instance of the *CustomPropertyToolPart* class provides access to the properties provided by the custom Web Part.

For implementations that override the *GetToolParts* method, the *CustomPropertyToolPart* must be added to the collection of *ToolParts* for it to be visible to the user. Calling code can customize the object as appropriate through the reference to the *CustomPropertyToolPart* object.

> **More Info**   If you would like to learn more about the classes discussed here, follow these links:
>
> *CustomPropertyToolPart* class: *http://msdn2.microsoft.com/en-us/library/microsoft.sharepoint. webpartpages.custompropertytoolpart.aspx*
>
> *WebPartToolPart* class: *http://msdn2.microsoft.com/en-us/library/ms950501.aspx*

Implementing Interfaces in Web Parts   I'm sure you are aware of the fact that .NET classes cannot participate in multiple inheritance. Although I carefully side-step the fiery debate, I acknowledge the fact that multiple inheritance does allow classes to extend functionality based on other classes. Fortunately for us, the .NET Framework supports multiple interface inheritance.

Using interface inheritance, a class can extend its functionality through a set of contracts. Classes that support these contracts can be used as building blocks in our architecture because we are guaranteed that they will honor at least the interface piece. How we choose to implement the details of these pieces is entirely up to us.

You can extend the functionality of any Web Part by implementing an appropriate interface. SharePoint Web Parts are no different, and they shouldn't benefit from any privileged treatment. Let's consider two examples that drive home this point. Our first example will walk you through a simple interface inheritance implementation so that you get the basic idea. The next example will be a bit more involved.

Create a class based on a Web Part template and that inherits from *IToolPaneControl*. We used IntelliSense to determine that an *IToolPaneControl* interface exists in the body of the code-beside file. Name the project **ExtendToolPane**. Visual Studio IntelliSense might be used to generate the interface implementation, which contains code that simply throws an exception to indicate that the property or method has not been implemented. The IntelliSense hint appears in Figure 6-32.

Figure 6-32   IntelliSense hint.

Consider Listing 6-17, which modifies the Web Part Gallery. We use IntelliSense to search for a suitable candidate property. We find a guinea pig in *IAddToGalleryWebPart*.

Listing 6-17   Modifying the Web Part Gallery through code.

```
C# Snippet
namespace AddToGallery
{
    [Guid("dff94de1-b6e4-4709-939e-f677dbfe6e04")]
    [DefaultProperty("Text"), ToolboxData("<{0}:IAddToGalleryWebPart runat=server>
    </{0}:IAddToGalleryWebPart">")]
    public class IAddToGalleryWebPart : Microsoft.SharePoint.WebPartPages.WebPart,
      Microsoft.SharePoint.WebPartPages.IAddtoGallery
    {
        private string _data = "Some internal data";
        // Create and return the XML fragment to define two menu commands.
        public string GalleryOptions
        {
            get
            {
                System.Text.StringBuilder gallerySchema =
                   new System.Text.StringBuilder(1024);
                gallerySchema.Append("<?xml version=\"1.0\"?>");
                gallerySchema.Append("<GalleryOptions>");
                gallerySchema.Append("<Option ID=\"{CAEAE2BB-56F8-426f-A279-
                   84E2465808B7}\">");
                gallerySchema.Append("<OptionName>Fire Event</OptionName>");
                gallerySchema.Append("<LinkValue>javascript:
                 alert('Event fired with data: " + _data + ".'));</LinkValue>");
                gallerySchema.Append("</Option>");
                gallerySchema.Append("</GalleryOptions>");

                return gallerySchema.ToString();
            }
        }
        #region IAddtoGallery Members
        string IAddtoGallery.GalleryOptions
        {
            get { return GalleryOptions; }
        }
        #endregion
    }
}

Visual Basic Snippet
Namespace AddToGallery
    <Guid("dff94de1-b6e4-4709-939e-f677dbfe6e04"), DefaultProperty("Text"),
      ToolboxData("<{0}: IAddToGalleryWebPart runat=server>
      </{0}:IAddToGalleryWebPart">")>
    Public Class IAddToGalleryWebPart
        Inherits Microsoft.SharePoint.WebPartPages.WebPart
        Implements Microsoft.SharePoint.WebPartPages.IAddtoGallery
        Private _data As String = "Some internal data"
        ' Create and return the XML fragment to define two menu commands.
        Public ReadOnly Property GalleryOptions() As String
            Get
                Dim gallerySchema As System.Text.StringBuilder = New
                   System.Text.StringBuilder(1024)
                gallerySchema.Append("<?xml version=""1.0""?>")
```

```
            gallerySchema.Append("<GalleryOptions>")
            gallerySchema.Append("<Option ID=""{CAEAE2BB-56F8-426f-A279-
                84E2465808B7}"">")
            gallerySchema.Append("<OptionName>Fire Event</OptionName>")
            gallerySchema.Append("<LinkValue>javascript: alert('Event fired with
                data: " & _data & ".'));</LinkValue>")
            gallerySchema.Append("</Option>")
            gallerySchema.Append("</GalleryOptions>")
            Return gallerySchema.ToString()
        End Get
    End Property

    #Region "IAddtoGallery Members"

    Private ReadOnly Property GalleryOptions() As String
        Implements IAddtoGallery.GalleryOptions
        Get
            Return GalleryOptions
        End Get
    End Property

    #End Region
    End Class
End Namespace
```

The code shown here allows the Web Part to hook into the Web Part Gallery and impose certain customizations. The mandatory implementation is the *GalleryOptions* method. In this method, we simply return the *GalleryOption* object that represents an XML fragment that will be used to construct the menu. (See Figure 6-33.)

Figure 6-33 Web Part Gallery link.

The *GalleryOption* fragment contains a special schema, which is described by Table 6-3.

Table 6-3 *GalleryOption* Schema

Element	Description
GalleryOptions	Describes the container element for the menu item definitions
Option	Contains the definition for a single menu item
OptionName	Indicates the text that will be displayed for the menu item
LinkValue	Specifies the JavaScript *onClick* action that will run when the user clicks the menu item

The fragment tells the run time the specific options and functionality that need to be rendered in the Advanced Web Part Gallery And Options page. The Advanced Web Part Gallery And Options link is shown in Figure 6-34. It is displayed at the bottom of the Web Part Gallery page when the Add Web Part link is clicked.

Figure 6-34   Advanced Web Part Gallery And Options link.

After the assembly is deployed and the Gallery pane displays, click the Browse button on the Gallery pane to display the new menu item as shown in Figure 6-35.

Figure 6-35   New Gallery menu option named Browse.

The menu item is fully functional and displays a message to the client passed in from the code-beside file running on the server. You can use these techniques to implement any one of the numerous interfaces present in SharePoint. You need to use a combination of IntelliSense, MSDN, and intuition to figure out which interface suits your need.

Summary

This chapter presented some advanced concepts, including object hosting and tool pane customizations. Tool pane customization allows the developer to brand a Web Part so that it is distinct. Branding is particularly important for companies that need their product offerings to stand out. In addition to branding, the Web Part architecture allows calling code to manipulate Web Part internals so that custom functionality can be built into an application.

The idea that Web pages are inherently limited to the Web is a popular but uninformed opinion that is loudly proclaimed. And, as is the typical case, opinions with significant volume often tend to represent themselves as truth. Web Parts can indeed have their functionality extended to reach onto the desktop. What's more interesting is that this improved functionality can occur in a way that is safe and controlled. And we have demonstrated this rather clearly in code.

Hopefully, the material here lights a fire of innovation underneath your applications that will shine brightly in the Web pages you build. Customers are drawn to applications that are sophisticated and polished while providing what the client requires. In this new breed of applications, you can expect to use Web Parts that contain embedded controls that offer all sorts of interesting functionality. In addition, you can cater to the demands of the knowledge worker by providing intimate control over the custom Web Parts that you build through the use of customizations to the tool pane and property pages.

Before you rush out to begin writing Web Parts, pause for a moment to consider this. The SharePoint architecture is built around the concept of Web Parts; it overshadows the fact that Web Parts aren't necessarily suited for all types of functionality. In particular, a Web Part was not designed to host an application. Rather, Web Parts specialize in displaying functional points of an application. You are still at liberty to develop ASP.NET Web pages and host these pages in SharePoint. The next chapter will walk you through this process.

Chapter 7

Advanced Concepts with Excel Services

Microsoft Office SharePoint Server (MOSS) was designed to offer enterprise-level solutions. As such, it cannot possibly be discussed in a vacuum, nor can code examples be confined solely to a SharePoint context. At least at the enterprise level, it makes sense to discuss SharePoint in a real-world context. After all, the concept of a software silo is dead. At the enterprise level, .NET applications such as Web Forms, Windows Forms, Web Services, and Distributed Applications extend, integrate, and complement SharePoint.

In that regard, I'll focus on the wider strategies that allow SharePoint to transition from a boxed product to a solid enterprise package with moving parts that address the needs of a functioning business. This chapter will raise the bar on what is possible and show you how best to massage the SharePoint product to fit your business need. Whether that need involves customizing sites to integrate with other Microsoft Office applications or building powerful custom .NET applications that integrate directly into the SharePoint experience, the concepts discussed will provide the final pieces of the puzzle that will help you build world-class applications.

SharePoint Web Parts Connections

Up until now, we have created only .NET Web Parts—that is, Web Parts that inherit from the *System.Web.UI.WebPart* base class. This is a recommended practice, and you must exercise the discipline to consistently follow this practice. However, you can also develop Web Parts that derive from a SharePoint base class, *Microsoft.SharePoint.WebPartPages.WebPart*. Later in this chapter, I'll broaden the concept to include full-blown Web pages that live on SharePoint. This will complement your arsenal of solutions that you can use to address enterprise-level problems.

Although it might seem like a simple rebasing exercise, there is more to the argument of inheriting from the SharePoint *WebPart* base class. Aside from the usual reusability and customization benefits, there are two other important reasons for creating SharePoint Web Parts:

- Data caching functionality
- Connections

The term *connection* is an umbrella concept that can be broken down further into these categories:

- Client-side connections
- Cross-page connections
- Cross-zone connections

The difference between these items lies in the location of the connection. Up until now, we have assumed that Web Parts are implicitly flat—that is, they exist on a single page. In the real world, Web Parts are three-dimensional—that is, they have depth. And this depth allows Web Parts to be placed in different locations either on a client, on the server, or on different pages in the same domain. Once Web Parts are physically isolated, you need to address the data exchange concerns.

Connecting Web Parts

There are some key types of functionality that you have not yet learned to perform. This covers areas such as data exchange between Web Parts, event notification across Web Parts, extensibility of existing Web Parts, and programming around existing limitations in Web Parts.

These are key parts of the enterprise puzzle that you will likely encounter and need to deal with when writing enterprise software. The next few examples will show you how to perform each of these activities.

Connecting two disparate Web Parts is often considered to be one of the more complicated features of SharePoint programming. That's not entirely true, as you will soon find out, but it is a popular belief. And there are some brownie points to be earned by top-tier developers who can connect Web Parts in SharePoint. For now, let's be indulgent and listen politely when these huge egos start talking up a storm about the complexities involved in connecting Web Parts. Later, when it's our turn to talk, we intend to scrub some of that gloss from those huge egos.

From a theoretical perspective, Web Parts that exchange data follow the publisher/subscriber design pattern, which is described in more detail at *http://msdn2.microsoft.com/en-us/library/w369ty8x(VS.80).aspx*. One Web Part defines its role as the publisher or provider, and the other becomes the subscriber or consumer.

In addition, a provider can also be a consumer, as long as it is not a consumer of its own services. That sort of behavior can lead to circular references and is explicitly forbidden by the compiler.

Web Parts based on SharePoint follow a set protocol. SharePoint provides a standard set of connection interfaces that define a contract between a publisher and a subscriber. Web Parts can be connected together only if they implement one or more of these interfaces.

The primary means of communication between Web Parts is through the event model. A publisher seeking to publish information fires a specific event that is caught and processed in the consumer or consumers. Before building a connected Web Part, you should first determine the interface that you need to implement. The determination is based on the type of data that you want to exchange. Consider Table 7-1, which shows the interfaces supported and the functionality that each supports.

Table 7-1   Connection Interfaces

Connection Interface	Description
IWebPartField	Supports a single-value item
IWebPartRow	Supports a single row or several rows of values
IWebPartTable	Supports an entire collection
IWebPartParameters	Supports negotiation between Web Parts

As you can see, the SharePoint Web Part requires some effort. You need to implement one or more of the interfaces in your consumer and provider. Once the code is in place, you deploy the Web Part and connect the provider to the consumer. The following link on MSDN will walk you through the process: *http://msdn2.microsoft.com/en-us/library/ms469765.aspx*. We won't rehash these concepts here. That's not the reason you purchased this book, and I won't shortchange you either. Instead, we will break new ground by examining radical approaches to connectable Web Parts using new techniques available with ASP.NET 2.0. Let's get started.

There are two approaches to developing connectable Web Parts that are not based on SharePoint Web Parts. One approach demonstrates how to connect Web Parts using the standard *System.Web.UI.WebPart* class. The other approach demonstrates how to develop connectable Web Parts based on user controls. A very basic example that demonstrates the first approach is outlined in Listing 7-1.

Listing 7-1   A connection-aware consumer Web Part based on the *System.Web.UI.WebControls.WebParts.WebPart* class.

```csharp
C# Snippet
public class ConsumerWebPart : System.Web.UI.WebControls.WebParts.WebPart
{
    Label lbl = null;
    [ConnectionConsumer("Display User Info")]
    public void GetUserData(string str)
    {
        EnsureChildControls();
        if (str != null)
            lbl.Text = "Select Value : " + str;
    }
}
```

```vb
Visual Basic Snippet
Public Class ConsumerWebPart
    Inherits System.Web.UI.WebControls.WebParts.WebPart
        Private lbl As Label = Nothing
        <ConnectionConsumer("Display User Info")> _
        Public Sub GetUserData(ByVal str As String)
            EnsureChildControls()
            If Not str Is Nothing Then
                lbl.Text = "Select Value : " & str
            End If
        End Sub
End Sub
```

To keep the example simple, the *Render* and *CreateChildControls* methods have been removed. The driving method is the *GetUserData* method. It is decorated with an attribute, *Connection-Consumer*, that allows the Web Part Connection menu to be visible in the Web Part. This allows the end user to connect one Web Part to another at run time. Notice that the *ConnectionConsumer* attribute uses a string parameter, *Display User Info*. This string appears in the Web Part Connection menu at run time.

If a connectable Web Part is available, data will be stored in the *str* variable of type *string*. Note that the *GetUserData* parameter can be of any type because it is a regular .NET method. The code example uses a single string parameter for simplicity.

A standard label control declared dynamically in the body of the code receives the data from the provider. At run time, when the Web Part is connected by the end user, data from the provider will be displayed in the Web Part on screen. Compare this to the 15-page MSDN provider walk-through and realize that our approach is less verbose and certainly less intimidating. However, the result is the same—that is, data is moved from one Web Part to another. The driving difference is that we connect based on pure ASP.NET 2.0 mechanisms. You don't need to be a hotshot developer to implement this approach, either.

Consider the code for the provider Web Part shown in Listing 7-2.

Listing 7-2   A connection-aware provider Web Part based on the *System.Web.UI.WebControls.Web-Parts.WebPart* class.

C# Snippet

```csharp
public class ProviderWebPart : System.Web.UI.WebControls.WebParts.WebPart
{
    TextBox txtbox = null;
    Button btn = null;
    private string str = "";
    protected override void CreateChildControls()
    {
        txtbox = new TextBox();
        btn = new Button();
        btn.Text = "Pass Value";
        btn.Click += new EventHandler(btn_Click);
        Controls.Add(txtbox);
        Controls.Add(btn);
    }
    void btn_Click(object sender, EventArgs e)
    {
        str = "New Value : " + DateTime.Now;
    }
    protected override void Render(HtmlTextWriter writer)
    {
        txtbox.RenderControl(writer);
        btn.RenderControl(writer);
        writer.Write("Provider1");
    }
    [ConnectionProvider("Information")]
    public string SetUserInfo()
    {
        return txtbox.Text   + DateTime.Now ;
    }
}
```

Visual Basic Snippet

```vb
Public Class ProviderWebPart
Inherits System.Web.UI.WebControls.WebParts.WebPart
    Private txtbox As TextBox = Nothing
    Private btn As Button = Nothing
    Private str As String = ""
    Protected Overrides Sub CreateChildControls()
        txtbox = New TextBox()
        btn = New Button()
        btn.Text = "Pass Value"
        AddHandler btn.Click, AddressOf btn_Click
        Controls.Add(txtbox)
        Controls.Add(btn)
    End Sub

    Private Sub btn_Click(ByVal sender As Object, ByVal e As EventArgs)
        str = "New Value : " & DateTime.Now
    End Sub
    Protected Overrides Sub Render(ByVal writer As HtmlTextWriter)
        txtbox.RenderControl(writer)
```

```
        btn.RenderControl(writer)
        writer.Write("Provider1")
    End Sub
    <ConnectionProvider("Information")> _
    Public Function SetUserInfo() As String
        Return txtbox.Text + DateTime.Now
    End Function
```

A short explanation will suffice here. The *CreateChildControls* method creates a new button dynamically and adds an event handler for the click event. Then the control is added to the *Controls* collection. The important method is *SetUserInfo*. It is decorated with a *ConnectionProvider* attribute that allows the provider Web Part to connect to another Web Part. When this function executes, the text in the *Textbox* control is concatenated with time information and passed to the connected Web Part. That's all there is to it. Figure 7-1 shows the connected Web Parts in action.

Figure 7-1   Connectable Web Parts at run time.

You'll notice that, in this particular implementation, the Web Part page does not inherit from the *SharePoint.WebPart* class. The example is crafted to demonstrate that this is not necessarily a requirement for connecting Web Parts. Web Parts can be connected based on the regular ASP.NET Web Part class. It's in your best interest to keep that bit of information away from the aforementioned hotshot developer to avoid bruised egos.

Don't be fooled by the simple attributes that decorate the key methods in the provider and consumer. The attributes are responsible for implementing the lion's share of the work. At run time, the framework calls both the provider's connection point method and the consumer's connection point method. Using the reference returned from these methods, the framework establishes a working connection.

Also note that both types of attributes, *ConnectionConsumer* and *ConnectionProvider*, can decorate any method in the source code. The functionality allows a Web Part to be both a consumer and a provider.

Creating Connection-Aware User Controls

The second approach involves creating connection-aware user controls. This is certainly the Holy Grail of user controls. The overall approach is the same in that it works with a consumer and a provider Web Part. However, the difference is that both the consumer and the provider are built using user control templates. The code to implement this is so short that you shouldn't blink during the discussion, lest you miss it entirely.

We can create the consumer based on any Visual Studio SharePoint template. For this exercise, we prefer to use the user control template because it lends us the Microsoft Visual Studio designer. In the Visual Studio designer, create a Web Part based on a Web Site template named Provider. Add a text box named **DisplayText** to the form. The code is shown in Listing 7-3. For brevity, the *Render* and *CreateChildControls* methods have been removed.

Listing 7-3 Creating the consumer user control.

```csharp
C# Snippet
public partial class Consumer : System.Web.UI.UserControl
{
    public string DisplayValue
    {
        get
        {
            return DisplayText.Text;
        }
        set
        {
            DisplayText.Text = value;
        }
    }
}
```

```vb
Visual Basic Snippet
Public Partial Class Consumer
    Inherits System.Web.UI.UserControl
    Public Property DisplayValue() As String
        Get
            Return DisplayText.Text
        End Get
        Set
            DisplayText.Text = Value
        End Set
    End Property
End Class
```

There's no point in a code discussion. Let's review the provider code (shown in Listing 7-4). It is built using a *Textbox* control and a button control, named *Transmit* and TransmitData, respectively. Change the text property of the TransmitData button to **Transmit Data** so that it is intuitive to the end user.

Listing 7-4 Provider user controls with public property.

```csharp
C# Snippet
public partial class Provider : System.Web.UI.UserControl
{
    public string ProvideData
    {
        get
        {
            return ProviderMsg.Text;
        }
        set
        {
            ProviderMsg.Text = value;
        }
    }

    protected void TransmitData_Click(object sender, EventArgs e)
    {
        ProvideData = ProviderMsg.Text;
    }
}
```

```vbnet
Visual Basic Snippet
Public Partial Class Provider
    Inherits System.Web.UI.UserControl
    Public Property ProvideData() As String
        Get
            Return ProviderMsg.Text
        End Get
        Set
            ProviderMsg.Text = Value
        End Set
    End Property

    Protected Sub TransmitData_Click(ByVal sender As Object, ByVal e
      As EventArgs)
        ProvideData = ProviderMsg.Text
    End Sub
End Class
```

The important method is the *TransmitData_Click* event handler. The event handler fires when the button, TransmitData, is clicked. The event handler's job is to move the text from the *Textbox* control to the public *ProvideData* property. The consumer Web Part will extract data from that public property as appropriate. Honestly, that was shamefully easy.

To finish off, we simply need to build the respective assemblies and publish them to a temporary directory using the Publish Website option of the Visual Studio Build menu. During the publish process, you need to sign the assembly using a strong name key. Figure 7-2 shows the relevant settings in the Publish Web Site dialog box.

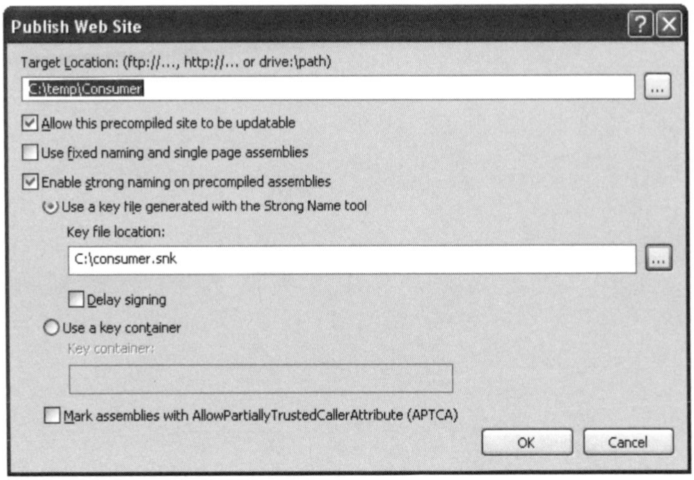

Figure 7-2   Connectable Web Part user control.

Then modify the regular Web Part code to load the consumer and provider *.ascx* files. We will do so as we have done in the past by creating a consumer and provider loader Web Part.

Creating the Consumer Loader Web Part

The consumer loader Web Part is responsible for loading the *consumer.ascx* file into SharePoint. Let's review the code (shown in Listing 7-5) since we have seen it a number of times before.

Listing 7-5   Consumer user controls with public property.

```csharp
C# Snippet
private Consumer usercontrol;
protected override void CreateChildControls()
{
    base.CreateChildControls();
    Controls.Clear();

    usercontrol = (Consumer)Page.LoadControl(@"/Connect/Consumer.ascx");
    Controls.Add(usercontrol);
}
protected override void Render(HtmlTextWriter writer)
{
    EnsureChildControls();
    usercontrol.RenderControl(writer);
}
[ConnectionConsumer("Display user Info")]
public void GetUserData(string str)
{
    EnsureChildControls();

    if (str != null)
    {
```

```
        usercontrol.DisplayValue = "Passed value: " + str;
    }
}
```
Visual Basic Snippet
```
Private usercontrol As Consumer
Protected Overrides Sub CreateChildControls()
    MyBase.CreateChildControls()
    Controls.Clear()

    usercontrol = CType(Page.LoadControl("/Connect/Consumer.ascx"), Consumer)
    Controls.Add(usercontrol)
End Sub
Protected Overrides Sub Render(ByVal writer As HtmlTextWriter)
    EnsureChildControls()
    usercontrol.RenderControl(writer)
End Sub
<ConnectionConsumer("Display user Info")> _
Public Sub GetUserData(ByVal str As String)
    EnsureChildControls()

    If Not str Is Nothing Then
        usercontrol.DisplayValue = "Passed value: " & str
    End If
End Sub
```

Notice the user control of type *Consumer* declared as a private variable. This will hold a reference to the consumer user control assembly at run time. With this reference, we can manipulate the contents of the *Consumer* user control object.

For the code to compile, add a reference to the consumer library. The path to the consumer library leads to the *.ascx* file on disk. This strategy is quite common in .NET development, so you should have no trouble adding the reference.

The consumer method *GetUserData* is decorated with a *ConnectionConsumer* attribute that allows the Web Part to be connection-aware. A connection-aware control allows the Web Part to display the Connection menu. The data that fills the *TextBox* control in the consumer Web Part will come from the *Textbox* control in the provider Web Part when the provider Web Part button is clicked.

Creating the Provider Loader Web Part

Let's focus on the provider. The provider loader Web Part's code (shown in Listing 7-6) is similar to code that we have seen in the consumer.

Listing 7-6   Creating the provider loader Web Part.

```csharp
C# Snippet
Public partial class Provider : System.Web.UI.UserControl, IWebPartField
{
        private Provider usercontrol;
        [ConnectionProvider("Information")]
        public string GetUserData()
        {
            EnsureChildControls();

            return usercontrol.ProvideData;
        }
}
```

```vb
Visual Basic Snippet
Friend Public Partial Class Provider
    Inherits System.Web.UI.UserControl
    Implements IWebPartField
        Private usercontrol As Provider
        <ConnectionProvider("Information")> _
        Public Function GetUserData() As String
            EnsureChildControls()

            Return usercontrol.ProvideData
        End Function
End Class
```

For clarity, the *Render* and *CreateChildControls* methods have been removed. *ProvideData* is a public property declared in the user control. (See Listing 7-6.) When this property is read or written, data will move from the provider to the consumer.

Deploying the Web Parts

To run the application, load both Web Parts into a page and place the SharePoint page in edit mode by clicking the Edit This Page link in the top, right corner of the Web page. Once the page is in edit mode, click on the Edit menu for the consumer Web Part. Use the Connection menu to connect one Web Part to the other. Now the Web Parts are connected. Enter some text in the provider, and click the Transmit Data button. You should see results similar to Figure 7-3.

Figure 7-3 shows the connected Web Part in action.

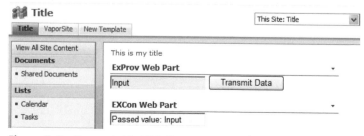

Figure 7-3   Connectable Web Part user control.

Guidelines for SharePoint Web Parts

As is the case with most bits of working code presented here, there are issues to watch out for, so let's enumerate a short list of them. Web Parts can run either on the server or the client. However, Web Parts can be connected only if they both reside in the same location. To clarify, a client-side Web Part cannot connect to a server-side Web Part. Further, a connected Web Part cannot switch to another location while it is connected. That would simply subvert the restriction.

As with any connection paradigm, there must be some fundamental rule to avoid circular connections. Therefore, a Web Part cannot connect to itself either directly or indirectly. You do not have to explicitly cater for this scenario in code; the Web Part makes that determination for you and informs you through the normal exception reporting mechanism.

I indicated earlier that a Web Part can be either a consumer or provider. This is misleading because there are no constraints imposed on the interface. A Web Part can be both a consumer and a provider as long as it does not consume itself either directly or indirectly; that would violate the previous rule. If you need to build this sort of Web Part, follow the same procedures presented earlier except apply both interface attributes to the same Web Part. An implementation is best left as an exercise for the reader to undertake.

SharePoint Web Part Caching

The basic concept of data caching is consistent across SharePoint and ASP.NET. However, SharePoint contains its own implementation of a cache that can be addressed programmatically using members of the cache enumeration type, which are listed in Table 7-2.

Table 7-2 Cache Enumeration Values

Member	Description
CacheObject	Stores cached property values using the ASP.NET *Cache* object.
Database	Stores cached property values in the SharePoint database.
None	No property values are cached.

These member values show that you can programmatically target either the ASP.NET cache infrastructure or the SharePoint database for caching values. There is no direct equivalent for such functionality in ASP.NET. The different state providers in ASP.NET must be configured at design time using the *web.config* file. In a typical case, these design-time settings are overridden at run time using code logic.

The same rules that apply with respect to performance and resource constraints for cached objects apply to SharePoint caching as well. For instance, an in-memory cache store will outperform a database store by at least 15 to 20 percent. However, the database will support caching for hundreds of thousands of sites. This number is usually unattainable for in-memory caches servicing real-world applications. You need to opt for the most appropriate storage location based on a number of factors, including site traffic, performance, and site availability.

Working with the Cache Mechanism

To configure caching for a particular store, open your *web.config* file and locate the *WebPart-Cache* node as shown in the following *web.config* blurb:

```
<WebPartCache Storage="CacheObject" />
```

Set the *Storage* attribute to the appropriate value, as shown in Table 7-2. Note that these values are case sensitive. Also note that adjusting values in the *web.config* file forces the application pool to be recycled. This behavior is no different from ASP.NET.

If you decide to use the cache, note that SharePoint provides functionality to allow calling code to invalidate the cache. Table 7-3 shows the cache validation methods.

Table 7-3   Cache Method Signatures

Member	Description
WebPart.PartCacheInvalidate ()	Marks all the contents of the Web Part cache as outdated
WebPart.PartCacheInvalidate (Storage)	Marks all contents of the specified storage type in the Web Part cache as outdated
WebPart.PartCacheInvalidate (Storage, String)	Marks the specified cache entries of the specified storage type in the Web Part cache as outdated

Listing 7-7 shows just the bare-bones code required to read and write to the SharePoint cache.

Listing 7-7   Creating the provider loader.

```
C# Snippet
//Read the cache
this.PartCacheRead(Storage.Shared, "AKey");
//Write to the cache
object o;
this.PartCacheWrite(Storage.Shared, "AKey", o, TimeSpan.FromSeconds(10));
Visual Basic Snippet
'Read the cache
Me.PartCacheRead(Storage.Shared, "AKey")
'Write to the cache
Dim o as object
TryCast(Me.PartCacheRead(Storage.Shared, "AKey"), o)
```

Notice that the cache allows calling code to set expiration policies on the items. In that regard, it behaves no differently from the ASP.NET caching that you are accustomed to.

The SharePoint cache does not allow calling code to set cached dependencies. If you need that type of functionality, consider building it using the *PartCacheInvalidate* method call to flush the cache. You can pair this approach with a file or directory monitoring object such as the *FileSystemWatcher* object available in .NET. An implementation example is trivial and best left as an exercise for the reader.

You can also extend the caching mechanism by creating an *IVaryByCustomHandler* interface. The concept borrows heavily from ASP.NET, so we need to concern ourselves only with the differences between the two. The implementation details follow the ASP.NET tradition of creating and registering a handler to intercept the browser input. Then use the input to influence the caching mechanism. An article describing the implementation details of ASP.NET output caching can be found at *http://msdn2.microsoft.com/en-us/library/ms972362.aspx*. The only difference worth noting is the registration step, which resembles the following code:

```
//Register the VaryByCustom string in the Global.asax file
<%@ Assembly Name="Microsoft.SharePoint"%>
<%@ Assembly Name="add_assembly_name_here"%>
<%@ Import Namespace="import_namespace_here" %>
<%@ Application Language="C#" Inherits=" add_assembly_name_here.CacheClass %>
```

Guidelines for Web Part Caching

ASP.NET caching such as the intrinsic session and cache objects is automatically disabled on MOSS 2007 as seen in the *web.config* blurb shown here:

```
<pages enableSessionState="false" enableViewState="true" enableViewStateMac="true"
validateRequest="false"
pageParserFilterType="Microsoft.SharePoint.ApplicationRuntime.SPPageParserFilter,
Microsoft.SharePoint, Version=12.0.0.0, Culture=neutral, PublicKeyToken=71e9bce111e9429c"
asyncTimeout="7">
```

Though you can turn session state on, you should resist this urge. Instead, you should use the caching infrastructure provided by MOSS 2007.

Important   SharePoint makes a context object available for use within the *Microsoft.SharePoint.SPContext* class. You can use this context object to gain access to view state and other intrinsic ASP.NET objects. As pointed out in Chapter 4, "Excel Calculation Service," session state is turned off by default. You can expect to suffer severe performance consequences under load with session state turned on. The reason for this performance consequence is that once session state is enabled, pages processed by the safe-mode parser are forced to use session state. These pages cannot opt out even with a page-level directive. What this means is that the performance optimization that dynamically compiled pages enjoy will no longer be available. As the site increases in load, the burden becomes increasingly unbearable on the SharePoint engine, resulting in degradation of performance.

As is the typical case, objects that need to be cached must be serializable. Intrinsic .NET types found in the Framework Class Library (FCL) are explicitly marked with the *serializable* attribute. However, custom types that you create need to be decorated with the attribute if they are to be stored in the cache.

Caching of objects incurs a performance cost as a result of overhead inherent in the serialization process. In some cases, this totally negates the performance benefit of caching. In those cases, you should prevent caching by using the appropriate member of the *CacheType* enumeration. Or accept the default cache value in the *web.config* file. The best way to determine application performance is to perform application instrumentation (that is, measure the performance). There are many suitable tools that can perform this function, including Perfmon.

If you are designing for performance, you might want to consider implementing Output caching. The Output caching mechanism used in MOSS 2007 is based on ASP.NET 2.0. The Output caching implementation in SharePoint is enhanced to incorporate cache profiles. Cache profiles are list-style cache settings that can be named and applied to pages, items, content types, sites, and site collections. Cache profiles provide a level of control that is suitable for caching data across groups, credentials, and access rights.

Code Access Security

Shout "Code Access Security" in a room full of .NET programmers and you are certain to cause a wild stampede for the exits! Why? Code Access Security (CAS) has received a very bad rap over the years. Developers walk the extra mile to avoid it, or simply ignore it whenever possible. It's time to change that way of thinking because CAS is tied to every piece of code that runs on the .NET platform, SharePoint being no exception.

 Caution   The following discussion assumes that you have more than a passing knowledge of Code Access Security, as well as a knowledge of its implementation in .NET and the various tools and strategies that are used to inspect, configure, and apply CAS. If you are weak on CAS, you might struggle with the concepts and exercises that follow. You can read up on CAS here: *http://en.wikipedia.org/wiki/Code_Access_Security*.

After the managed user control exercises in Chapter 6, "Advanced Web Parts Programming," you've probably found out the hard way that you need to gain more than a passing familiarity with CAS to build some types of SharePoint applications. But this is a hard lesson that pays huge dividends. There's more to the story, though. ASP.NET runs with full trust on its assemblies. SharePoint, built on top of ASP.NET, does not run with full trust. You are all but certain to run into security issues if you play with SharePoint long enough.

Configuring CAS Policy for Managed User Controls

In Chapter 6, I demonstrated how to write a managed user control that enumerates registry keys to a control on screen. To get this control to work in Chapter 6, you had to turn CAS policy off on the machine. You might have found out that this approach was problematic. For instance, the configuration database intermittently refuses to service requests, Visual Studio does not open and load any projects. This is by design. Visual Studio and Microsoft SQL Server 2005 use .NET Code Access Security in their implementation. The only valid reason for turning CAS policy off on a machine is to troubleshoot permissions errors. The solution is to configure CAS appropriately rather than turn it off completely.

> **Tip** To turn CAS policy off successfully and enable the managed user control to load, you need to click the Web Part's Add A Web Part button and select the Managed User Control Web Part. Navigate to the Add Web Parts–Webpage dialog box, turn off CAS policy at the command prompt, and then click the Add button. It's all a matter of timing.

As it turns out, the default CAS policy on the machine is too strict to permit managed user controls to load. We need to loosen the restrictions to allow these types of applications to work. Ideally, we want to provide only the bare minimum permissions that are required by the run time to load the control.

To find the bare minimum permissions, simply deploy the Web Part and add it to the page. If the control renders correctly in the Web Part, the default permission set is sufficient and there is nothing more that needs to be done. This is most likely not the case. In the typical case, the control will not render at all. We troubleshoot the permission issue in the next section.

Resolving Permissions Issues that Result from Caching

Whenever the common language runtime (CLR) tries unsuccessfully to bind to a managed user control assembly, the requesting page or Web Part renders a small, empty box that represents the location where the managed user control should be rendered. The CLR writes a temporary file to disk containing a stack trace of the assembly bind error. To view the contents of this file, open your temporary file cache in your browser and click the View Files button. The highlighted item, shown in Figure 7-4, contains the error log information.

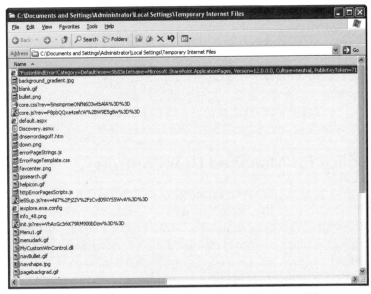

Figure 7-4 Assembly bind failure log in Internet Explorer 7.0.

Open the file in Notepad by dragging and dropping the file into Notepad through Windows Explorer. The contents show a stack trace with the error message that prevents the assembly from being loaded. Notice that the stack trace indicates that there was an unsatisfied request for File IO permissions. This is the minimum permission required by the CLR to load the control. Figure 7-5 shows a stack trace of an assembly bind failure.

Figure 7-5   Stack trace for assembly bind failure.

To fix this, you need to add the required permissions to the appropriate code group using the .NET configuration utility. Run the .NET 2.0 mscorcfg.msc at a Visual Studio 2005 command prompt. Navigate to the Runtime Security Policy level represented by the appropriately named TreeView node. Create a permission set named **BareMinimum** by clicking on the Machine node, selecting the Machine TreeView node and then the permissions set level, and then selecting Create Permissions Set in the left window pane.

For our particular example, Figure 7-6 shows the bare-minimum permissions that are required to allow the managed user control to function correctly. The File IO item requires unrestricted access to the file system. The registry permission does not require unrestricted access, and you might want to limit access to just the registry hives that need to be enumerated.

Next, create a code group called **MyWinControls** as a child of the All_Code group, and assign the custom permission set to it. Click the Membership tab, and choose the URL condition type for the assembly. Enter the URL to the assembly as **http://<*servername:port*>/Controls/ MyCustomWinControl.dll**. That's all, in terms of configuration. However, you need to add declarative demands for the permissions that the assembly requires. The modified code is shown in Listing 7-8.

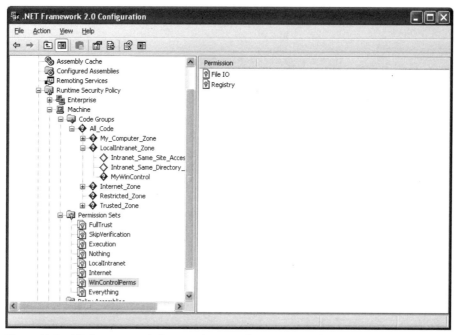

Figure 7-6 Minimum permission requirement for UserControl1.

Listing 7-8 Declarative security in an assembly.

```csharp
C# Snippet
[FileIOPermission(SecurityAction.Assert, Unrestricted = true)]
[RegistryPermission(SecurityAction.Assert,Unrestricted = true)]
public partial class UserControl1 : UserControl
{
        [FileIOPermission(SecurityAction.Assert, Unrestricted = true)]
        [RegistryPermission(SecurityAction.Assert, Unrestricted = true)]
        public UserControl1()
        {
        }
        [RegistryPermission(SecurityAction.Assert, Unrestricted = true)]
        public void PopulateRegistryKeys(string key, TreeView yourKeys)
        {
        }
}
```

```vbnet
Visual Basic Snippet
<FileIOPermission(SecurityAction.Assert, Unrestricted := True),
RegistryPermission(SecurityAction.Assert,Unrestricted := True)> _
Public Partial Class UserControl1
    Inherits UserControl
        <FileIOPermission(SecurityAction.Assert, Unrestricted := True),
          RegistryPermission(SecurityAction.Assert,
```

```
            Unrestricted := True)> _
        Public Sub New()
        End Sub
        <RegistryPermission(SecurityAction.Assert, Unrestricted := True)> _
        Public Sub PopulateRegistryKeys(ByVal key As String, ByVal yourKeys
          As TreeView)
        End Sub
    End Class
```

I'll formalize a discussion of the code in the next section.

> **Best Practices**   It is possible to nest your control underneath any one of the other code groups displayed in Figure 7-6 so that your control can inherit the parent permissions. This arrangement allows you to increase the permissions granted to your assembly without reconfiguring the custom permission set. For instance, you can simply drag your custom permission group, MyWinControl, and drop it underneath LocalIntranetZone. The custom permission group then inherits the permissions from the parent LocalIntranetZone.

CAS and Internet Browsers

Code Access Security is a road less traveled. As is typical with those types of roads, the ride is often bumpy. Let's discuss one bump in the road. When a Windows user control is delivered to the client, the CLR must first create an application domain to house the managed assembly. Application domains must be created with security policy that governs the executing assembly. Because the assembly isn't yet loaded, the CLR really has no way to determine what type of permissions the assembly will require. The CLR assigns the permissions to the *AppDomain* based on what it knows about the assembly it loads, which is Zone and URL permissions.

These default permissions are often inadequate for real-world use, and they result in the assembly failing to load even though you might have specifically configured a custom group that provides the necessary required permissions. Remember, that the permissions *Demand* is occurring before the assembly is loaded, so the CLR cannot yet associate your assembly permissions with the custom code group because the CLR does not trust your assembly.

There are two ways to work around this. One approach involves elevating permissions at the All_Code group because this code group governs access to all code running on the machine. You can either provide full trust or create a permission set and add the necessary permission to satisfy the permission request—*FileIOPermissions*, in our case. When the *AppDomain* is created, it uses the elevated permission and the user control renders correctly.

At the enterprise level, this is a corrosive approach to developing secure software because it provides code with more permissions than it requires. Elevated permissions corrode the principle of *least privilege*, resulting in software that is susceptible to attack. Further, any control running on the machine now receives elevated permission. In this regard, it is only marginally better than an ActiveX control. Code running with full trust is inherently dangerous!

> **More Info**   You can read more about the doctrine of least privilege at *http://en.wikipedia.org/wiki/Principle_of_least_privilege*.

The second approach involves strong-naming the assembly. From the point of view of the CLR, a strong-named assembly is implicitly trusted. However, it still does not work around the limitation of insufficient *AppDomain* privilege. When a stack walk commences for *FileIOPermission*, for instance, the request is satisfied at the assembly level because it is strong-named and trusted. However, the request fails at the *AppDomain* level because the *AppDomain* loaded by the browser is partially trusted and won't necessarily have these elevated permissions.

> **Note**   Visual Studio 2005 Extensions for SharePoint implicitly strong-names every assembly by default. If you do not use this tool, you need to manually perform strong-naming using the sn.exe utility that ships with the .NET Framework. An example is provided in Chapter 3, "Excel Web Access."

The simple yet elegant solution is to stop the stack walk from reaching the *AppDomain*. The *assert* statement essentially vouches for the remaining callers on the stack so that this particular permission request will not reach the *AppDomain*. You need to perform declarative demands for the specific permissions that your assembly requires at all entry points in your class. This is the reason for decorating the class, constructor, and methods with the security attributes in Listing 7-8.

The solution just presented is acceptable at the enterprise level because custom permission sets can be used to govern access to executing code. And no piece of code receives more permission than it requires. Further, you cannot assert permissions that you don't have in the first place. The reason why we asserted only for the *FileIOPermission* and *RegistryPermission* objects is because these were granted in our custom permission set, *BareMinimum*.

One drawback to this approach is that you need to configure each client desktop with the updated CAS policy. Another drawback to this approach is that the executing code is representing to the CLR that it implicitly trusts the callers in the stack. What if one of the callers in the stack is a rogue assembly? The CLR does not care at this point because you vouched for its authenticity. Asserts are potentially dangerous and leave your code vulnerable to luring attacks.

The next version of Visual Studio handles this situation a bit differently. Embedded controls are allowed to request the required permissions when the *AppDomain* is being created. The permissions request is implemented within a configuration file so that it can occur long before code execution. This approach negates the need to configure client CAS policy.

CAS and UDFs

Chapter 4 presented the user-defined function (UDF) concept within Excel Services. UDFs run on the server and are implemented as a regular .NET assembly with a few decorations that allow Excel to find and load the assembly. There's a whole lot more to the concept, and we'll revisit these issues in a bit more detail here.

To configure CAS policy for UDFs, apply the same principles discussed previously to the managed assembly in the bin directory of the Web application. As I noted in Chapter 4, if the assembly requires full trust, you should strong-name the assembly and place it in the global assembly cache (GAC). If the assembly requires partial trust, you can use CAS configuration techniques to configure permissions on the assembly.

I won't bother rehashing the exact details here; instead, I'll provide a simple overview of the process. First, you need to create a Code Group that you want to associate with your UDF. Scope the Code Group to the UDF assembly using the URL condition or some other appropriate condition. Finally, create a Permission Set with the bare-minimum permissions, and assign the Permission Set to the new Code Group.

> **Tip**   Note that you can strong-name an assembly and deploy it outside of the GAC. Strong-naming is a way of signing an assembly. It just so happens that the GAC imposes this requirement on assemblies that it contains.

Configuring CAS Policy for XLL

The UDFs that we examined all run on the server. Excel is also able to load assemblies that reside on the client. These XLL assemblies perform the same function as server UDFs. However, XLL add-ins are built in a format that can be natively consumed by Microsoft Office Excel 2007. Recall that the UDFs developed in Chapter 4 could not be natively consumed and resulted in a #NAME error in the cell. XLL assemblies enjoy a significant performance boost over server UDFs.

Although a thorough inspection of XLL add-ins is outside the scope of this discussion, note that the CAS configuration process is identical to that presented earlier. You need to perform two simple steps. First, you need to create a .NET wrapper for the XLL because the XLL is typically built using unmanaged code. Then apply CAS policy to the wrapper. As a prerequisite, your security policy must grant the permission to call native code.

Note here that as soon as the managed code is granted the permission to call unmanaged code and the code within the assembly begins to execute, the thread of execution transitions across the unmanaged boundary. At that point, CAS policy settings no longer apply until the thread of execution transitions back into managed code.

Once the thread of execution is in unmanaged territory, only Operating System Role based security applies. In that regard, managed UDFs reap a security benefit over that of the XLL add-ins. It is important to understand that this is a potential vulnerability that cannot possibly be repaired by CAS policy.

The semantics of the unmanaged permission look like this:

```
[assembly: SecurityPermission(SecurityAction.RequestMinimum, UnmanagedCode=true)]
```

CAS Policy Deployment Strategies

The final steps involved in applying CAS policy relate to the actual deployment of the policy files. The policy files are XML files residing on a disk that is protected by a Domain Control List. For instance, administrative permissions are required to manipulate CAS policy. As we shall soon see, the permission requirement is problematic from a deployment perspective.

Admittedly, there are very few resources available for information on deploying CAS policy. In most cases, the available resources fail to address the real-world problems associated with policy updates. Let's walk through these issues and figure out solutions as we go.

As a developer or administrator, you have the responsibility to provide the correct CAS policy to enable your assembly to function correctly on the server or client. Using the .NET 2.0 configuration utility, you can create the appropriate policy file by first configuring CAS policy on your machine to enable your control to work. Once you have arrived at a suitable configuration that works well, navigate to the Runtime Security Policy level and right-click the node. Click Create A Deployment Package. The action triggers the Deployment Package Wizard. Walk through the wizard to produce an MSI package that contains the updated CAS policy.

There are a few things to note during the walk-through. The wizard creates a snapshot of the CAS policy on your machine. The wizard allows you to create policy for the Enterprise, Machine, or User level. The Enterprise level is geared toward large organizations with a defined structure. Mid-sized to small shops that have less of a defined structure should use the Machine level. Otherwise, the User level should be used. A defined structure accommodates a workplace that has been structured into computer workgroups that have defined user accounts and domains, and that has one or more administrative policies governing the use of software and hardware for each employee.

The MSI package created by the wizard can be distributed to desktops through either a pull or push mechanism. A push mechanism is a deployment process that is either developed by a third party or organically grown. A pull mechanism allows end users to perform an installation by clicking on an installation package. In every case, a deployment always overwrites existing policy–that is, unless you roll your own code, there is no way to version CAS policy. Without due diligence, there is a very real possibility that a new CAS policy can break existing applications. I'll show some code to work around this issue later on.

For the pull mechanism, the developer or administrator must make the MSI package available to the end user by deploying the package to a common site. As a one-time setup cost, the end user will navigate to the location of the MSI package and perform the installation by copying the MSI package locally and running it. The end user requires administrative privileges for this step. Running the MSI package remotely installs CAS policy on the remote machine. This is not the desired effect.

Pulling works well with small to medium-sized deployments, where the average user might have administrative privileges on the client machine. But, note here, that some small shops do contain well-defined structures with locked-down accounts where the end user does not have administrative privileges. In these cases, a pull mechanism will not work.

For scenarios where it is not feasible to pull, you should consider a push mechanism. In the typical case, pushing is reserved for large enterprises. Consider a large financial institution or government establishment containing 50,000 desktops sitting in different geographical locations, each with varying degrees of privileges to the local system. In these cases, the organizations usually have their own deployment strategy based either on a third-party product, organically grown deployment mechanisms, or deployment based on an existing Microsoft technology.

The policy files can be pushed to the enterprise using Windows Group Policy Objects (GPOs). GPOs allow the MSI package to be installed when the end user logs in or reboots the machine. One benefit of a GPO is that, because it is based on Windows Active Directory, it can target user profiles. As an example, an administrator is able to push the policy files to select desktops—only to project managers, for instance.

Third-party and organically developed packages work in roughly the same way—that is, administrative privilege is not required by the end user because the files are pushed to the desktop in a deployment process that already contains the required administrative privilege.

Customizing the Deployment Process

If you intend to use a push mechanism and need to make customizations to the deployment package, one strategy is to build the CAS policy file dynamically using managed code that hooks into the Windows installer. Custom-built code can then provide any type of functionality required by the enterprise. For instance, instead of overwriting policy, custom code can append policy to the client machine.

Examine the code shown in Listing 7-9, which allows the Windows installer to activate an assembly that installs the required CAS policy on a machine.

Listing 7-9 Dynamic code group creation.

```csharp
C# Snippet
using System;
using System.Collections;
using System.ComponentModel;
using System.Configuration.Install;

using System.Security;
using System.Security.Policy;
using System.Security.Permissions;

[RunInstaller(true)]
public class MyInstallPackage : System.Configuration.Install.Installer
{
    private System.ComponentModel.Container components = null;

    string permissionName        = "MyCustomWinControlsPermissions";
    string permissionDescription= "Custom permissions for my control.";
    string codeGroupName         = "MyCustomGroup";
    string codeGroupDescription = "Grants permissions that allow a managed
      control to work.";
    // this code will run when the MSI file is installed
    public override void Install(IDictionary stateSaver)
    {
        //find the machine policy,
        PolicyLevel machinePolicy = PolicyLevel("Machine");

        // add a named permission set
        NamedPermissionSet nps = new NamedPermissionSet(permissionName,
          PermissionState.None);
        nps.Description = permissionDescription;
        nps.AddPermission(new FileIOPermission(PermissionState.Unrestricted));
        try
        {
            machinePolicy.AddNamedPermissionSet(nps);
        }
        catch
        {
            //there is a duplicate name, so let's update instead
            machinePolicy.ChangeNamedPermissionSet(nps.Name, nps);
        }

        CodeGroup cg = new UnionCodeGroup(new UrlMembershipCondition("http://
          <servername>/controls/mycustomwincontrols.dll"), new PolicyStatement(nps,
          PolicyStatementAttribute.Nothing));
        cg.Name = codeGroupName;
        cg.Description = codeGroupDescription;

        // add new code group
        machinePolicy.RootCodeGroup.AddChild(cg);

        //save all changes
        SecurityManager.SavePolicyLevel(machinePolicy);
    }
}
```

```
    PolicyLevel PolicyLevel(string target)
    {
        IEnumerator policyEnumerator = SecurityManager.PolicyHierarchy();
        PolicyLevel found = null;
        while (policyEnumerator.MoveNext())
        {
            PolicyLevel level = (PolicyLevel)policyEnumerator.Current;
            if (target == level.Label)
            {
                found = level;
            }
        }
        return found;
    }
}
```

Visual Basic Snippet

```
Imports System
Imports System.Collections
Imports System.ComponentModel
Imports System.Configuration.Install

Imports System.Security
Imports System.Security.Policy
Imports System.Security.Permissions

<RunInstaller(True)> _
Public Class MyInstallPackage
    Inherits System.Configuration.Install.Installer
    Private components As System.ComponentModel.Container = Nothing

    Private permissionName As String = "MyCustomWinControlsPermissions"
    Private permissionDescription As String= "Custom permissions for my
      control."
    Private codeGroupName As String = "MyCustomGroup"
    Private codeGroupDescription As String = "Grants permissions that allow a
      managed control to work."
    ' this code will run when the MSI file is installed
    Public Overrides Sub Install(ByVal stateSaver As IDictionary)
        'find the machine policy,
        Dim machinePolicy As PolicyLevel = PolicyLevel("Machine")
        ' add a named permission set
        Dim nps As NamedPermissionSet = New NamedPermissionSet(permissionName,
          PermissionState.None)
        nps.Description = permissionDescription
        nps.AddPermission(New FileIOPermission(PermissionState.Unrestricted))
        Try
            machinePolicy.AddNamedPermissionSet(nps)
        Catch
            'there is a duplicate name, so let's update instead
            machinePolicy.ChangeNamedPermissionSet(nps.Name, nps)
        End Try
        Dim cg As CodeGroup = New UnionCodeGroup(New UrlMembershipCondition ("http://
          <servername>/controls/mycustomwincontrols.dll"), New PolicyStatement(nps,
          PolicyStatementAttribute.Nothing))
```

```
        cg.Name = codeGroupName
        cg.Description = codeGroupDescription
        ' add new code group
        machinePolicy.RootCodeGroup.AddChild(cg)

        'save all changes
        SecurityManager.SavePolicyLevel(machinePolicy)
    End Sub

    Private Function PolicyLevel(ByVal target As String) As PolicyLevel
        Dim policyEnumerator As IEnumerator =
          SecurityManager.PolicyHierarchy()
        Dim found As PolicyLevel = Nothing
        Do While policyEnumerator.MoveNext()
            Dim level As PolicyLevel = CType(policyEnumerator.Current,
              PolicyLevel)
            If target = level.Label Then
                found = level
            End If
        Loop
        Return found
    End Function
End Class
```

Let's briefly walk through the code. To compile this example, you need to add a reference to the *System.Configuration.Installer* assembly. Inherit your class from the *Installer* class, and override the *install* and *uninstall* methods. These methods are called by the installer package automatically. The *uninstall* method performs the reverse of the *install* method and has been removed to keep the example simple.

The installation creates a custom Permission Set and a custom Code Group. For the custom Permission Set, a URL provides the evidence. The Code Group is assigned the custom permission. This example is roughly identical to the steps performed earlier.

Think carefully about the strategy that you will employ to distribute policy files, especially if you are pushing to an enterprise organization. A 1-percent failure rate for a push to 50,000 desktops can result in 500 support calls from distressed clients. Support staff can become quickly overwhelmed by the deluge of support incidents.

Guidelines for Applying CAS to UDFs

Let's mention some best practices around granting managed code the permission to call unmanaged code. First, as I mentioned, there is an inherent security risk in the process. Only grant this permission to code that you have a reason to trust.

We have discussed sandboxing within the context of permissions. And you must have the discipline to sandbox unmanaged code. Part of the process is already provided for you when you implement a managed wrapper around the unmanaged XLL add-in. Close the loop, and protect your intellectual property by applying CAS policy to these managed wrappers to govern the access to system resources.

At the code level, perform a permission demand for the unmanaged code in your wrapper class. Whatever the unmanaged code can perform, callers in the stack should have that permission set as well.

It's also a good practice to visually inspect code through a code review process for code that requires elevated privilege. Manual inspection can catch issues before policy files are released to production.

> **Troubleshooting**   The CAS policy techniques shown here can be used to resolve all sorts of permissions issues, such as SQL Server permissions issues, Web services permissions problems from Web Part calling code, and issues related to sandboxing any assembly executing on the client or server. It's important to note that these techniques are not specific to SharePoint but apply to .NET applications in general.

Beyond SharePoint Programming

A large majority of resources today address Excel Services in isolation. This approach is handicapped when considered within a real-world context. Applications are not developed in isolation and SharePoint is no exception. In the real world, applications need to be massaged to work alongside existing infrastructure, which often includes disparate back ends and a colorful mix of execution platforms.

This resource specifically services the need to write applications in a real-world context so that you can break free from the vacuum of developing applications that exist only in SharePoint. We walk through asynchronous Web Parts next.

Asynchronous Web Parts

At the time of this writing, AJAX is not supported within MOSS 2007. You might be a bit confused because we have already examined an example in Chapter 3 that performed asynchronous calls within the context of sorting and paging. And this is AJAX. It stands to reason that the support statement I just made does not mean that AJAX implementations will not work with SharePoint; it simply means that Microsoft Product Support will not service these support requests. If you care to service your own support requests, you can AJAX-enable your Web Parts. Otherwise, you should not.

It is possible to develop Web Parts that support asynchronous processing similar to the model we followed in Chapter 3. Developing an example along these lines would therefore be a more prudent investment of time and resources. First, the asynchronous calls occur within the context of a user control, and user controls are in fact supported within SharePoint. It's a gray area that we can exploit to our advantage, confident in the knowledge that Microsoft Product Support will support the code if we falter. Full-blown AJAX development with the Microsoft toolkit will not be considered here for obvious reasons.

From a high level, we simply need to create a user control and inherit from the *ICallback-EventHandler* interface. This interface is used to indicate that a control can be the target of a callback event on the server. We then provide some basic script to the calling page and launch the Web Part. The client script then queries the server for the time of day, and the results are returned to the client. It's a pretty simple concept, but it demonstrates all the nuts and bolts of enterprise applications. Finally, you should note that the *ICallbackEventHandler* interface also supports validation, but we won't consider it here.

There isn't much going on in the server-side code, so we can simply present the entire source in Listing 7-10.

Listing 7-10 Implementing AJAX in SharePoint.

```csharp
C# Snippet
using System;
using System.Web;
using System.Web.UI;

namespace AJAX
{
    public partial class WebUserControl1 : System.Web.UI.UserControl,
      ICallbackEventHandler
    {
        public string _callbackArg;

        void Page_Load(object sender, System.EventArgs e)
        {
            ClientScriptManager csm = Page.ClientScript;
            String cbReference = csm.GetCallbackEventReference(this,
              "","ReceiveServerData", "");
            String callbackScript = "function CallServer() {" + cbReference + "; }";
            csm.RegisterClientScriptBlock(this.GetType(),"CallServer",
              callbackScript, true);
        }

        public string GetCallbackResult()
        {
            return _callbackArg;
        }

        public void RaiseCallbackEvent(string eventArgument)
        {
            this._callbackArg = DateTime.Now.ToString("hh:mm:ss");
        }
    }
}
```

```vb
Visual Basic Snippet
Imports System
Imports System.Web
Imports System.Web.UI

Namespace AJAX
    Public Partial Class WebUserControl1
        Inherits System.Web.UI.UserControl
        Implements ICallbackEventHandler
        Public _callbackArg As String

        Private Sub Page_Load(ByVal sender As Object, ByVal e As
          System.EventArgs)
            Dim csm As ClientScriptManager = Page.ClientScript
            Dim cbReference As String = csm.GetCallbackEventReference(Me,
              "","ReceiveServerData", "")
            Dim callbackScript As String = "function CallServer() {" &
              cbReference & "; }"
            csm.RegisterClientScriptBlock(Me.GetType(),"CallServer",
              callbackScript, True)
        End Sub

        Public Function GetCallbackResult() As String Implements
          ICallbackEventHandler.GetCallbackResult
            Return _callbackArg
        End Function

        Public Sub RaiseCallbackEvent(ByVal eventArgument As String)
          Implements
          ICallbackEventHandler.RaiseCallbackEvent
            Me._callbackArg = DateTime.Now.ToString("hh:mm:ss")
        End Sub
    End Class
End Namespace
```

The important piece of the ACSX control is shown here:

```html
<script type="text/javascript">
    function ReceiveServerData(arg, context)
    {
        Message.innerText = arg;
    }
</script>
<input type="button" value="Callback" onclick="CallServer()"/>
<span id="Message"></span>
```

The implementation of *RaiseCallbackEvent* actually performs the server-side processing. *GetCallbackEvent* returns the callback result to the client. The ASPX page contains three client script functions responsible for performing the actual request to the server. That's basically all there is to implementing AJAX. Notice that we have implemented the functionality in a way that honors the product support agreement.

Working with SharePoint Features

Features are new for Windows SharePoint Services 3.0 (WSS). Features allow WSS 3.0 to encapsulate functionality in definition containers. These containers, or *definition files*, are stored by default in *<Drive>:\Program Files\Common Files\Microsoft Shared\Web Server Extensions\12\TEMPLATE\FEATURES*. Exactly one *feature.xml* file resides in the each feature subfolder. The *feature.xml* file is an XML file that defines the base properties of the features that are available.

> **Important** Because features extend the SharePoint functionality, these files are protected by SharePoint security. For features that are created manually, you need to explicitly set folder-level permissions; otherwise, a security exception is thrown on first access.

Before we look at the specific types of functionality that can be implemented with features, let's spend a moment reviewing the object hierarchy shown in Figure 7-7.

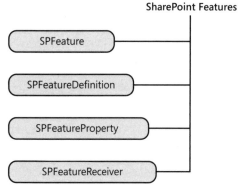

Figure 7-7 SharePoint feature object hierarchy.

Table 7-4 shows definitions of the key objects.

Table 7-4 Feature Object Hierarchy

Object	Description
SPFeature	Represents an activated feature on the server farm, Web application, site collection, or Web site levels. The absence of an *SPFeature* object indicates that the object has not been activated.
SPFeatureDefinition	Contains the base definition of a feature, including its name, ID, scope, and version.
SPFeatureProperty	Is used to install and activate a feature in the server farm.
SPFeatureReceiver	A base abstract class that can be overridden to provide access to a feature. Uses the *SPFeatureReceiver* class to trap events that are raised after the feature installation, uninstallation, activation, or deactivation action has been performed. *SPFeatureReceiver* events are asynchronous in nature.

> **Important**   Upon reading these descriptions, you might have noticed that the terminology differentiates between installation and activation. Let's formalize a definition for those before moving forward. *Installing* a feature makes its definition and elements known throughout a server farm. *Activating* a feature makes it available at a particular scope. Activation requires installation. Installation is not dependent on activation.

A feature can consist of one or more bits of functionality. The feature developer has precise control over the range and scope of the feature. For instance, features can be implemented with the *feature.xml* file that I mentioned earlier. Or features can be implemented programmatically. A feature can provide a customized list, a menu to a site, or a hook that allows an ASP.NET application to run inside SharePoint. The possibilities are endless.

Creating a Feature

A feature is implemented inside a *feature.xml* file. The *feature.xml* file is located within a custom directory given by the file path *<Drive>:\Program Files\Common Files\Microsoft Shared\Web Server Extensions\12\TEMPLATE\FEATURES*. If you care to examine this directory, you will find numerous folders, each containing an XML file implementing a feature on SharePoint.

To create a new feature, one approach is to copy the *feature.xml* file found in any of the subfolders in the Features directory into your own folder and hand edit the *feature.xml* file as appropriate. To assist you in the manual edit, add a SharePoint schema to Visual Studio 2005. The schema can be found in the directory with file path *<Drive>:\Program Files\Common Files\Microsoft Shared\Web Server Extensions\12\TEMPLATE\FEATURES\wss.xsd*.

The contents of the *feature.xml* file are shown here:

```
<?xml version="1.0" encoding="utf-8" ?>
<Feature Title="New Site Actions Link"
  Scope="Web"
  Id="ECE4C8D8-6CBA-431d-A820-4D902A781AE0"
  xmlns="http://schemas.microsoft.com/sharepoint/">
    <ElementManifests>
        <ElementManifest Location="Elements.xml" />
    </ElementManifests>
</Feature>
```

The *feature.xml* file contains an *ElementManifest* node that points to the location of *Elements.xml*. The *Feature* element is used in a *feature.xml* file to define a feature and to specify the location of assemblies, files, dependencies, or properties that support the feature. *Elements.xml* appears next and implements the action for the link:

```
<?xml version="1.0" encoding="utf-8" ?>
<Elements xmlns="http://schemas.microsoft.com/sharepoint/">
    <CustomAction
      GroupId = "SiteActions"
      Location="Microsoft.SharePoint.StandardMenu"
```

```
        Sequence="1000"
        ShowInLists="TRUE"
        Title="Site Features">
    </CustomAction>
    <CustomAction
      GroupId="SiteActions"
      Location="Microsoft.SharePoint.StandardMenu"
      Sequence="1001"
      Title="Check Mail">
        <UrlAction Url="/_layouts/WinOutlooker/CheckMail.aspx"/>
    </CustomAction>
</Elements>
```

The menu items are added using a *CustomAction* tag. The attributes are easy to figure out and don't require an extended explanation. The *GroupId* attribute indicates to SharePoint that the new link must be placed in the *SiteActions* menu. This menu can be found in the Standard Menu location. The link appears with a description given by the text attribute. The click action invokes the page pointed to by the *UrlAction* attribute.

Deploying Features   To deploy a feature, you need to create a folder called **SimpleFeature** in the Feature directory, which is found at this location: *<Drive>:\Program Files\Common Files\Microsoft Shared\Web Server Extensions\12\TEMPLATE\FEATURES*. Although the folder name is arbitrarily chosen, there are some limitations. Pay special attention to the folder name that you provide for the feature. WSS 3.0 does not support low-order ASCII characters (non-printable) in folder names. There is no support for folder or file names that contain spaces.

Folders created by using Windows Explorer do not have inherited permissions by default. This lack of permissions can cause some Windows SharePoint Services 3.0 pages to throw an exception. The problem can be remedied by removing the *uninherited* permissions from the newly created folder in Windows Explorer.

Installation and Activation of Features   Assuming that you have implemented and deployed a feature, you can install and activate the feature by using code or through the use of the stsadm tool. Listing 7-11 shows the code to install and activate a feature.

Listing 7-11   Feature installation and activation with code.

C# Snippet
```csharp
SPFeatureDefinitionCollection featureDefinitions = SPFarm.Local.FeatureDefinitions;
Guid guid = new Guid("ECE4C8D8-6CBA-431d-A820-4D902A781AE0");
SPFeatureDefinition featureDefinition =
  featureDefinitions.Add(@"Feature1\feature.xml", guid);
SPFeatureCollection websiteFeatures = SPContext.Current.Site.AllWebs["Site"].Features;
SPFeature myFeature = websiteFeatures.Add(guid);
```

Visual Basic Snippet
```vb
Dim featureDefinitions As SPFeatureDefinitionCollection =
SPFarm.Local.FeatureDefinitions
Dim guid As Guid = New Guid("ECE4C8D8-6CBA-431d-A820-4D902A781AE0")
Dim featureDefinition As SPFeatureDefinition =
  featureDefinitions.Add("Feature1\feature.xml", guid)
```

```
Dim websiteFeatures As SPFeatureCollection =
  SPContext.Current.Site.AllWebs("Site").Features
Dim myFeature As SPFeature = websiteFeatures.Add(guid)
```

Because features can be implemented only in a subfolder of a specific directory, the code uses a partial path *Feature1\feature.xml* in the *Add* method. The *feature.xml* file contains the required elements that drive the new functionality. Each feature being installed requires a GUID. The GUID can be generated using the Guidgen tool that ships with .NET. The remainder of the code scopes the feature to the site level and installs and activates it.

Here is the command-line call with appropriate arguments to first install and then activate a feature using the stsadm tool:

```
stsadm -o installfeature -filename SimpleFeature\Feature.xml
stsadm -o activatefeature -filename SimpleFeature\Feature.xml -url http://Server/Site/
Subsite
```

Important   After performing the feature installation and activation, you need to perform a Microsoft Internet Information Services (IIS) reset (IISReset from the command prompt). The *installfeature* might require the *–force* option to force a re-installation of the feature if the feature is already installed. There is no *–force* option for activation. You need to use the deactivate command to deactivate the feature. Then perform an activation.

Figure 7-8 shows the feature in action. The feature adds two items in the Site Actions menu. If you examine the *element.xml* file, the first item doesn't have an action associated with it. The second item, Check Mail, calls a Web FormWeb Form that is able to perform some type of custom action. I'll return to its implementation in the next section.

Figure 7-8   Site Actions menu item added using a feature.

Tip   You don't always have to program a snazzy piece of functionality using features. You can use features simply to perform mundane tasks such as implementing shortcuts to frequently used pages.

Office Automation with SharePoint

In Chapter 6, we implemented a property that was able to invoke a custom ASPX page to get client input. The example did not show how to build the ASPX page. Although adding ASCX user control files is relatively painless, adding ASPX or ASMX pages to SharePoint is not as straightforward as you might have been led to believe.

There are two approaches to doing this correctly. The magic wand approach is simply to use SharePoint Designer 2007. The tool allows you to add a Web Form to a site. Behind the scenes, SharePoint Designer is hard at work hooking up the internal plumbing to make everything work. If you don't have SharePoint Designer, you have to put a bit more effort into it. Let's outline some basic steps.

First, you need to create an ASPX page and deploy the page to the _Layouts folder. Because this is an advanced chapter, I won't bother with a standard "Hello, world" page; these pages scarcely reflect enterprise application requirements. Let's walk through an example that launches a custom Web Form tied to the Check Mail item in the Features section presented in the previous section.

The features part is already implemented for us, so we will simply wire up custom functionality to the click event. When the Check Mail item is clicked, we expect to be redirected to a Web Form, CheckMail.aspx, that allows us to check our mail using Microsoft Office Outlook.

Technically, the process of invoking one application from another application is referred to as *automation*. Part of the automation involves iterating the Mail folder on the client and displaying the mail items that are available. This is difficult but not impossible because Outlook is running on the client while the feature is implemented on the server. If we can pull this off, it will show us how to automate Office applications from SharePoint, something I promised earlier. You can then extend this concept to automate any client application from within SharePoint.

Listing 7-12 shows the Outlook automation code. Before the code will compile, you need to add a reference to the Microsoft Outlook 12 Object Library. You can find this underneath the COM tab in the Add Reference option of Visual Studio 2005 property pages. The Outlook 11 Object Library can be used as a substitute as well.

Listing 7-12   Office Outlook automation code.

```
C# Snippet
private void GetMail()
{
    //let's create an Outlook object in the client process space
    //we can piggyback on the current user session and grab the related data
    Microsoft.Office.Interop.Outlook._Application olApp = new
      Microsoft.Office.Interop.Outlook.ApplicationClass();
    Microsoft.Office.Interop.Outlook._NameSpace olNS =
      olApp.GetNamespace("MAPI");
```

```csharp
Microsoft.Office.Interop.Outlook._Folders oFolders = olNS.Folders;

if (oFolders.Count > 0)
{
    Microsoft.Office.Interop.Outlook.MAPIFolder oPublicFolder = oFolders["Personal
        Folders"];
    oFolders = oPublicFolder.Folders;

    Microsoft.Office.Interop.Outlook.MAPIFolder oAllPFolder = oFolders["Inbox"];
        oFolders = oAllPFolder.Folders;

    if (oFolders.Count < 1)
    {
        OutlookTreeView.Nodes.Clear();
        OutlookTreeView.Nodes.Add("No new Email.");
        }
        else
        {
        OutlookTreeView.Nodes.Clear();
        for (int i = 1; i < oFolders.Count; i++)
        {
            Microsoft.Office.Interop.Outlook.MailItem mi = oFolders[i].Items as
                Microsoft.Office.Interop.Outlook.MailItem;
            OutlookTreeView.Nodes.Add(mi.Subject);
        }
    }
    }
}
}
```

Visual Basic Snippet

```vbnet
Private Sub GetMail()
'let's create an Outlook object in the client process space
'we can piggyback on the current user session and grab the related data
    Dim olApp As Microsoft.Office.Interop.Outlook._Application = New
        Microsoft.Office.Interop.Outlook.ApplicationClass()
    Dim olNS As Microsoft.Office.Interop.Outlook._NameSpace =
        olApp.GetNamespace("MAPI")
    Dim oFolders As Microsoft.Office.Interop.Outlook._Folders = olNS.Folders
    If oFolders.Count > 0 Then
        Dim oPublicFolder As Microsoft.Office.Interop.Outlook.MAPIFolder =
            oFolders("Personal Folders")
        oFolders = oPublicFolder.Folders
        Dim oAllPFolder As Microsoft.Office.Interop.Outlook.MAPIFolder =
            oFolders("Inbox")
        oFolders = oAllPFolder.Folders

        If oFolders.Count < 1 Then
            OutlookTreeView.Nodes.Clear()
            OutlookTreeView.Nodes.Add("No new Email.")
        Else
            OutlookTreeView.Nodes.Clear()
            Dim i As Integer = 1
            Do While i < oFolders.Count
            Dim mi As Microsoft.Office.Interop.Outlook.MailItem =
```

```
              TryCast(oFolders(i).Items,
              Microsoft.Office.Interop.Outlook.MailItem)
                OutlookTreeView.Nodes.Add(mi.Subject)
                i += 1
          Loop
       End If
    End If
```

Let's walk through this beauty. We first need to create an instance variable of type *OutlookApplicationClass*. We then use MAPI to attach to the currently logged-on user session and query the public folder on the server. The code requires an active session, so if Microsoft Outlook is not running on the client, the run time attempts to start Outlook. If this fails, an exception is thrown and the application terminates.

If the attempt to start Outlook is successful, the server is queried for mail items. If mail items exist, the subject of each mail item is added to a Windows *TreeView* control. Depending on how the Outlook server was configured, it's quite possible that strings such as *["Personal Folders"]* might be different than what is presented here. If that is the case, an exception will be thrown. As a workaround, you can use an index instead of the string, as long as the index is greater than zero and less than the size of the collection.

The automation code presented here is best placed in a user control because it needs to perform automation on the client. It can't simply be placed in a Web Form because a Web Form does not have access to the desktop. Create a user control called **WinOutlooker**, and place a *TreeView* control named **OutlookTreeView** on the design surface. Place the *GetMail* method call in the *Load* event handler for the control so that the code can execute once the control is completely loaded. Compile the control, and test it using the ActiveX Control Test Container to make sure that it works correctly. This is no different from the Web Part approach.

Adding a Custom Web Form to SharePoint

The code presented earlier demonstrates how to automate Microsoft Office on the client, something I talked rather boldly about in previous chapters. Until now, however, we lacked sufficient knowledge to throw an end-to-end example together. You need to create an ASPX page that acts as a hosting container for the user control. In the source of the ASPX page, add an object tag that points to a user control that contains the automation code. Here is an example:

```
<object id="myControl1" name="myControl1" classid="/Controls/
WinOutlooker.dll#WinOutlooker.UserControl1"> </object>
```

Notice that the code is reusing the controls directory that we are familiar with. That's it for the heavy lifting; we simply need to perform some configuration steps. Open IIS Manager, and create a virtual directory named **WinOutlooker** pointing to the project that contains the ASPX file. (See Figure 7-9.)

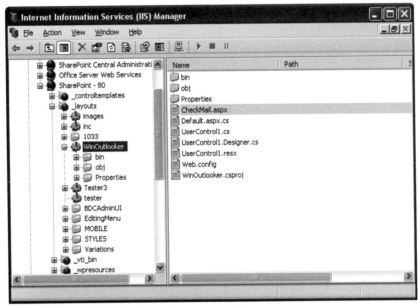

Figure 7-9   Creating a virtual directory in IIS Manager.

Invoke the Virtual Directory Creation Wizard by right-clicking on the WinOutlooker directory, and choosing New Virtual Directory on the context menu. Walk through the wizard. Add the necessary permissions in the Virtual Directory Creation Wizard as shown in Figure 7-10.

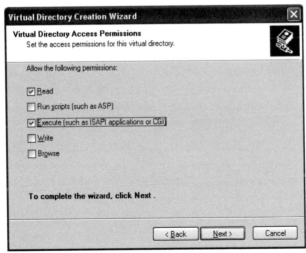

Figure 7-10   Virtual Directory Access Permissions page in the Virtual Directory Creation Wizard.

After the directory is created, right-click on it and select Properties. Click the Virtual Directory tab as shown in Figure 7-11. Verify that your settings resemble those of Figure 7-11.

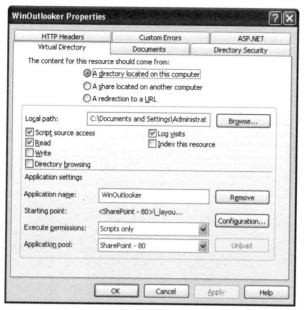

Figure 7-11   Internet Information Services (Inetmgr) permissions configuration.

Place the compiled WinOutlooker.dll assembly in the controls directory of the SharePoint Web application on the server. We won't be using events or a code-beside file for this example, so remove the reference from the CheckMail.ASPX file. The source in the CheckMail.ASPX file should resemble the following line:

```
<%@ Page Language="C#" %>
```

Exercise the application from SharePoint. You should receive a security exception. These types of applications require a CAS policy. I won't rehash the approach to configuring permissions here again because these have been addressed earlier in the chapter. Apply the same approach to resolve the security issue. Once the application successfully executes, you will see the mail items displayed in the *TreeView* control in the Web Form.

> **Note**   In some cases, the CLR might throw an exception because the Office Interop DLL cannot be found. That situation occurs only if you do not have the Outlook Primary Interop Assemblies (PIA) installed. The quick fix for this condition is to place the Outlook Interop assembly in the root folder of the Web server. I do not claim to know why this solution works, because the automation is occurring on the client and not the server.

COM Automation Events in SharePoint   Most enterprise applications fire and handle events. For Web applications, these events can fire on the server, on the client, or both. user controls are no different. Wiring event code to a user control is relatively pain free. For this example, we will graft an event onto the automation code in the previous example. If you recall, the code iterates the Outlook Inbox and displays mail in a *TreeView* control on the client.

Our modification involves catching errors related to the Outlook automation and passing the entire error object to client script running inside the browser. First, you need to wire the object in the browser for events. Here is the code:

```javascript
<script type="text/javascript" for="myControl1" event="ErrorEvent(e)" language="javascript">
    function myControl1::ErrorEvent(e)
    {
        //Be sure to turn your popup blocking software off
        alert(e.Message);
    }
</script>
```

Place the code after the closing object tag but before the *<form>* tag. Save the file. The code essentially calls a method, *ErrorEvent*, defined on the control and displays information to the screen via an alert message box.

Troubleshooting   IntelliSense will indicate that the *for* and *event* tags are invalid. You can safely ignore those. They will be resolved at run time.

For the code-beside modifications, first add a reference to *System.Runtime.InteropServices*. Then add a delegate inside the class. Here is the code:

```csharp
C#
public delegate void ErrorEventHandler(object e);
VB
Public Delegate Sub ErrorEventHandler(ByVal e As Object)
```

Next, you need to declare the COM events that the browser will handle. Place the code before the class method *UserControl1*. The code is shown in Listing 7-13.

Listing 7-13   Interface events declaration.

```csharp
C# Snippet
[GuidAttribute("9819EE05-86A4-43a8-AF62-A7AFFA69AB1B")]
[InterfaceTypeAttribute(ComInterfaceType.InterfaceIsIDispatch)]
public interface ControlEvents
{
    //Add a DispIdAttribute to any members in the source interface
    [DispIdAttribute(0x60020000)]
    void ErrorEvent(object e);
}
```

```
Visual Basic Snippet
<GuidAttribute("9819EE05-86A4-43a8-AF62-A7AFFA69AB1B"),
InterfaceTypeAttribute(ComInterfaceType.InterfaceIsIDispatch)> _
Public Interface ControlEvents
  'Add a DispIdAttribute to any members in the source interface
  <DispIdAttribute(&H60020000)> _
  Sub ErrorEvent(ByVal e As Object)
End Interface
```

The *ErrorEvent* method is the same method being called by the script code presented earlier. The signatures must match exactly; otherwise, the script code will not be invoked and will result in a page error in the browser.

The *UserControl* class is a managed class, but it needs to be able to fire COM events, so we need to decorate the class appropriately. Add this piece of code to the class definition:

```
[ClassInterface(ClassInterfaceType.None), ComSourceInterfaces(typeof(ControlEvents))]
```

We now need to declare an event variable that we can map to our delegate. Let's also implement the *IObjectSafety* interface while we are at it.

> **Best Practices** *IObjectSafety* should be implemented by objects that have interfaces that support *untrusted* clients. *IObjectSafety* allows the owner of the object to specify which interfaces need to be protected from *untrusted* use.

This indicates to the browser that the control is safe for scripting. It is not required for the example to run, but it is a good practice. Note that the implementation of the *IObjectSafety* interface is not related to Code Access Security but rather to the way in which the browser perceives ActiveX controls. The code is shown in Listing 7-14.

Listing 7-14 Event declaration and *IObjectSafety* implementation.

```
C# Snippet
//event declaration for browser
event WinOutlooker.ErrorEventHandler ErrorEvent;

// Constants for implementation of the IObjectSafety  interface.
private const int INTERFACESAFE_FOR_UNTRUSTED_CALLER = 0x00000001;
private const int INTERFACESAFE_FOR_UNTRUSTED_DATA = 0x00000002;
private const int S_OK = 0;
// Implementation of the IObjectSafety  methods.
int IObjectSafety.GetInterfaceSafetyOptions(ref Guid riid, out int
pdwSupportedOptions, out int pdwEnabledOptions)
{
     pdwSupportedOptions = INTERFACESAFE_FOR_UNTRUSTED_CALLER |
        INTERFACESAFE_FOR_UNTRUSTED_DATA;
```

```
        pdwEnabledOptions = INTERFACESAFE_FOR_UNTRUSTED_CALLER |
          INTERFACESAFE_FOR_UNTRUSTED_DATA;

        return S_OK;   // return S_OK
}


//except for advanced scenarios, just return ok
int IObjectSafety.SetInterfaceSafetyOptions(ref Guid riid, int
  dwOptionSetMask, int dwEnabledOptions)
{
        return S_OK;   // return S_OK
}
```

Visual Basic Snippet

```
'event declaration for browser
Event ErrorEvent As WinOutlooker.ErrorEventHandler
' Constants for implementation of the IObjectSafety  interface.
Private Const INTERFACESAFE_FOR_UNTRUSTED_CALLER As Integer = &H00000001
Private Const INTERFACESAFE_FOR_UNTRUSTED_DATA As Integer = &H00000002
Private Const S_OK As Integer = 0


' Implementation of the IObjectSafety  methods.
Private Function GetInterfaceSafetyOptions(ByRef riid As Guid,
  <System.Runtime.InteropServices.Out()> ByRef pdwSupportedOptions As Integer,
  <System.Runtime.InteropServices.Out()> ByRef pdwEnabledOptions As Integer)
  As Integer Implements IObjectSafety.GetInterfaceSafetyOptions
    pdwSupportedOptions = INTERFACESAFE_FOR_UNTRUSTED_CALLER Or
      INTERFACESAFE_FOR_UNTRUSTED_DATA
    pdwEnabledOptions = INTERFACESAFE_FOR_UNTRUSTED_CALLER Or
      INTERFACESAFE_FOR_UNTRUSTED_DATA

    Return S_OK ' return S_OK
End Function

'except for advanced scenarios, just return ok
Private Function SetInterfaceSafetyOptions(ByRef riid As Guid, ByVal
  dwOptionSetMask As Integer, ByVal dwEnabledOptions As Integer) As Integer Implements
IObjectSafety.SetInterfaceSafetyOptions
    Return S_OK ' return S_OK
End Function
```

The code needs to be placed inside the *UserControl1* class. You then need to inherit the *IObjectSafety* interface at the class level.

Finally, we fire the event in response to some error. You can trigger the error by entering an invalid folder name in the automation code. Simply wrap the automation code with a *try/catch* block, and poison the input by changing the string *"Inbox"* to *"NoboxAtAll"*. When the automation code executes this new line of code, *oFolders["NoboxAtAll"]*, Outlook will throw an exception and the *catch* block will handle the exception. Listing 7-15 shows the code.

Listing 7-15   Exception-handling code firing event.

```
C# Snippet
catch (Exception ex)
{
    //throw the exception so that it is caught in the client browser
    if (ErrorEvent != null)
    {
        ErrorEvent(ex);
    }
}
Visual Basic Snippet
Catch ex As Exception
    'throw the exception so that it is caught in the client browser
    If Not ErrorEvent Is Nothing Then
        ErrorEvent(ex)
    End If
End Try
```

Let's wire an event handler that listens for events that are fired in response to exceptions thrown. Listing 7-16 shows the load event handler code.

Listing 7-16   Event wire-up.

```
C# Snippet
private void UserControl1_Load(object sender, EventArgs e)
{
    ErrorEventHandler(RaiseMyEvent);
    ErrorEvent += myDelegate;

    GetMail();
}
public void RaiseMyEvent(object e)
{
    System.Exception ex = e as System.Exception;
    OutlookTreeView.Nodes.Add("Failed with error: " + ex.Message);
}
Visual Basic Snippet
Private Sub UserControl1_Load(ByVal sender As Object, ByVal e As EventArgs)
    ErrorEventHandler(RaiseMyEvent)
    ErrorEvent += myDelegate

    GetMail()
End Sub
Public Sub RaiseMyEvent(ByVal e As Object)
    Dim ex As System.Exception = TryCast(e, System.Exception)
    OutlookTreeView.Nodes.Add("Failed with error: " & ex.Message)
End Sub
```

When the user control loads, the event listeners are attached and the *GetMail* method is called. Recall that this method is poisoned with an invalid folder name. We expect the code to choke on the poisoned input firing an exception. Because the assembly is COM visible, it will fire an event in the managed assembly calling the *RaiseMyEvent* method, which will display a message in the *TreeView* control. Then the event will transition to unmanaged code, where it will be caught in the browser. The browser code will extract the error message and display it on the screen.

There's one final step in the dance. You need to enable the managed assembly for COM Interop. It is not enabled by default. To enable it, navigate to the Build option on the WinOutlooker tab. In the Output section, select the Register For Com Interop check box as shown in Figure 7-12.

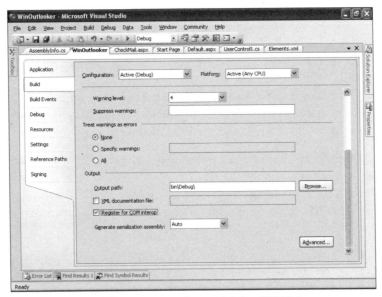

Figure 7-12   Enabling a managed assembly for COM Interop.

Go ahead, give it a whirl. You should see a message box with an error message being displayed in the browser similar to Figure 7-13.

Figure 7-13   Client error being generated using events notification.

Words fail to describe the endless possibilities that are now available to you with this type of programming. In case you missed it, you now have a technique that can essentially allow script to subscribe to automation code running in the managed user control. And this technique can be used for non-automation code as well. It is also cross-browser compliant, meaning that it will work in non–Internet Explorer browsers.

This last piece of code completes the circle in SharePoint development. You can now write applications that start in a SharePoint context and reach out to the client, exchanging data and firing events in a way that is seamless to the end user. And this is the power of ASP.NET and SharePoint!

Guidelines for Developing Custom Web Forms with SharePoint

If you chose to skip the complicated parts of this chapter and preferred to implement a simple HelloWorld custom Web Form, you need to point the virtual directory to the location containing the custom Web Form. Also, you don't need to remove the *AutoEventWireUp*, *CodeBehind*, and *Inherits* directives from the ASPX page because these are required to cause the code-beside file to respond to events correctly. Use either a feature or a link from your portal to invoke the Web page.

The example assumes that Outlook 2007 is installed on the client. A valid installation of Microsoft Outlook adds the required Outlook 12 Object Library to the client machine. You do not need to deploy the Outlook assembly on the server because the client already has the assembly installed. If there are any other assembly dependencies in the project, they need to be deployed in the controls folder of the Web application as well.

When debugging these types of applications, you should prefer to attach the debugger to the Iexplorer.exe process. Avoid attaching to the w3wp.exe worker process. In some cases, the attachment effort might succeed but the breakpoint will not fire. You also need to copy the Program Database (PDB) files to the same folder where the user control lives so that the run time can load the debugging symbols.

In some rare instances, managed user controls embedded in Internet Explorer can actually leak memory. The exact details are described in this article: *http://support.microsoft.com/default.aspx?scid=kb;en-us;555916*. Bear this in mind when you develop these types of controls.

Programming with Accessibility in Mind

Let's unwind from this rather steep climb by discussing accessibility. Accessibility is a legal requirement in most countries. Accessibility refers to applications that cater to the needs of individuals with disabilities. It makes sense to build applications that cater to the needs of all users, not just users without disabilities because your application should target the widest possible audience.

The accessibility-related improvements are supported in the following areas:

Tables   Table heading tags are now added by default. TH tags provide information to screen-reader software, which results in a better audible experience for screen-reader users.

Navigation   Navigation links, such as Skip To Main Content, help visually impaired users quickly jump to the most important content without having to tab through navigation links. Also, SharePoint adds navigation breadcrumbs to assist with site navigation.

Keyboard   All user-interface (UI) controls in SharePoint are keyboard accessible. Also, the tab order of the keyboard is more intuitive.

Images   All images expose ALT description tags. Custom images also allow for a UI-based way to define custom ALT text for that image so that blind users can interpret what the uploaded images are. Warnings, as appropriate, are provided for links that will open a new window.

High contrast   High contrast testing is implemented for low-vision scenarios. SharePoint does not rely on the use of color alone to convey information.

HTML controls   SharePoint includes a special accessible mode that allows users with special needs to identify themselves so that the software can change the way dynamic content is rendered. For instance, form controls are rendered as standard HTML controls so that they will be better recognized by the accessible technology.

With regard to accessibility, SharePoint has improved support that far surpasses previous versions. However, the product is still not 100-percent compliant with accessibility requirements. You should test your application to see if it works well with screen-reader software by running Microsoft Accessibility Checker on your Web Parts and custom Web Forms. The Accessibility Checker will point out the parts of the application that need to be addressed to work well with screen-reading software.

Visual Studio 2005 Extensions Templates

For the most part, I have ignored the other options of the Visual Studio Extensions templates. Let's walk through some simple scenarios. As you know, the extensions are templates that can be used to develop Web Parts, site definitions, and list definitions.

The extensions also ship with a SharePoint Solution Generator. This standalone program generates a Site Definition project from an existing SharePoint site. SharePoint Solution Generator enables developers to use the browser and Microsoft Office SharePoint Designer 2007 to customize the content of their sites before creating code by using Visual Studio. That sort of functionality is especially handy for teams that contain defined roles, such as developers and user-interface designers.

Visual Studio 2005 Extensions templates also allow the developer to make additions to the standard set of templates through items. The following items can be added into an existing project:

- Web Part
- Custom field
- List definition

- Content type
- Module

For the list definition and content types, item templates can include optional event receivers.

Building Team Site Definitions for SharePoint

Site definitions are collections of physical files located in *<Drive>:\Program Files\Common Files\Microsoft Shared\Web Server Extensions\12\TEMPLATE*. These files provide the definition for a SharePoint site.

In the past, it was certainly not a trivial task to create these files manually. The Team Site Definition template now performs this task for you. The process involves selecting the Team Site Definition template as shown in Figure 7-14.

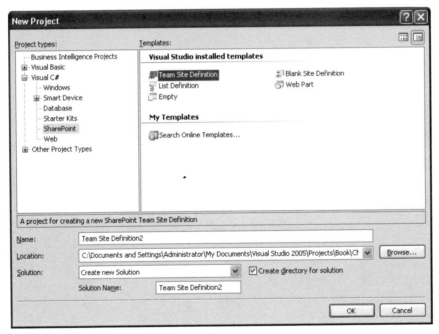

Figure 7-14   Team Site Definition template.

Figure 7-15 shows the relevant files associated with the project.

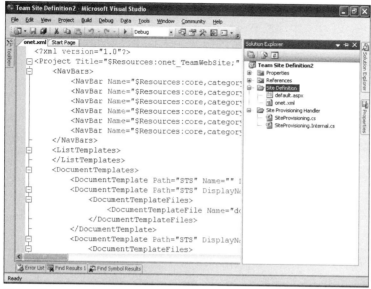

Figure 7-15   Default files created by the Team Site Definition template.

Building List Site Definitions for SharePoint

Internally, SharePoint represents most items as a list. A list must therefore be very generic in form and function because it must cater to a wide variety of needs, such as wikis, document libraries, picture libraries, announcements, and so on.

Because of this underlying commonality in the infrastructure, you can port your knowledge from one user-interface piece to the other. For instance, throughout the book, you have been working exclusively with lists, document libraries, and Web Parts. However, it requires very little effort to work with a wiki or discussion board because they share the underlying list base. Wikis are increasing in importance, especially in business environments. Consider that a wiki may be used between legal departments to draft a legal document without the hassle of faxing documents around or e-mailing PDF documents.

The Visual Studio Extensions templates allow you to create definitions based on existing lists. In that way, you can build upwards from a SharePoint platform. To create a site definition or list definition project, create a new project and select the appropriate template as shown in Figure 7-14.

Deploying Definitions to SharePoint

After you have built a new list definition or created a team site definition, you might be eager to see what it looks like in SharePoint. The extensions also allow you to deploy these definitions directly to SharePoint by pressing F5. The process is exactly the same as deploying a Web Part.

After deploying the list or team site definition to SharePoint using the Visual Studio 2005 Extensions deployment process, navigate to your site and select the Create item from the Site Actions menu. For a team site, click the Site Definitions link. In the page that comes up next, add a suitable description and title for the team site. Base your new site on the template that was deployed by clicking on the Development tab as shown in Figure 7-16.

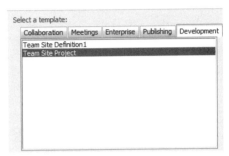

Figure 7-16   Site options on the Development tab.

Navigate to your team site by entering the URL into the browser address bar that you configured earlier for the team site. Figure 7-17 shows a site based on a custom site definition.

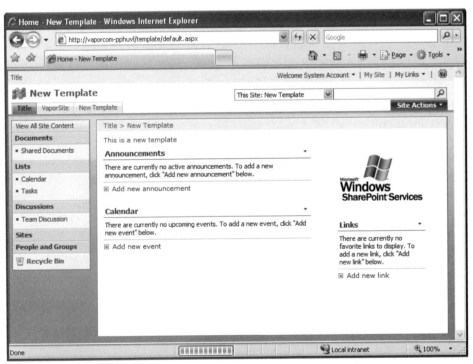

Figure 7-17   Web Form created using the Team Site Definition template.

Customization of site definition files works rather well when data is stored directly on the Web servers. In fact, certain types of customization to sites or lists require the use of site definitions, such as introducing new file types, defining view styles, or modifying the drop-down Edit menu.

Site definition customization does have a few disadvantages. For instance, theming is not supported. Also, tweaking site definitions after deployment is difficult but not impossible. If you need to tweak them, you will require access to the file system on the server.

Core Schema Files in SharePoint

It's time to formalize a discussion of core schema files in SharePoint. SharePoint chooses to represent core files using XML for the various benefits inherent in XML. Each XML file uses Collaborative Application Markup Language (CAML). CAML is described in complete detail on Microsoft Developer Network (MSDN):

The feature.xml file has been presented earlier and will not be rehashed here. Three other files, WEBTEMP.XML, ONET.XML, and SCHEMA.XML are important for site customization.

The WEBTEMP.XML file specifies the various configurations available for creating sites. When you begin customizations, make a backup of the WEBTEMP.XML file and rename the target file to a string containing WEBTEMP in its title. At run time, WSS 3.0 merges the contents of all files that match WEBTEMP*.XML when showing available configurations on the Template Selection page. To remove your customizations, simply delete this file.

The ONET.XML file performs several functions. It defines the top navigation and Quick Launch areas, specifies which list types are available on the Create page, and specifies document templates and their file types. It defines the base types for lists, which include Generic List, Document Library, Discussion Forum, Vote Or Survey, and Issues List. It defines the configurations and modules in the site definition.

 Note   A *configuration* specifies the set of lists and modules that are included when a site is created, and a *module* specifies the file or files to include during site creation and the location where they are stored.

The SCHEMA.XML file defines the views, forms, toolbar, and any special fields for a list type. It's important to always create a new site definition when implementing new functionality. Default site definition files can be overwritten during SharePoint repairs or service pack updates, resulting in broken applications.

If you care to look at the files in a new site definition project, you will notice that the core schema files are created automatically for you, along with a handful of ASPX files. You can then begin customizing this set of files to enhance the client experience in SharePoint.

> **More Info**   Take a look at the bin folder in the *<Drive>:\inetpub\wwwroot* directory and containing subdirectories—you will not find any binary files. This is fundamentally different from ASP.NET virtual directories that store binary assemblies in the bin folder of the virtual directory. For ASP.NET, the relevant files are compiled into an assembly on demand, stored in process, and made available to service requests that address that particular virtual directory. These assemblies can be cached to disk as appropriate, usually in a temporary directory well known to ASP.NET. In SharePoint, assemblies are loaded from the virtual bin directory that is explicitly mapped to *<Drive>:\Program Files\Common Files\Microsoft Shared\Web Server Extensions\12\isapi* directory for customized pages. Uncustomized pages compile assemblies as needed and store those in temporary folders similar to ASP.NET.

Summary

This chapter presented several new concepts. In particular, you learned how to connect Web Parts and how to configure CAS to allow managed user controls to function correctly. The chapter also walked through the creation and deployment of ASP.NET Web pages in SharePoint. A number of considerations need to be observed to get this to work correctly. However, the end justifies the means in that you can now integrate your disparate ASP.NET applications in SharePoint.

SharePoint ships with a new feature called a *feature*. There is absolutely no pun intended here. The text discussed the various uses and strategies for implementing, deploying, and activating features across a farm. What is important is that a feature can be combined with code to extend and improve the end user experience. For instance, I showed how to use a feature to fire Office automation code. You can use similar approaches to burst through the SharePoint silo to connect disparate .NET applications into SharePoint or to dribble functionality in from disparate platforms such as UNIX and Java.

Finally, I discussed the improvements made with respect to accessibility and wrapped up with a look at the various templates that are available for use in the Visual Studio 2005 Extensions for SharePoint. These templates take the effort out of developing customized solutions so that you can focus on implementing business logic. And this is where you, as a developer, can add value!

Index

A

access control lists (ACLs), 50
Accessibility Checker, 289
accessibility features, 288
ACLs (access control lists), 50
activation
    compared to installation, 275
    features, 275–276
    Web Parts, 82
ActiveX Control Test Container utility, 206, 280
ActiveX objects
    ActiveX COM objects, 193–194, 284
    automating in Web Parts, 201–202
    charts as, 199
    Excel object rendering and, 5
    guidelines for, 200–201
    legacy objects, 201
Actor property, 65
add-ins, Excel, 140, 265–266, 270
administration object model, 172–177
administrative ports
    number, 26
    security, 168
administrative privileges
    CAS and, 208
    MOSS deployment and, 18
administrative site best practices, 28
administrators groups
    access to IIS metabase, 169
    role assignments, 168
Advanced installation option, 20
Advanced properties, 227
Advanced Web Part Gallery, 83, 243
AJAX, 271–273
alerts
    message text, 163
    stop and continue alerts, 64–67
AllowMinimize property, 226
AllowPartialTrustedCallers (APTC), 76
AllowUnsafeUpdates property, 159
AllUsers property, 148
ALT description tags, 289
anonymous access, 127
Appearance properties, 227
application pool identity, 23
ApplyChanges method, 237
APTC (AllowPartialTrustedCallers), 76
arguments in formulas, 61
arrays
    indexing into, 49

iterating, 52
jagged, 52
parameter, 143
single-dimension, 143
two-dimensional, 143
ASCX files
    loading into SharePoint, 253, 278
    user controls and, 95
ASMX files
    displaying list of, 68
    Excel Web Services configuration, 36
    loading into SharePoint, 278
ASP.NET 2.0
    assembly locations, 294
    caching in, 256, 258
    Code Access Security and, 259
    compared to managed user controls, 206
    connecting Web Parts, 247
    developer expectations for, 2
    developer perspectives for, 2
    Excel Services architecture and, 1
    managed user controls in, 205
    safe-mode parser and, 178
    searching SharePoint sites from, 160
    timesheet Web Parts application, 99–110
    Web Part class, 75
    Web Parts, 95. See also SharePoint Web Parts; Web Parts
ASP.NET Web Parts. See also SharePoint Web Parts; Web Parts
    approaches to, 95
    connecting, 247
    EWA Web Parts and, 71
    timesheet application, 99–110
    Web Part class, 75
ASPX files
    hosting user controls in, 280
    loading into SharePoint, 278
    loading spreadsheets, 186
    xlViewer modifications, 187
assemblies
    compared to .dwp files, 220–221
    declarative security, 262
    directory locations, 294
    extracting, 182
    for Internet Explorer, 207
    registering, 140, 151–153
    retrieving data about, 77
    signing UDFs, 134
    signing Web Parts, 75–79

S

X

XLL add-ins, 265–266, 270
.xlsb extension, 40
.xlsx extension, 40
xlViewer object, 184–189
XML files
  core schema files in SharePoint, 293
  .webpart files, 222
XML serializer, 167
XML strings, search queries as, 162

Y

yellow screen of death, 87

Z

Zone permissions, 263

Alvin J. Bruney

Alvin Bruney is a consultant for one of the big four financial institutions in North America, where he trains personnel and provides guidance and best practices on using the .NET platform. Alvin started out writing taxation software using C++ for leading companies in the tax industry before moving on to .NET. This is Alvin's third book on .NET technology. Alvin writes about topics that interest him and that allow him to draw on several years of working experience with .NET and several more years of experience developing software for server farms containing more than 1000 servers. For several years now, Alvin has also been a Microsoft ASP.NET MVP and counts this as one of his major accomplishments.